AMERICAN FICTION
TO 1900

AMERICAN LITERATURE, ENGLISH LITERATURE, AND WORLD LITERATURES IN ENGLISH: AN INFORMATION GUIDE SERIES

Series Editor: Theodore Grieder, Curator, Division of Special Collections, Fales Library, New York University, New York, New York

Associate Editor: Duane DeVries, Assistant Professor, Polytechnic Institute of New York, Brooklyn, New York

Other books on American Literature in this Series:

AMERICAN FICTION, 1900-1950—*Edited by James Woodress*

AMERICAN DRAMA TO 1900—*Edited by Walter J. Meserve**

AMERICAN DRAMA, 1900-1950—*Edited by Paul Hurley**

AMERICAN PROSE AND CRITICISM TO 1820—*Edited by Donald Yannella and John Roch**

AMERICAN PROSE AND CRITICISM, 1820-1900—*Edited by Elinore H. Partridge**

AMERICAN POETRY TO 1900—*Edited by Bernice Slote**

AMERICAN POETRY, 1900-1950—*Edited by William White and Artem Lozynsky**

THE LITERARY JOURNAL IN AMERICA TO 1900—*Edited by Edward Chielens*

THE LITERARY JOURNAL IN AMERICA, 1900-1950—*Edited by Edward Chielens**

CONTEMPORARY FICTION IN AMERICA AND ENGLAND, 1950-1970— *Edited by Afred F. Rosa and Paul A. Eschholz*

CONTEMPORARY DRAMA IN AMERICA AND ENGLAND, 1950-1970— *Edited by Richard Harris**

CONTEMPORARY POETRY IN AMERICA AND ENGLAND, 1950-1970— *Edited by Calvin Skaggs**

*in preparation

The above series is part of the
GALE INFORMATION GUIDE LIBRARY

The Library consists of a number of separate Series of guides covering major areas in the social sciences, humanities, and current affairs.

General Editor: Paul Wasserman, Professor and former Dean, School of Library and Information Services, University of Maryland

AMERICAN FICTION
TO 1900

A GUIDE TO INFORMATION SOURCES

*Volume 4 in the American Literature, English
Literature, and World Literatures in English
Information Guide Series*

David K. Kirby

*Associate Professor and Director of Writing Programs
Florida State University*

Gale Research Company
Book Tower, Detroit, Michigan 48226

**Library of Congress
Cataloging in Publication Data**

Kirby, David K.
   American fiction to 1900.

   (American literature, English literature, and world literatures in
English; v.4) (Gale information guide library)
   1. American fiction--19th century--Bibliography. 2. American
fiction--19th century--History and criticism--Bibliography. I. Title.
Z1231.F4K57   016.813'008   73-16982
ISBN 0-8103-1210-7

To my father

THOMAS A. KIRBY

VITA

David K. Kirby received his B.A. from Louisiana State University and his Ph.D. from Johns Hopkins University, where he wrote a dissertation on the fictional technique of Henry James. Since 1969 he has been teaching at Florida State University (including six months at the F.S.U. Study Center in Florence, Italy), where he is now Associate Professor and Director of Writing Programs in the Department of English. His writings have appeared in a variety of learned journals and literary quarterlies. He has given public talks and readings in the United States and Australia and has conducted workshops and seminars for elementary school children, prison inmates, and other groups. With Kenneth H. Baldwin, he is co-editor of INDIVIDUAL AND COMMUNITY: VARIATIONS ON A THEME IN AMERICAN FICTION, a _Festschrift_ for Charles R. Anderson published by Duke University Press. At present he is engaged in a study of Louisiana author Grace King.

CONTENTS

Contents

Contents

HOW TO USE THIS BOOK

This book is divided into two parts. The first and shorter part is entitled GEN-
ERAL AIDS and includes the following items:

(1) HANDBOOKS. Listed are the most useful reference works
which pertain to American fiction and American authors to 1900.

(2) BIBLIOGRAPHIES AND CHECKLISTS. Included under this head-
ing are the various guides to works by American fiction writers to
1900 as well as guides to critical and biographical studies of these
authors and their writings.

(3) PERIODICALS AND SERIALS. The periodicals and serials that
are essential to a study of American fiction to 1900 are listed here.
Journals devoted to particular authors are listed in the second section of the book.

(4) GENERAL CRITICAL STUDIES. A highly selective group of
studies is included in this section. Each deals with some aspect of
American fiction to 1900 and each treats more than one author;
works that deal with a single author only are listed under the
CRITICAL STUDIES in the part that follows.

The second and longer part of this book is entitled INDIVIDUAL AUTHORS.
Included are forty-one authors; in the case of each, the following items are
included:

(1) PRINCIPAL WORKS. First American editions (exclusive of
prepublication or copyright issues and serial publications) are cited.
This section has two purposes: (a) to provide a convenient guide to
the reader who needs to make a quick check of exact titles, dates,
etc., without going to the author's standard bibliography, and (b) to
suggest the scope of an author's career--types of writing, frequency
of publication, and so on. The list is necessarily selective, in
most cases; the reader who is not sure which works by a given author are important is advised to examine the section on the CRITI-
CAL STUDIES of that author to see which works have attracted the
most attention.

(2) COLLECTED WORKS. Of the available collected editions of a particular author's works, the most reliable are listed here. In some cases, of course, no collected edition is available.

(3) LETTERS. An author's principal collection or collections of letters are listed here; where there are many collections involved, the principal ones are listed and the reader is advised where to look to find out more about the others.

(4) BIBLIOGRAPHY. When available, one or more reliable bibliographies of works by the author are listed. Blanck (see item 12) is the single best source of bibliographical information.

(5) CHECKLIST. When available, one or more checklists of biographical and critical studies of the author are listed. In certain cases, I have not listed checklists because my own listings of biographical and critical studies are more extensive.

(6) JOURNAL. Several authors in this guide have journals dedicated entirely to them and their works; these are listed and they supplement the list of less specialized PERIODICALS AND SERIALS in the first part of this book.

(7) BIOGRAPHY and (8) CRITICAL STUDIES. These two sections may be discussed together, since the same principles of selection operate in both. It is difficult to select fifty or sixty works from the hundreds that have been written on a particular author and his writings. I have tried to pick the most useful studies; at the same time, I have tried to make my selections in a way that will give the reader a broad picture of the present state of scholarship on the author and his works. Biographical-critical studies pose a problem which I have resolved for the most part by putting the standard biography or biographies under BIOGRAPHY and the critical works which contain biographical material under CRITICAL STUDIES.

Many of the annotations are evaluative, but most are merely descriptive. As often as possible, I have quoted from the book or article under consideration. In order to leave more room for annotations, I have omitted, where possible, superfluous bibliographical information (such as page numbers within books that have indices).

Because of the method of producing this volume, it was impossible to include diacritical marks. The author regrets any confusion that this might create.

ACKNOWLEDGMENTS

I should like to express my thanks to all of those who patiently answered my letters and phone calls, lent me books and other materials, and contributed in other ways to the preparation of this guide. Those to whom I am especially grateful are George Arms, R. Bruce Bickley, Jr., Robert Bush, Dedria Bryfonski, Myrtle Carroll, Jerry Cebelak, Duane DeVries, Clayton L. Eichelberger, Richard W. Etulain, Theodore Grieder, Judy K. Kirby, Thomas A. Kirby, Joseph R. McElrath, Jr., Griffith T. Pugh, Jay Simpson, and Joseph W. Slade.

I made extensive use of the interlibrary loan service of the Robert Manning Strozier Library at Florida State University, and I should like to thank the interlibrary loan staff, particularly Ann L. Lo and Anne Page Mosby. In addition, I am grateful to the libraries that lent me materials; these include the libraries of the following institutions: Auburn University, Cornell University, Duke University, Florida Atlantic University, Harvard University, Louisiana State University, Mississippi State University, Rutgers University, Southern Illinois University, Tulane University, University of Florida, University of Maine, University of Miami (Florida), University of Mississippi, University of Virginia, and Washington University (St. Louis). I am grateful also to the Jacksonville Public Library.

I owe a special debt to the humanities librarians at Strozier Library, particularly Louise Clay. Finally, I am grateful to George M. Harper for suggesting this project to me in the first place.

ABBREVIATIONS OF PERIODICAL AND SERIAL TITLES

ABC	AMERICAN BOOK COLLECTOR
AH	AMERICAN HERITAGE
AHR	AMERICAN HISTORICAL REVIEW
AL	AMERICAN LITERATURE
ALR	AMERICAN LITERARY REALISM
AmRev	AMERICAN REVIEW
AN&Q	AMERICAN NOTES AND QUERIES
AQ	AMERICAN QUARTERLY
AR	ANTIOCH REVIEW
ArielE	ARIEL: A REVIEW OF INTERNATIONAL ENGLISH LITERATURE
ArQ	ARIZONA QUARTERLY
ASch	AMERICAN SCHOLAR
ASp	AMERICAN SPEECH
BB	BULLETIN OF BIBLIOGRAPHY
BNYPL	BULLETIN OF THE NEW YORK PUBLIC LIBRARY
BuR	BUCKNELL REVIEW
CE	COLLEGE ENGLISH
CEAAN	CENTER FOR EDITIONS OF AMERICAN AUTHORS NEWSLETTER
CL	COMPARATIVE LITERATURE
CLAJ	COLLEGE LANGUAGE ASSOCIATION JOURNAL
CLQ	COLBY LIBRARY QUARTERLY
ColQ	COLORADO QUARTERLY
CritQ	CRITICAL QUARTERLY
DR	DALHOUSIE REVIEW
ECS	EIGHTEENTH-CENTURY STUDIES
EIC	ESSAYS IN CRITICISM
ELH	JOURNAL OF ENGLISH LITERARY HISTORY
ES	ENGLISH STUDIES
ESQ	EMERSON SOCIETY QUARTERLY
GaR	GEORGIA REVIEW
HLB	HARVARD LIBRARY BULLETIN
HLQ	HUNTINGTON LIBRARY QUARTERLY
HudR	HUDSON REVIEW
IMH	INDIANA MAGAZINE OF HISTORY
JAmS	JOURNAL OF AMERICAN STUDIES
JGE	JOURNAL OF GENERAL EDUCATION
JSH	JOURNAL OF SOUTHERN HISTORY
KanQ	KANSAS QUARTERLY

KR	KENYON REVIEW
LaHist	LOUISIANA HISTORY
LaHistQ	LOUISIANA HISTORICAL QUARTERLY
LondM	LONDON MERCURY
MarkR	MARKHAM REVIEW
MASJ	MIDCONTINENT AMERICAN STUDIES JOURNAL
MFS	MODERN FICTION STUDIES
MH	MINNESOTA HISTORY
MHM	MARYLAND HISTORICAL MAGAZINE
MHSB	MISSOURI HISTORICAL SOCIETY BULLETIN
MissQ	MISSISSIPPI QUARTERLY
MJ	MIDWEST JOURNAL
MLJ	MODERN LANGUAGE JOURNAL
MLN	MODERN LANGUAGE NOTES
MLQ	MODERN LANGUAGE QUARTERLY
MLR	MODERN LANGUAGE REVIEW
MP	MODERN PHILOLOGY
MQ	MIDWEST QUARTERLY
MVHR	MISSISSIPPI VALLEY HISTORICAL REVIEW
NALF	NEGRO AMERICAN LITERATURE FORUM
N&Q	NOTES AND QUERIES
NAR	NEW AMERICAN REVIEW
NCF	NINETEENTH-CENTURY FICTION
NCHR	NORTH CAROLINA HISTORICAL REVIEW
NEQ	NEW ENGLAND QUARTERLY
NMQ	NEW MEXICO QUARTERLY
NR	NEW REPUBLIC
NY	NEW YORKER
NYH	NEW YORK HISTORY
PBSA	PAPERS OF THE BIBLIOGRAPHICAL SOCIETY OF AMERICA
PLL	PAPERS ON LANGUAGE AND LITERATURE
PMLA	PUBLICATIONS OF THE MODERN LANGUAGE ASSOCIATION OF AMERICA
PQ	PHILOLOGICAL QUARTERLY
PR	PARTISAN REVIEW
PW	PUBLISHERS' WEEKLY
QJS	QUARTERLY JOURNAL OF SPEECH
RRel	REVIEW OF RELIGION
SA	STUDI AMERICANI
SAQ	SOUTH ATLANTIC QUARTERLY
SatR	SATURDAY REVIEW
SB	STUDIES IN BIBLIOGRAPHY
SCR	SOUTH CAROLINA REVIEW
SF	SOCIAL FORCES
SFQ	SOUTHERN FOLKLORE QUARTERLY
SHR	SOUTHERN HUMANITIES REVIEW
SIR	STUDIES IN ROMANTICISM
SLJ	SOUTHERN LITERARY JOURNAL
SN	STUDIA NEOPHILOLOGICA
SNNTS	STUDIES IN THE NOVEL (NORTH TEXAS STATE)
SoQ	SOUTHERN QUARTERLY
SoR	SOUTHERN REVIEW

SP	STUDIES IN PHILOLOGY
SR	SEWANEE REVIEW
SSF	STUDIES IN SHORT FICTION
SWR	SOUTHWEST REVIEW
TCL	TWENTIETH-CENTURY LITERATURE
THQ	TENNESSEE HISTORICAL QUARTERLY
TLS	TIMES LITERARY SUPPLEMENT
TQ	TEXAS QUARTERLY
TSE	TULANE STUDIES IN ENGLISH
TSL	TENNESSEE STUDIES IN LITERATURE
TSLL	TEXAS STUDIES IN LITERATURE AND LANGUAGE
TWA	TRANSACTIONS OF THE WISCONSIN ACADEMY OF SCIENCES, ARTS, AND LETTERS
UCPES	UNIVERSITY OF CALIFORNIA PUBLICATIONS, ENGLISH STUDIES
UKCR	UNIVERSITY OF KANSAS CITY REVIEW
UMSE	UNIVERSITY OF MISSISSIPPI STUDIES IN ENGLISH
UTQ	UNIVERSITY OF TORONTO QUARTERLY
UWP	UNIVERSITY OF WYOMING PUBLICATIONS
VMHB	VIRGINIA MAGAZINE OF HISTORY AND BIOGRAPHY
WAL	WESTERN AMERICAN LITERATURE
WHR	WESTERN HUMANITIES REVIEW
WMH	WISCONSIN MAGAZINE OF HISTORY
WMQ	WILLIAM AND MARY QUARTERLY
WPennHM	WESTERN PENNSYLVANIA HISTORICAL MAGAZINE
YR	YALE REVIEW
YULG	YALE UNIVERSITY LIBRARY GAZETTE

Other abbreviations

comp(s).	compiler(s), compiled by
ed(s).	editor(s), edition, edited by
enl.	enlarged
no.	number
n.s.	new series
p(p).	page(s)
[pseud.]	pseudonym
rev.	revised
trans.	translated by, translator
vol(s).	volume(s)

Suggestions for additions to this guide as well as corrections should be sent to me in care of the English Department, Florida State University, Tallahassee, Fla. 32306.

GENERAL AIDS

HANDBOOKS

1. Curley, Dorothy Nyren, et al., eds. A LIBRARY OF LITERARY CRITICISM:
    MODERN AMERICAN LITERATURE. 4th ed. 3 vols. New York: Fred-
    erick Ungar, 1969.

    An extremely useful collection of excerpts from critical works
    on individual American authors (who are listed alphabetically).
    Unfortunately, only authors from the twentieth century are
    treated (including, of the writers treated in the present volume,
    Bierce, Chopin, Clemens, Crane, Frederic, Garland, Howells,
    James, and Norris).

2. Hart, James D. THE OXFORD COMPANION TO AMERICAN LITERA-
    TURE. 4th ed. New York: Oxford University Press, 1965.

    Short biographies and bibliographies of American authors, more
    than 1000 summaries of American literary works, entries on
    literary schools and movements, etc. Its scope, balance, read-
    ability, and the alphabetical arrangement of entries make this
    a useful "companion" indeed.

3. Herzberg, Max J. THE READER'S ENCYCLOPEDIA OF AMERICAN LIT-
    ERATURE. New York: Thomas Y. Crowell, 1962.

    "The most comprehensive reference book on its subject in exis-
    tence..., it includes entries on authors, titles, characters,
    periodicals, literary groups, historical personages, and other
    topics related to literature."

4. Johnson, Allen, et al., eds. DICTIONARY OF AMERICAN BIOGRAPHY.
    22 vols. New York: Charles Scribner's Sons, 1928-58.

    Includes 14,870 biographies, each written by a specialist, of
    "Americans who have made memorable contributions to our
    national life."

5. Magill, Frank N., ed. MASTERPLOTS: AMERICAN FICTION SERIES
    New York: Salem Press, 1964.

Includes 262 plot summaries from the best American fiction.

6. Spiller, Robert E., et al., eds. LITERARY HISTORY OF THE UNITED STATES: HISTORY [thus designated to distinguish it from the BIBLIOG-RAPHY; see 29]. 4th ed. rev. New York: Macmillan, 1974; London: Collier-Macmillan, 1975.

> An indispensable handbook. Spiller is also the author of a companion volume to LHUS, a book entitled THE CYCLE OF AMERICAN LITERATURE (New York: The Free Press; London: Collier-Macmillan, 1967), which is "the distillation in one mind of the knowledge and wisdom of the fifty-five scholar-contributors to [the] larger work."

7. Thrall, W. F., Addison Hibbard and C. Hugh Holman. A HANDBOOK TO LITERATURE. 3rd ed. Indianapolis, Ind., and New York: Odyssey Press, 1972.

> The best of such handbooks. Over 1360 entries in alphabetical order; in addition to the usual definitions (e.g., "short story"), this guide also includes concise articles on broader topics (e.g., "Realistic Period in American Literature, 1865-1900").

4

BIBLIOGRAPHIES AND CHECKLISTS

8. ABSTRACTS OF ENGLISH STUDIES. 1958- .

    Brief summaries of articles (including ones on American litera-
    ture) appearing in scholarly journals; in 1972, AES began to
    cover monographs as well. Published ten times a year by the
    National Council of Teachers of English, 1111 Kenyon Road,
    Urbana, Ill. 61801.

9. AMERICAN LITERARY REALISM. 1967- .

    This quarterly is indispensable because of its thorough biblio-
    graphical studies of works by and about the American Realists.
    Address: Department of English, University of Texas at Arling-
    ton, Arlington, Tex. 76010.

10. AMERICAN LITERATURE. 1929- .

    Each issue of this quarterly includes a listing of "Articles on
    American Literature Appearing in Current Periodicals." (In
    addition, the book reviews published in each issue of AL are
    consistently reliable.) Published by Duke University Press, P.
    O. Box 6697, College Station, Durham, N.C. 27708.

11. AMERICAN LITERATURE ABSTRACTS. 1967- .

    Brief summaries of articles on American literature appearing in
    scholarly journals. Published semiannually by the Department
    of English, San Jose State College, San Jose, Cal. 95114.

12. Blanck, Jacob, comp. BIBLIOGRAPHY OF AMERICAN LITERATURE. 6
    vols. to date. New Haven, Conn.: Yale University Press, 1955- .

    A multivolume attempt to describe bibliographically American
    literary works which "enjoyed something resembling recognition."
    The most detailed and authoritative work of its kind. Its many
    author bibliographies are highly detailed and largely definitive.

13. BOOK REVIEW DIGEST. 1905- .

> The student of American fiction (or any other subject) is well advised to use this compilation of short excerpts from book reviews. Appears monthly except in February and July. Published by H. W. Wilson Co., 950 University Avenue, Bronx, N.Y. 10452.

14. CHARLES E. MERRILL CHECKLISTS. Matthew J. Bruccoli and Joseph Katz, general editors. Columbus, Ohio: Charles E. Merrill Publishing Co.

> Each checklist includes information on works both by and about the author. There are checklists on Melville, Poe, Harold Frederic, Hawthorne, Frank Norris, James, and Crane. Unfortunately, these first-rate bibliographical tools, which seem to have appeared in 1969 and 1970, are inexplicably out of print.

15. Clark, Harry Hayden, comp. AMERICAN LITERATURE: POE THROUGH GARLAND. New York: Appleton-Century-Crofts, 1971.

> Includes major and lesser American writers; a handy supplement to 21. Not fully annotated.

16. Davis, Richard Beale, comp. AMERICAN LITERATURE THROUGH BRYANT, 1585-1830. New York: Appleton-Century-Crofts, 1969.

> Includes entries on Brackenridge, Brockden Brown, Cooper, Irving, Paulding, and other fiction writers of the early period. Not fully annotated.

17. Eichelberger, Clayton L., comp. A GUIDE TO CRITICAL REVIEWS OF UNITED STATES FICTION, 1870-1910. Metuchen, N.J.: Scarecrow, 1971.

> This book will be extremely useful to those interested in the reception of a particular book of fiction at the time of its publication.

18. Gerstenberger, Donna and George Hendrick, comps. THE AMERICAN NOVEL 1789-1959: A CHECKLIST OF TWENTIETH-CENTURY CRITICISM (Denver, Col.: Alan Swallow, 1961) and THE AMERICAN NOVEL: A CHECKLIST OF TWENTIETH CENTURY [sic] CRITICISM ON NOVELS WRITTEN SINCE 1789; VOLUME II: CRITICISM WRITTEN 1960-1968 (Chicago, Ill.: The Swallow Press, 1970).

> Each of these two volumes is divided into two sections: (1) individual authors (where criticism is listed under three categories: individual novels, general studies, and bibliographies), and (2) criticism of the American novel as a genre. N.B.: only novels are treated; thus, under "Poe," only studies of his single novel THE NARRATIVE OF A. GORDON PYM are listed.

6

19. Gohdes, Clarence. BIBLIOGRAPHICAL GUIDE TO THE STUDY OF THE LITERATURE OF THE U.S.A. 3rd ed., rev. Durham, N.C.: Duke University Press, 1970.

This book treats, rather than works on individual authors, thirty-five broad areas of interest (such as poetry, fiction, drama), as well as backgrounds (such as American history, biography, art, philosophy, religion), and other topics.

20. Havlice, Patricia Pate, comp. INDEX TO AMERICAN AUTHOR BIBLIOG-RAPHIES. Metuchen, N.J.: Scarecrow, 1971.

Somewhat misleading in title, this nonetheless useful compilation includes only those bibliographies which have been published in periodicals, not books. It includes both bibliographies of authors' works as well as checklists of criticism about individual authors. Especially useful for minor authors.

21. Holman, C. Hugh, comp. THE AMERICAN NOVEL THROUGH HENRY JAMES. New York: Appleton-Century-Crofts, 1966.

Includes major and lesser American novelists as well as sections on other aspects of American fiction (e.g., books about the form of the novel); these latter sections are especially useful. Largely unannotated, this bibliography is nonetheless essential. See also 15.

22. Jones, Howard Mumford and Richard M. Ludwig. GUIDE TO AMERICAN LITERATURE AND ITS BACKGROUNDS SINCE 1890. 4th ed. Cambridge, Mass.: Harvard University Press, 1972.

The first half of this book deals mainly with social and intellectual backgrounds; the second consists of fifty-two reading lists organized by topic (e.g., "Historical Romance," "The Forces of Naturalism," etc.). It is to be hoped that the scope of this useful book will be expanded.

23. Jones, Joseph, et al., comps. AMERICAN LITERARY MANUSCRIPTS: A CHECKLIST OF HOLDINGS IN ACADEMIC, HISTORICAL, AND PUBLIC LIBRARIES IN THE UNITED STATES. Austin: University of Texas Press, 1960.

A useful tool for the patient student; since the entries are limited (a typical entry notes only that there is a significant collection of Henry James manuscripts in the New York Public Library), the reader will have to write or visit the individual libraries for more specific information.

24. Leary, Lewis G., comp. ARTICLES ON AMERICAN LITERATURE, 1900-1950 (1954); ARTICLES ON AMERICAN LITERATURE, 1950-1967 (1970). Durham, N.C.: Duke University Press.

Although the bulk of each volume is devoted to articles on the works of individual authors, there are also sections on general topics (such as "Fiction").

25. Marsh, John L. A STUDENT'S BIBLIOGRAPHY OF AMERICAN LITERATURE. Dubuque, Iowa: Kendall/Hunt, 1971.

    A selected, unannotated bibliography which concentrates on "the major literary genres and the most frequently anthologized figures in our literature."

26. MLA INTERNATIONAL BIBLIOGRAPHY OF BOOKS AND ARTICLES ON THE MODERN LANGUAGES AND LITERATURES. 1921- .

    An annual bibliography of books and articles (including ones on American literature). Abstracts of many of the articles may be found in MLA ABSTRACTS OF ARTICLES IN SCHOLARLY JOURNALS (an annual which begins with the year 1970). Both collections are published by the Modern Language Association of America, 62 Fifth Avenue, New York, N.Y. 10011.

27. Rees, Robert A. and Earl N. Harbert, eds. FIFTEEN AMERICAN AUTHORS BEFORE 1900. Madison: University of Wisconsin Press, 1971.

    Bibliographic essays on research and criticism about Cooper, Crane, Howells, Irving, Norris, and others.

28. Rubin, Louis D., Jr., ed. A BIBLIOGRAPHICAL GUIDE TO THE STUDY OF SOUTHERN LITERATURE. Baton Rouge: Louisiana State University Press, 1969.

    A guide to criticism on dozens of general topics and individual authors, including many minor pre-1900 fiction writers.

29. Spiller, Robert E., et al., eds. LITERARY HISTORY OF THE UNITED STATES: BIBLIOGRAPHY. 4th ed. rev. New York: Macmillan, 1974; London: Collier-Macmillan, 1975.

    Four main sections: a guide to bibliographical resources, bibliographies of literature and culture, bibliographies of movements and influences, and bibliographies of 207 individual authors. See also 6.

30. Stovall, Floyd, ed. EIGHT AMERICAN AUTHORS. Rev. ed. New York: W. W. Norton, 1971.

    Includes bibliographical essays on Poe, Hawthorne, Melville, Twain, and James.

31. STUDIES IN SHORT FICTION. 1963- .

    Publishes "an annual bibliography of interpretive material on short fiction in English." Address: Newberry College, Newberry, S.C. 29108. A quarterly.

32. Thurston, Jarvis, et al., comps. SHORT FICTION CRITICISM: A CHECK-LIST OF INTERPRETATION SINCE 1925 OF STORIES AND NOVELETTES (AMERICAN, BRITISH, CONTINENTAL), 1800-1958. Denver, Col.: Alan Swallow, 1960.

The annual bibliography in STUDIES IN SHORT FICTION (see 31) is intended to serve as a continuation of this bibliography.

33. Turner, Darwin T., comp. AFRO-AMERICAN WRITERS. New York: Appleton-Century-Crofts, 1970.

   Includes lists of works by and about pre-1900 black writers.

34. Walker, Warren S., comp. TWENTIETH-CENTURY SHORT STORY EX-PLICATION: INTERPRETATIONS, 1900-1966, OF SHORT FICTION SINCE 1800. 2nd ed. [Hamden, Conn.]: Shoe String Press, 1967.

   "A bibliography of short story explication published from 1900 through 1966 in books, monographs, and periodicals."

35. Whiteman, Maxwell. A CENTURY OF FICTION BY AMERICAN NEGROES, 1853-1952: A DESCRIPTIVE BIBLIOGRAPHY. Philadelphia, Pa.: privately printed, 1955.

   Designed to offer "as complete as possible a record of fiction by American Negroes."

36. Woodress, James, ed. AMERICAN LITERARY SCHOLARSHIP: AN AN-UAL / 1963- . Durham, N.C.: Duke University Press, 1965.

   Essays by various hands "summarizing the year's work in some segment of American literary scholarship."

37. _____, comp. DISSERTATIONS IN AMERICAN LITERATURE, 1891-1966. 3rd ed. Durham, N.C.: Duke University Press, 1968.

   Includes 4700 dissertations, listed under individual authors as well as topics (such as "Fiction") and subtopics (such as "Novel Before 1900"). Includes dissertations written in other countries.

38. Wright, Lyle H. AMERICAN FICTION, 1774-1850: A CONTRIBUTION TOWARD A BIBLIOGRAPHY (2nd rev. ed., 1969); AMERICAN FICTION, 1851-1875: A CONTRIBUTION TOWARD A BIBLIOGRAPHY (1957); AMERICAN FICTION, 1876-1900: A CONTRIBUTION TOWARD A BIBLIOG-RAPHY (1966). San Marino, Calif.: Huntington Library.

   Designed to serve "as a guide to the books rather than as a complete bibliographical description of them."

39. THE YEAR'S WORK IN ENGLISH STUDIES. 35 (1954)-

   Previously devoted solely to British literature, this bibliographi-cal annual added a chapter on American literature in 1954; be-ginning with the 1968 volume (and continuing to the present), there are separate chapters on American literature to 1900 and twentieth-century American literature.

PERIODICALS AND SERIALS

40. ABSTRACTS OF ENGLISH STUDIES.

     See 8 for annotation.

41. AMERICAN LITERARY REALISM.

     See 9 for annotation.

42. AMERICAN LITERATURE.

     See 10 for annotation.

43. AMERICAN LITERATURE ABSTRACTS.

     See 11 for annotation.

44. MODERN FICTION STUDIES. 1955- .

     A quarterly which occasionally publishes "special numbers" (which include useful checklists of criticism) on Melville, James, Twain, Howells, and other American novelists. Published by the Department of English, Purdue University, Lafayette, Ind. 47907.

44a. NINETEENTH-CENTURY FICTION. 1945- .

     This quarterly covers British and American fiction of the nineteenth century. Published by the University of California Press, 2223 Fulton Street, Berkeley, Calif. 94720.

45. NOVEL. 1967- .

     Of particular interest to students of critical theory. Appears thrice yearly. Address: Box 1984, Brown University, Providence, R.I. 02912.

46. STUDIES IN AMERICAN FICTION. 1973- .

     Articles, notes, reviews, occasional interviews, bibliographies, exchanges. Appears twice yearly. Published by Northeastern University, Boston, Mass. 02115.

47. STUDIES IN SHORT FICTION.

    See 31 for annotation.

48. STUDIES IN THE NOVEL. 1969- .

    Address: P.O. Box 12706, N. T. Station, Denton, Tex.
    76203. A quarterly.

49. UNIVERSITY OF MINNESOTA PAMPHLETS ON AMERICAN WRITERS.
    Minneapolis: University of Minnesota Press, 1959- .

    More than a hundred useful pamphlets on individual authors
    (each of which includes critical and biographical information
    as well as a bibliography) and special topics such as "The
    American Short Story." See also 59.

GENERAL CRITICAL STUDIES

50. Ahnebrink, Lars. THE BEGINNINGS OF NATURALISM IN AMERICAN FICTION. New York: Russell & Russell, 1961.

    Treats the works of Garland, Crane, and Norris.

51. Berthoff, Warner. THE FERMENT OF REALISM: AMERICAN LITERATURE 1884-1919. New York: Free Press, 1965.

    An intellectual and literary history of the years 1884-1919.

52. Cady, Edwin H. THE LIGHT OF COMMON DAY: REALISM IN AMERI-CAN FICTION. Bloomington: Indiana University Press, 1971.

    A collection of interrelated essays which deal with the concept of literary realism and with Twain, Hawthorne, Howells, Crane, Owen Wister, and others.

53. Chase, Richard. THE AMERICAN NOVEL AND ITS TRADITION. Garden City, N.Y.: Doubleday, 1957.

    Discusses the work of Brockden Brown, Cooper, Hawthorne, Melville, James, Twain, Cable, Norris, and others.

54. Cohen, Hennig, ed. LANDMARKS OF AMERICAN WRITING. New York and London: Basic Books, 1969.

    Essays by specialists on selected works by Irving, Cooper, Poe, Hawthorne, Melville, Twain, Crane, James, Bellamy, and others.

55. Cowie, Alexander. THE RISE OF THE AMERICAN NOVEL. New York: American Book Co., 1951.

    An attempt "to indicate the evolution of the American novel by means of comparatively full treatments of representative figures: all the major novelists, most of the secondary figures, and a considerable sprinkling of writers whose absolute value is very slight."

56. Falk, Robert P. THE VICTORIAN MODE IN AMERICAN FICTION 1865-1885. East Lansing: Michigan State University Press, 1965.

A study of the period 1865-85 and of the writings of James, Howells, De Forest, and Twain.

57.   Feidelson, Charles, Jr.   SYMBOLISM AND AMERICAN LITERATURE. Chicago: University of Chicago Press, 1953.

Considers Hawthorne, Melville, and Poe (among others) as modern symbolists rather than romantic egoists.

58.   Fiedler, Leslie A.   LOVE AND DEATH IN THE AMERICAN NOVEL. Rev. ed.   New York: Stein and Day, 1966.

Not "a conventional scholarly book...but a kind of gothic novel (complete with touches of black humor) whose subject is the American experience as recorded in our classic fiction," this book is probably best known for its discussion of the archetypal image (found in MOBY DICK, HUCKLEBERRY FINN, the Leatherstocking romances of Cooper, and elsewhere) of "a white and a colored American male [fleeing] from civilization into each other's arms."

59.   Foster, Richard, ed.   SIX AMERICAN NOVELISTS OF THE NINETEENTH CENTURY: AN INTRODUCTION.   Minneapolis: University of Minnesota Press, 1968.

Includes, under one cover, the UMPAW monographs (see 49) on Cooper, Hawthorne, Melville, Twain, Howells, and James.

60.   Frederick, John T.   THE DARKENED SKY: NINETEENTH-CENTURY AMER-ICAN NOVELISTS AND RELIGION.   Notre Dame, Ind.: University of Notre Dame Press, 1969.

Treats Cooper, Hawthorne, Melville, Twain, Howells, and James.

61.   Hoffman, Daniel G.   FORM AND FABLE IN AMERICAN FICTION.   New York: Oxford University Press, 1961.

Myths and folktales in the writings of Irving, Hawthorne, Melville, and Twain.

62.   Kaul, A. N.   THE AMERICAN VISION: ACTUAL AND IDEAL SOCIETY IN NINETEENTH-CENTURY FICTION.   New Haven, Conn., and London: Yale University Press, 1963.

Examines the dialectic between actual and ideal societies in the writings of Cooper, Hawthorne, Melville, and Twain.

63.   Kolb, Harold H.   THE ILLUSION OF LIFE: AMERICAN REALISM AS A LITERARY FORM.   Charlottesville: The University Press of Virginia, 1969.

A narrow focus (the writings of Twain, James, and Howells, 1884-86) yields some wide-ranging implications for the study of American literary realism.

64. Lawrence, D. H. STUDIES IN CLASSIC AMERICAN LITERATURE. New York: Viking, 1964.

   Provocative, impressionistic commentary on the works of Cooper, Poe, Hawthorne, Melville, and others.

65. Leisy, Ernest E. THE AMERICAN HISTORICAL NOVEL. Norman: University of Oklahoma Press, 1950.

   Comments on individual novels are grouped together according to particular historical periods (e.g., Colonial America, the Revolution, etc.).

66. Levin, Harry. THE POWER OF BLACKNESS: HAWTHORNE, POE, AND MELVILLE. New York: Alfred A. Knopf, 1958.

   Symbolism in the fiction of Hawthorne, Poe, and Melville.

67. Lynen, John F. THE DESIGN OF THE PRESENT: ESSAYS ON TIME AND FORM IN AMERICAN LITERATURE. New Haven, Conn., and London: Yale University Press, 1969.

   Lynen's theory--that an author's sense of time serves to organize a poem or novel--is employed "to illuminate the distinctive merits of American literature" (including the works of Irving, Cooper, Poe, and others).

68. Martin, Jay. HARVESTS OF CHANGE: AMERICAN LITERATURE, 1865-1914. Englewood Cliffs, N.J.: Prentice-Hall, 1967.

   A comprehensive--indeed, exemplary--study of a particularly rich period in American literary history.

69. Matthiessen, F. O. AMERICAN RENAISSANCE: ART AND EXPRESSION IN THE AGE OF EMERSON AND WHITMAN. London: Oxford University Press, 1941.

   Includes lengthy discussions of the works of Hawthorne and Melville.

70. Maxwell, D. E. S. AMERICAN FICTION: THE INTELLECTUAL BACKGROUND. New York: Columbia University Press, 1963.

   An uneven book which discusses certain writers at length and neglects others, this study still offers illuminating comments on the works of Poe, Hawthorne, Melville, and Twain.

71. Pattee, Fred Lewis. THE DEVELOPMENT OF THE AMERICAN SHORT STORY. New York and London: Harper & Brothers, 1923.

   From Washington Irving to the early twentieth century.

72. Petter, Henri. THE EARLY AMERICAN NOVEL. Columbus: Ohio State University Press, 1971.

   A comprehensive "descriptive and critical survey of the American novel up to the year 1820."

73. Pizer, Donald. REALISM AND NATURALISM IN NINETEENTH-CENTURY AMERICAN LITERATURE. Carbondale and Edwardsville: Southern Illinois University Press, 1966.

>   This book is largely concerned with describing Realism and Naturalism in nineteenth-century American fiction and the relationship of literary criticism to these movements; however, there are individual chapters on selected novels by Howells, Crane, and Norris.

74. Porte, Joel. THE ROMANCE IN AMERICA: STUDIES IN COOPER, POE, HAWTHORNE, MELVILLE, AND JAMES. Middletown, Conn.: Wesleyan University Press, 1969.

>   Argues that these five writers wrote according to "a theory of stylized art" which enabled each to explore the "large questions" of life.

75. Quinn, Arthur Hobson. AMERICAN FICTION: AN HISTORICAL AND CRITICAL SURVEY. New York: Appleton-Century-Crofts, 1936.

>   A study of both the novel and short story (excluding dime novels, detective stories, and juvenile fiction) through 1920.

76. Schneider, Robert W. FIVE NOVELISTS OF THE PROGRESSIVE ERA. New York and London: Columbia University Press, 1965.

>   "An analysis of the concepts of man held by representative novelists during the Progressive period" (1890-1917). Treats Howells, Crane, Norris, Dreiser, and Winston Churchill.

77. Shapiro, Charles, ed. TWELVE ORIGINAL ESSAYS ON GREAT AMERICAN NOVELS. Detroit: Wayne State University Press, 1958.

>   Essays by various hands on novels by Cooper, Hawthorne, Melville, Twain, Crane, James, and others.

78. Spiller, Robert E. THE CYCLE OF AMERICAN LITERATURE. New York: The Free Press; London: Collier-Macmillan, 1967.

>   See 6 for annotation.

79. Stegner, Wallace, ed. THE AMERICAN NOVEL FROM JAMES FENIMORE COOPER TO WILLIAM FAULKNER. New York and London: Basic Books, 1965.

>   Essays by various hands on novels by Cooper, Hawthorne, Melville, De Forest, James, Twain, Howells, Crane, Norris, and others.

80. Taylor, Gordon O. THE PASSAGES OF THOUGHT: PSYCHOLOGICAL REPRESENTATION IN THE AMERICAN NOVEL 1870-1900. New York: Oxford University Press, 1969.

>   Treats selected major works by James, Howells, Crane, Norris, and Dreiser.

81. Van Doren, Carl. THE AMERICAN NOVEL, 1789-1939. Rev. and enl. ed. New York: Macmillan, 1940.

    A comprehensive "record of the national imagination in the progress of native fiction."

82. Wagenknecht, Edward. CAVALCADE OF THE AMERICAN NOVEL. New York: Henry Holt and Co., 1952.

    A history of the American novel from Charles Brockden Brown to the novelists of the 1930's.

83. Walcutt, Charles Child. AMERICAN LITERARY NATURALISM, A DIVIDED STREAM. Minneapolis: University of Minnesota Press, 1956.

    Walcutt believes that naturalism is the child of Transcendentalism. At the end of the nineteenth century, the "mainstream of transcendentalism" divided, producing "two rivers of thought," one concerned with Spirit, the other with Nature. Both rivers flow through the naturalistic movement, and Walcutt's book explores the tension that results.

84. Wilson, Edmund. PATRIOTIC GORE: STUDIES IN THE LITERATURE OF THE AMERICAN CIVIL WAR. New York: Oxford University Press, 1962.

    An eminently readable study of some thirty authors who wrote about the Civil War (including Stowe, Tourgee, Cable, Chopin, Page, Bierce, and De Forest).

INDIVIDUAL AUTHORS

JAMES LANE ALLEN (1849-1925)

Principal Works

FLUTE AND VIOLIN, 1891   Stories
THE BLUE-GRASS REGION OF KENTUCKY, 1892   Sketches
A KENTUCKY CARDINAL, 1894   Novel
AFTERMATH, 1896   Novel (a continuation of A KENTUCKY CARDINAL)
SUMMER IN ARCADY, 1896   Novel
THE CHOIR INVISIBLE, 1897   Novel
THE REIGN OF LAW, 1900   Novel
THE METTLE OF THE PASTURE, 1903   Novel
THE BRIDE OF THE MISTLETOE, 1909   Novel
THE DOCTOR'S CHRISTMAS EVE, 1910   Novel
THE LAST CHRISTMAS TREE, 1914   Prose Poem
THE SWORD OF YOUTH, 1915   Novelette
THE ALABASTER BOX, 1923   Story
THE LANDMARK, 1925   Stories

Collected Works

85.   A KENTUCKY CARDINAL, AFTERMATH, AND OTHER SELECTED WORKS
BY JAMES LANE ALLEN. Ed. William K. Bottorff. New Haven, Conn.:
College and University Press, 1967.

Letters

86.   Clemens, Cyril. "An Unpublished Letter from James Lane Allen." AL,
9 (1937), 355-56.

> There is no separate edition of Allen's letters, although many
> of them are reproduced in Townsend's biography (see 90).

Bibliography

87.   See 89 and 92.

James Lane Allen

Checklist

88.   Bottorff, William K. "James Lane Allen (1849-1925)." ALR, 2 (1969), 121-24.

A brief overview of the current status of Allen scholarship; includes suggestions for further study.

Biography

89.   Knight, Grant C. JAMES LANE ALLEN AND THE GENTEEL TRADITION. Chapel Hill: University of North Carolina Press, 1935.

First full-length biography. Knight treats Allen as "the last champion of the genteel tradition" in American letters. Includes bibliography of works by and about Allen.

90.   Townsend, John Wilson. JAMES LANE ALLEN: A PERSONAL NOTE. Louisville, Ky.: Courier-Journal Job Printing Co., 1927.

A less than adequate biography which relies heavily on Allen's letters, reproduced here extensively.

Critical Studies

91.   Bottorff, William K. "Introduction" to A KENTUCKY CARDINAL, AFTERMATH, AND OTHER SELECTED WORKS BY JAMES LANE ALLEN. New Haven, Conn.: College and University Press, 1967.

A compact introduction. Allen, a romanticist in an age of realism, criticized Howells and his "satellites" in an essay printed here.

92.   _____. JAMES LANE ALLEN. New York: Twayne, 1964.

A thoroughgoing analysis of Allen's work based on the "archetypal" critical approach. Includes a useful "Selected Bibliography" of works by and about Allen which supplements Knight (see 89).

93.   Hancock, Albert E. "The Art of James Lane Allen." OUTLOOK, 74 (1903), 953-55.

Favorable review of THE METTLE OF THE PASTURE.

94.   Henneman, John Bell. "James Lane Allen: A Study." In SHAKESPEAREAN AND OTHER PAPERS. Sewanee, Tenn.: The University Press, 1911.

Best early treatment of Allen. Deals with autobiographical elements in his fiction.

95.   Marcosson, Isaac F. "The South in Fiction." THE BOOKMAN, 32 (1910), 360-70.

Similar to Maurice (see 96), although other authors are included in addition to Allen.

96. Maurice, A. B. "James Lane Allen's Country." THE BOOKMAN, 12 (1900), 154-62.

Includes pictures and descriptions of the actual scenes in which Allen's stories and novels are set.

97. Payne, Leonidas W., Jr. "The Stories of James Lane Allen." SR, 8 (1900), 45-55.

The author considers Allen's first book, FLUTE AND VIOLIN, his best.

98. Toulmin, Harry Aubrey, Jr. "James Lane Allen." In SOCIAL HISTORIANS. Boston, Mass.: R. G. Badger, 1911.

Deals primarily with Allen's skill as a local colorist.

EDWARD BELLAMY (1850-1898)

Principal Works

SIX TO ONE; A NANTUCKET IDYL, 1878   Travel
DR. HEIDENHOFF'S PROCESS, 1880   Novel
MISS LUDINGTON'S SISTER, 1884   Novel
LOOKING BACKWARD 2000-1887, 1888   Novel
EQUALITY, 1897   Novel (a sequel to LOOKING BACKWARD)
THE BLINDMAN'S WORLD AND OTHER STORIES, 1898
THE DUKE OF STOCKBRIDGE, 1900   Novel
TALKS ON NATIONALISM, 1938   Essays
THE RELIGION OF SOLIDARITY, 1940   Essay Fragment

Collected Works

99.   EDWARD BELLAMY: SELECTED WRITINGS ON RELIGION AND SOCI-
       ETY. Ed. Joseph Schiffman. New York: Liberal Arts Press, 1955.

Letters

100.   Schiffman, Joseph. "Mutual Indebtedness: Unpublished Letters of Edward
       Bellamy to William Dean Howells." HLB, 12 (1958), 363-74.

       First publication of thirteen letters from Bellamy to Howells.

Bibliography

101.   See 103 and 104.

Checklist

102.   Bowman, Sylvia. "Edward Bellamy (1850-1898)." ALR, 1 (1967), 7-12.

       Covers books and articles about Bellamy as well as reprints
       of his writings; includes suggestions for future studies.

Biography

103. Bowman, Sylvia. THE YEAR 2000: A CRITICAL BIOGRAPHY OF ED-
WARD BELLAMY   New York: Bookman Associates, 1958.

    A thoroughly-researched study of Bellamy's life and personal-
    ity. Includes bibliography.

104. Morgan, Arthur. EDWARD BELLAMY. New York: Columbia University
Press, 1944.

    First full-length biography; includes bibliography.

Critical Studies

105. Aaron, Daniel and Harry Levin. EDWARD BELLAMY, NOVELIST AND
REFORMER. Schenectady, N.Y.: Union College, 1968.

    This short pamphlet includes separate essays by Aaron and
    Levin; both are reconsiderations of Bellamy's Utopianism.

106. Becker, George J. "Edward Bellamy: Utopia, American Plan." AR,
14 (1954), 181–94.

    Identifies in LOOKING BACKWARD two main ideas (economic
    abundance and equality) and a corollary (that human nature
    changes with the material environment).

107. Blau, Joseph. "Bellamy's Religious Motivation for Social Reform: A
Review Article." RRel, 21 (1957), 156–66.

    From Schiffman's collection (see 99), it is evident that Bellamy
    exemplified the combination of two forms of romanticism, one
    religious, the other political.

108. Bleich, David. "Eros and Bellamy." AQ, 16 (1964), 445–59.

    A reading of LOOKING BACKWARD in terms of Freud and
    Marcuse.

109. Boggs, W. Arthur. "LOOKING BACKWARD at the Utopian Novel,
1888-1900." BNYPL, 64 (1960), 329–36.

    Discusses six types of Utopian fiction which originated with
    LOOKING BACKWARD; includes bibliography of fiction in-
    fluenced by Bellamy. See 114 and 120.

110. Bowman, Sylvia. "Bellamy's Missing Chapter." NEQ, 31 (1958), 47–
65.

    The missing chapter in EQUALITY probably contained radical
    ideas on sex and marriage.

111. Bowman, Sylvia E., ed. EDWARD BELLAMY ABROAD: AN AMERICAN
PROPHET'S INFLUENCE. New York: Twayne, 1962.

An impressive collection of essays and bibliographical material dealing with Bellamy's international influence.

112. Cooperman, Stanley. "Utopian Realism: The Futurist Novels of Bellamy and Howells." CE, 24 (1963), 464-67.

LOOKING BACKWARD and A TRAVELER FROM ALTRURIA are valuable as "cultural diagnosis" rather than "aesthetic experience."

113. Dudden, Arthur P. "Edward Bellamy: LOOKING BACKWARD, 2000-1887." In LANDMARKS OF AMERICAN WRITING, ed. Hennig Cohen. New York and London: Basic Books, 1969.

"Despite the radicalism of [the novel's advocacy of utopian society],. LOOKING BACKWARD reflects the underlying conservatism of American society and was constructed to reinforce its native values and traditions."

114. Forbes, A. B. "The Literary Quest for Utopia, 1880-1900." SF, 6 (1927), 179-89.

A useful article in that it places LOOKING BACKWARD in relation to the other Utopian writings of the era. Includes a bibliography of "American Utopias." See 109 and 120.

115. Franklin, John Hope. "Edward Bellamy and the Nationalist Movement." NEQ, 11 (1938), 739-72.

An interesting history of the Nationalist movement (of which LOOKING BACKWARD "may accurately be called the textbook") and Bellamy's relation to it.

116. Levi, Albert W. "Edward Bellamy: Utopian." ETHICS, 55 (1945), 131-44.

Analyzes LOOKING BACKWARD in order to show that Bellamy is an "American Radical," one who believes in progressive social change yet values national tradition.

117. McNair, E. E. EDWARD BELLAMY AND THE NATIONALIST MOVEMENT, 1889-1894. Milwaukee, Wis.: Fitzgerald, 1957.

A thoroughly documented but overwritten study of the Nationalist Movement and of Bellamy's work as a social reformer.

118. Madison, C. A. "Edward Bellamy, Social Dreamer." NEQ, 15 (1942), 444-66.

The facts of Bellamy's life argue against the assumption that (as Bellamy himself wrote) LOOKING BACKWARD began as " 'a mere literary fantasy.' "

119. Parrington, Vernon L. "Edward Bellamy and 'Looking Backward.' " In MAIN CURRENTS IN AMERICAN THOUGHT, vol. 3. New York: Harcourt, Brace, 1930.

Discusses LOOKING BACKWARD in context with EQUALITY and Bellamy's other works.

120. Parrington, Vernon L., Jr. "Bellamy and His Critics." In AMERICAN DREAMS: A STUDY OF AMERICAN UTOPIAS. Providence, R.I.: Brown University Press, 1947; New York: Russell & Russell, 1964.

A useful discussion of the various utopian novels that resulted from the publication of LOOKING BACKWARD. See 109 and 114.

121. Sadler, Elizabeth. "One Book's Influence: Edward Bellamy's LOOK-ING BACKWARD." NEQ, 17 (1944), 530-55.

A thorough if somewhat overwritten history of the rise and fall in influence of LOOKING BACKWARD, which was "greater than that of any American book of the last half century."

122. Sanford, Charles. "Classics of American Reform Literature." AQ, 10 (1958), 295-311.

Places Bellamy in relation to other American reform writers, including Thoreau, Hawthorne, Twain, Steffens, and Steinbeck.

123. Schiffman, Joseph. "Edward Bellamy's Altruistic Man." AQ, 6 (1954), 195-209.

A learned discussion of Bellamy's ideas concerning the " 'illimitable possibilities of human nature' " which ran counter to the prevailing Darwinian theories of the day.

124. _____. "Edward Bellamy's Religious Thought." PMLA, 68 (1953), 716-32.

Religion is "a major genetic factor in Edward Bellamy's social thought and in modern American intellectual history."

125. Shurter, Robert L. "The Literary Work of Edward Bellamy." AL, 5 (1933), 229-34.

Bellamy began as a strictly literary man and became a social reformer. LOOKING BACKWARD is his last literary accomplishment; his later work must be regarded as economics.

126. _____. "The Writing of LOOKING BACKWARD." SAQ, 38 (1939), 255-61.

A brief and general discussion of the novel in its social and biographical context.

127. Taylor, Walter Fuller. "Edward Bellamy." In THE ECONOMIC NOVEL IN AMERICA. Chapel Hill: University of North Carolina Press, 1942.

A thorough discussion of LOOKING BACKWARD.

AMBROSE BIERCE (1842-1914?)

Principal Works

THE FIEND'S DELIGHT, 1873   Sketches (published under the pseudonym
of Dod Grile)
NUGGETS AND DUST PANNED OUT IN CALIFORNIA, 1873   Sketches
(also by "Dod Grile")
COBWEBS FROM AN EMPTY SKULL, 1874   Sketches
THE DANCE OF DEATH, 1877   Satire (a collaboration with T. A. Harcourt
published under the joint pseudonym of William Herman)
TALES OF SOLDIERS AND CIVILIANS, 1891   Stories (reissued in 1892 as
IN THE MIDST OF LIFE)
THE MONK AND THE HANGMAN'S DAUGHTER, 1892   Translation of
the work by Richard Voss (with G. A. Danziger)
BLACK BEETLES IN AMBER, 1892   Poems
CAN SUCH THINGS BE?, 1893   Stories
FANTASTIC FABLES, 1899   Homilies
SHAPES OF CLAY, 1903   Poems
THE CYNIC'S WORD BOOK, 1906   Definitions (retitled THE DEVIL'S
DICTIONARY in 1911)
THE SHADOW ON THE DIAL, 1909   Essays
WRITE IT RIGHT, 1909   Essay

Collected Works

128. THE COLLECTED WORKS OF AMBROSE BIERCE. 12 vols. New York:
Neale Publishing Co., 1909-12.

129. THE COLLECTED WRITINGS OF AMBROSE BIERCE. Ed. Clifton Fadiman.
New York: The Citadel Press, 1946.

130. THE COMPLETE SHORT STORIES OF AMBROSE BIERCE. Ed. Ernest
Jerome Hopkins. Garden City, N.Y.: Doubleday, 1970.

Letters

131. LETTERS OF AMBROSE BIERCE. Ed. Bertha C. Pope. San Francisco:

The Book Club of California, 1922. Reprinted by the Gordian Press in 1967.

Includes a memoir by Bierce's protege, George Sterling.

132. TWENTY-ONE LETTERS OF AMBROSE BIERCE. Ed. Samuel Loveman. Cleveland, Ohio: George Kirk, 1922.

Bibliography

133. Gaer, Joseph. AMBROSE GWINETT [sic] BIERCE, BIBLIOGRAPHY AND BIOGRAPHICAL DATA. San Francisco: California Literary Research Monograph No. 4, State Emergency Relief Association, 1935; New York: Burt Franklin, 1968.

   A curious collection of primary and secondary bibliographical materials which includes brief critical estimates and a biographical sketch.

134. Grenander, M. E. "Ambrose Bierce, John Camden Hotten, THE FIEND'S DELIGHT and NUGGETS AND DUST." HLQ, 28 (1965), 353-71.

   A history of two books which Bierce published under the pseudonym of Dod Grile; replete with bibliographical detail.

135. Starrett, Vincent, ed. AMBROSE BIERCE: A BIBLIOGRAPHY. Philadelphia, Pa.: The Centaur Book Shop, 1929.

Checklist

136. Fatout, Paul. "Ambrose Bierce." ALR, 1 (1967), 13-19.

   Covers biographical as well as critical studies of Bierce.

137. Forfenberry, George E. "Ambrose Bierce (1842-1914?): A Critical Bibliography of Secondary Comment." ALR, 4 (1971), 11-56.

   Annotated. Concludes with a note suggesting some fresh approaches to Bierce.

Biography

138. De Castro, Adolphe. PORTRAIT OF AMBROSE BIERCE. New York: Century Co., 1929.

   Probably the least useful of four Bierce biographies published in 1929 (see 140, 141, and 142).

139. Fatout, Paul. AMBROSE BIERCE, THE DEVIL'S LEXICOGRAPHER. Norman: University of Oklahoma Press, 1951.

   A thoroughgoing biography marred by a clumsy style.

140. Grattan, Clinton Hartley. BITTER BIERCE. Garden City, N.Y.: Doubleday, 1929.

> An attempt at definitive biography. (Also contains sections on Bierce's "Literature" and "Ideas.")

141. McWilliams, Carey. AMBROSE BIERCE. New York: A. & C. Boni, 1929; Hamden, Conn.: Archon, 1967.

> Useful as a source book as well as a biography. The chapter on fiction is weak.

142. Neale, Walter J. LIFE OF AMBROSE BIERCE. New York: Walter Neale, 1929.

> A collection of reminiscences.

143. O'Connor, Richard. AMBROSE BIERCE: A BIOGRAPHY. Boston, Mass.: Little, Brown, 1967.

> Brisk and readable, though it adds little to previous accounts.

144. Starrett, Vincent. AMBROSE BIERCE. Chicago, Ill.: W. M. Hill, 1920.

> An early (and brief) appraisal of Bierce's life and work.

145. Sterling, George. "Introduction" to IN THE MIDST OF LIFE. New York: Modern Library, 1927.

> Largely biographical; emphasizes Bierce's misanthropy.

146. Wilt, Napier. "Ambrose Bierce and the Civil War." AL, 1 (1929), 260-85.

> "A complete [and] orderly account of Bierce's army life," intended to supplement the biographical volumes that had appeared earlier.

Critical Studies

Note: Aspects of Bierce's colorful life are often included in studies that would be strictly critical if they dealt with any other author; the annotations will help the reader distinguish between works that contain biographical material and those that deal solely with Bierce's writings.

147. Bahr, Howard W. "Ambrose Bierce and Realism." SoQ, 1 (1963), 309-31.

> Deals with the difficulties in assigning Bierce to any particular literary school.

148. Boynton, Percy H. "Ambrose Bierce." In MORE CONTEMPORARY AMERICANS. Chicago: University of Chicago Press, 1927.

A general study in which the author expresses puzzlement at
the general reader's neglect of Bierce.

149. Brooks, Van Wyck. "The Letters of Ambrose Bierce." In EMERSON
AND OTHERS. New York: E. P. Dutton, 1927.

Praises the letters for revealing Bierce's unique quality, his
"dry" but "whole-souled" enthusiasm.

150. Cooper, Frederick Taber. "Ambrose Bierce." In SOME AMERICAN
STORY TELLERS. New York: Holt, Rinehart & Winston, 1911; Freeport, N.Y.: Books for Libraries Press, 1968.

The author finds Bierce "entitled to hearty recognition as an
enduring figure in American letters" even though "his writings
have too much the flavor of the hospital and the morgue."

151. Fatout, Paul. AMBROSE BIERCE AND THE BLACK HILLS. Norman:
University of Oklahoma Press, 1956.

Deals with what has been hitherto "an obscure interval in
[Bierce's] life," the months in 1880 when he was an employee
of the Black Hills Placer Mining Company.

152. Goldstein, Jesse Sidney. "Edwin Markham, Ambrose Bierce, and THE
MAN WITH THE HOE." MLN, 58 (1943), 165-75.

A detailed account of Bierce's literary and personal relationship with his onetime disciple Markham.

153. Grenander, M. E. AMBROSE BIERCE. New York: Twayne, 1971.

Biographical and critical; concludes with suggestions for future
investigations'. Includes "Selected Bibliography" of works by
and about Bierce.

154. _____. "Bierce's Turn of the Screw: Tales of Ironical Terror." WHR,
11 (1957), 257-64.

Argues against the prevailing thesis that Bierce is an imitator
of Poe. See 158 and 164.

155. Harding, Ruth Guthrie. "Mr. Boythorn Bierce." THE BOOKMAN, 61
(1925), 636-43.

A refreshingly unorthodox and realistic appraisal which begins
by damning most of the early essays on Bierce.

156. Jordan-Smith, Paul. "Ambrose Bierce." In ON STRANGE ALTARS.
London: Brentano's, 1923.

Biographical and critical; the author considers Bierce "the
greatest writer of the short story this country has yet pro-
duced."

157. Klein, Marcus. "San Francisco and Her Hateful Ambrose Bierce." HudR,

7 (1954), 392-407.

A comprehensive attempt to place Bierce in relation to
the literary and cultural context of the day.

158. Miller, Arthur E. "The Influence of Edgar Allen Poe on Ambrose Bierce."
AL, 4 (1932), 130-50.

Argues that Bierce never questioned the literary method of Poe,
whose influence on him was "far-reaching." See 154 and 164.

159. Monaghan, Frank. "Ambrose Bierce and the Authorship of THE MONK
AND THE HANGMAN'S DAUGHTER." AL, 2 (1931), 337-49.

Despite the claims of both Bierce and his collaborator, their
version of Richard Voss's work is largely a literal translation
and not a substantial rewriting.

160. Nations, Leroy J. "Ambrose Bierce: The Gray Wolf of American Letters." SAQ, 25 (1926), 253-58.

Useful as an introduction to Bierce, though not characterized
by any particularly original insights.

161. Noel, Joseph. FOOTLOOSE IN ARCADIA. A PERSONAL RECORD OF
JACK LONDON, GEORGE STERLING, AND AMBROSE BIERCE. New
York: Carrick & Evans, 1940.

Noel is perhaps too worshipful, but his recollections are entertaining and useful as source materials.

162. Partridge, Eric. "Ambrose Bierce." LondM, 16 (1927), 625-38.

A rarity among the early appraisals of Bierce in that it deals
with specific works instead of rehashing the biographical data.

163. Smith, Edward H. "The Ambrose Bierce Irony." In MYSTERIES OF THE
MISSING. New York: Dial Press, 1927.

A rehearsal of the various accounts of Bierce's disappearance
together with critical remarks.

164. Snell, George. "Poe Redivivus." ArQ, 1 (1945), 49-57.

Bierce "fell far short of his predecessor's vision or eloquence."
See 154 and 158.

165. Walker, Franklin. AMBROSE BIERCE, THE WICKEDEST MAN IN SAN
FRANCISCO. San Francisco, Calif.: Colt Press, 1941.

A sketch of Bierce's journalistic experiences in San Francisco.

166. _____. "The Town Crier." In SAN FRANCISCO'S LITERARY FRON-
TIER. New York: Alfred A. Knopf, 1939.

A study of the milieu in which Bierce operated.

167. Wiggins, Robert A. AMBROSE BIERCE. Minneapolis: University of Minnesota Press, 1964.

A brief but adequate introduction to the life and works.

168. Wilson, Edmund. "Ambrose Bierce on the Owl Creek Bridge." In PATRIOTIC GORE: STUDIES IN THE LITERATURE OF THE AMERICAN CIVIL WAR. New York: Oxford University Press, 1962.

169. Woodruff, Stuart C. THE SHORT STORIES OF AMBROSE BIERCE. Pittsburgh, Pa.: University of Pittsburgh Press, 1964.

First full-length study of Bierce's fiction; close readings of a few representative stories.

HUGH HENRY BRACKENRIDGE (1748-1816)

Principal Works

A POEM, ON THE RISING GLORY OF AMERICA, 1772   (a collaboration
   with Philip Freneau)
A POEM ON DIVINE REVELATION, 1774
THE BATTLE OF BUNKERS-HILL, 1776   Drama
THE DEATH OF GENERAL MONTGOMERY, 1777   Drama
SIX POLITICAL DISCOURSES, 1778   Sermons
MODERN CHIVALRY, 1792-1805   Novel (the first extended description
   of backwoods life in American fiction)
INCIDENTS OF THE INSURRECTION IN THE WESTERN PARTS OF PENNSYL-
   VANIA, 1795   History
LAW MISCELLANIES, 1814   Essays

Collected Works

170.   A HUGH HENRY BRACKENRIDGE READER, 1770-1815. Ed. Daniel
       Marder. Pittsburgh, Pa.: University of Pittsburgh Press, 1970.

       Essays, journalism, excerpts from the longer works.

Bibliography

171.   Heartman, Charles F. A BIBLIOGRAPHY OF THE WRITINGS OF HUGH
       HENRY BRACKENRIDGE PRIOR TO 1825. New York: C. F. Heartman,
       1917; New York: Burt Franklin, 1968.

Biography

172.   Newlin, Claude M. THE LIFE AND WRITINGS OF HUGH HENRY
       BRACKENRIDGE. Princeton, N.J.: Princeton University Press, 1932.

       A just appraisal which quotes lavishly from the works of
       Brackenridge.

Critical Studies

173. Haviland, T. P. "The Miltonic Quality of Brackenridge's POEM ON DIVINE REVELATION." PMLA, 56 (1941), 588-92.

>   A careful reading of the poem reveals that the author's debt to Milton is "large."

174. Marder, Daniel. HUGH HENRY BRACKENRIDGE. New York: Twayne, 1967.

>   A biographical-critical study which deals with Brackenridge's place in American literary history, including his relation to "later literary modes such as local color and realism." Includes a useful "Selected Bibliography" of works by and about Brackenridge.

175. Martin, Wendy. "On the Road with the Philosopher and Profiteer: A Study of Hugh Henry Brackenridge's MODERN CHIVALRY." ECS, 4 (1971), 241-56.

>   "The problem of artistic self-definition in a society which denies the value of art" is seen in the efforts of Captain Farrago, the protagonist, "to survive the levelling influence of the mob and counteract the confused values of the new democracy."

176. Nance, William L. "Satiric Elements in Brackenridge's MODERN CHIV-ALRY." TSLL, 9 (1967), 381-89.

>   An attempt "not to conceal the artistic weaknesses of MOD-ERN CHIVALRY but to make more evident its artistic strengths," which consist largely of its elements of burlesque and irony.

177. Smeall, J. F. S. "The Evidence That Hugh Brackenridge Wrote 'The Cornwalliad.' " PMLA, 80 (1965), 542-48.

>   An argument that does not convince the reader so much as it overwhelms him with scholarly apparatus.

CHARLES BROCKDEN BROWN (1771-1810)

Brown is variously described as America's first professional author, first professional novelist, and first professional literary critic.

Principal Works

ALCUIN; A DIALOGUE, 1798   Treatise on the rights of women (a second
        part was published in 1815)
WIELAND, 1798   Novel
ARTHUR MERVYN, 1799   Novel (a second part was published in 1800)
ORMOND, 1799   Novel
EDGAR HUNTLY, 1799   Novel
CLARA HOWARD, 1801   Novel (published in England as PHILIP STANLEY)
JANE TALBOT, 1801   Novel
MEMOIRS OF CARWIN, THE BILOQUIST, 1815   (sequel to WIELAND;
        unfinished)

Collected Works

178.   THE NOVELS OF CHARLES BROCKDEN BROWN. 7 vols. Boston,
        Mass.: S. G. Goodrich, 1827.

179.   THE NOVELS OF CHARLES BROCKDEN BROWN. 6 vols. Philadelphia,
        Pa.: M. Polock, 1857.

180.   CHARLES BROCKDEN BROWN'S NOVELS. 6 vols. Philadelphia, Pa.:
        David McKay, 1887; Port Washington, N.Y.: Kennikat Press, 1963.

181.   THE RHAPSODIST AND OTHER UNCOLLECTED WRITING. Ed. Harry R.
        Warfel. New York: Scholars' Facsimiles and Reprints, 1943.

181a.   THE WORKS OF CHARLES BROCKDEN BROWN. Ed. Sidney J. Krause,
        et al. 8 vols. projected. Kent, Ohio: Kent State University Press,
        1969- .

        In progress.

Bibliography

182. Krause, Sidney J. "Charles Brockden Brown." CEAAN, 1 (1968), 13-14.

    Survey of available editions and manuscripts.

183. Krause, Sidney J. and Jane Nieset. "A Census of the Works of Charles Brockden Brown." THE SERIF, 3 (1966), 27-55.

Checklist

184. Hemenway, Robert E. and Dean H. Keller. "Charles Brockden Brown, America's First Important Novelist: A Checklist of Biography and Criticism." PBSA, 60 (1966), 349-62.

    Invaluable to any serious student of Brown.

Biography

185. Clark, David L. CHARLES BROCKDEN BROWN, PIONEER VOICE OF AMERICA. Durham, N.C.: Duke University Press, 1952.

    Chiefly useful in that it contains heretofore unpublished material.

186. Dunlap, William. THE LIFE OF CHARLES BROCKDEN BROWN. 2 vols. Philadelphia, Pa.: James P. Parke, 1815.

    First full-length biography; uncritical and therefore thoroughly typical of its day.

187. Hemenway, Robert. "Daniel Edward Kennedy's Manuscript Biography of Charles Brockden Brown." THE SERIF, 3 (1966), 16-18.

    Kennedy (1879-1960) intended to write the first definitive biography of Brown. In spite of defects, the 635,000-word manuscript that resulted from his research adds much to our knowledge of Brown.

188. Prescott, William Hickling. "Memoir of Charles Brockden Brown, the American Novelist." In BIOGRAPHICAL AND CRITICAL MISCELLANIES. Philadelphia, Pa.: J. B. Lippincott, 1865.

    Also appears in CHARLES BROCKDEN BROWN'S NOVELS (see 180).

189. Warfel, Harry R. CHARLES BROCKDEN BROWN, AMERICAN GOTHIC NOVELIST. Gainesville: University of Florida Press, 1949.

    The most reliable and readable of the three full-length biographies.

Critical Studies

190. Aldridge, A. O. "Charles Brockden Brown's Poem on Benjamin Franklin." AL, 38 (1966), 230-35.

   Brown's poem, which appears to be an elaborate compliment, is actually a cleverly disguised satire.

191. Bernard, Kenneth. "Charles Brockden Brown." In MINOR AMERICAN NOVELISTS, ed. Charles Alva Hoyt. Carbondale: Southern Illinois University Press, 1971.

   A brief introduction to Brown, the key to whom is "an awareness of the tension between utopianism and a puritan pessimism that infused his life and his work."

192. _____. "Charles Brockden Brown and the Sublime." THE PERSONALIST, 45 (1964), 235-49.

   His champions' opinions to the contrary, Brown's descriptions of the American scene are based largely on conventional eighteenth-century notions of the sublime and the picturesque.

193. Berthoff, W. B. "Adventures of the Young Man: An Approach to Charles Brockden Brown." AQ, 9 (1957), 421-34.

   EDGAR HUNTLY, STEPHEN CALVERT, and ARTHUR MERVYN are stories of initiation. (ARTHUR MERVYN is discussed in detail.)

194. _____. "Brockden Brown: The Politics of the Man of Letters." THE SERIF, 3 (1966), 3-11.

   Discusses Brown's "liberalism" in terms of the pre-nineteenth-century definition of that concept. See 200.

195. _____. " 'A Lesson on Concealment': Brockden Brown's Method in Fiction." PQ, 37 (1958), 45-57.

   Examines a Brown story in order to prove that even though his fiction "is forbiddingly bare of entertaining graces," nonetheless it succeeds as "a fiction of ideas."

196. Blake, Warren Barton. "Brockden Brown and the Novel." SR, 18 (1910), 431-43.

   Brown is a transitional figure between the early and modern novel.

197. Brancaccio, Patrick. "Studied Ambiguities: ARTHUR MERVYN and the Problem of the Unreliable Narrator." AL, 42 (1970), 18-27.

   A close study of the novel reveals that Brown was "far more interested and successful with the techniques of fiction than has been generally recognized."

198. Erskine, John. "Charles Brockden Brown." In LEADING AMERICAN
      NOVELISTS New York: Henry Holt and Co., 1910; Freeport, N.Y.:
      Books for Libraries Press, 1966.

      A general biographical and critical survey.

199. Haviland, Thomas P. "Preciosite [sic] Crosses the Atlantic." PMLA,
      59 (1944), 131–41.

      Deals with the influence of the French heroic romance on
      C. B. Brown and W. H. Brown.

200. Hintz, Howard W. "Charles Brockden Brown." In THE QUAKER IN-
      FLUENCE IN AMERICAN LITERATURE. New York: Fleming H. Revell,
      1940.

      The roots of Brown's liberalism "spring unmistakably from his
      Quaker backgrounds." See 194.

201. Justus, James H. "ARTHUR MERVYN, American." AL, 42 (1970), 304–14.

      It was the creation of a new kind of hero--the successful and
      moral American--that made Brown "a significant precursor to
      the great fiction writers who followed him."

202. Kimball, Arthur G. "Savages and Savagism: Brockden Brown's Dramatic
      Irony." SIR, 6 (1967), 214–25.

      In several works Brown protests against Enlightenment optimism
      and suggests that man is capable of "savagery" as well as
      good.

203. Levine, Paul. "The American Novel Begins." ASch, 35 (1965–66),
      134–48.

      A convincing attempt both to define the American novel and
      to establish Brown's importance as the first professional nov-
      elist.

204. Loshe, Lillie D. "The Gothic and the Revolutionary." In THE EARLY
      AMERICAN NOVEL. New York: Columbia University Press, 1907;
      New York: F. Ungar, 1958.

      A perceptive essay, largely historical in nature.

205. McDowell, Tremaine. "Scott on Cooper and Brockden Brown." MLN,
      45 (1930), 18–20.

      The English novelist admired Cooper but thought that Brown
      was too greatly influenced by " 'bad examples.' "

206. Manly, William M. "The Importance of Point of View in Brockden
      Brown's WIELAND." AL, 35 (1963), 311–21.

      This essay adds a new dimension to the criticism of WIELAND
      by seeing it as "a powerful psychological experience" and not
      merely "a mine of literary-cultural materials."

207. Marble, Annie Russell. "Charles Brockden Brown and Pioneers in Fiction." In HERALDS OF AMERICAN LITERATURE. Chicago, Ill.: University of Chicago Press, 1907.

A general biographical and critical essay.

208. Marchand, Ernest C. "The Literary Opinions of Charles Brockden Brown." SP, 31 (1934), 541-66.

An admirable and thorough study which recognizes Brown's shortcomings as a novelist and critic as well as his strengths.

209. Morris, Mabel. "Charles Brockden Brown and the American Indian." AL, 18 (1946), 244-47.

A study of EDGAR HUNTLY and other writings by Brown indicates that his attempt to portray the Indian was honest and sympathetic.

210. Prescott, F. C. "WIELAND and FRANKENSTEIN." AL, 2 (1930), 172-73.

Suggests that a passage from WIELAND may be the germ for FRANKENSTEIN.

211. Ridgely, J. V. "The Empty World of WIELAND." In INDIVIDUAL AND COMMUNITY: VARIATIONS ON A THEME IN AMERICAN FICTION, ed. Kenneth H. Baldwin and David K. Kirby. Durham, N.C.: Duke University Press, 1975.

The complications in WIELAND are attributable to the physical and psychic isolation of the main characters; only Clara and Pleyel are saved, and their salvation is made possible by their movement toward a larger social context.

212. Ringe, Donald A. CHARLES BROCKDEN BROWN. New York: Twayne, 1966.

The best critical work on Brown. Includes a useful "Selected Bibliography" of primary and secondary sources.

213. _____. "Charles Brockden Brown." In MAJOR WRITERS OF EARLY AMERICAN LITERATURE, ed. Everett Emerson. Madison: University of Wisconsin Press, 1972.

A study of Brown's major novels in terms of his use of three fictional forms: the sentimental romance, the Gothic tale, and the novel of purpose.

214. Schulz, Dieter. "EDGAR HUNTLY as Quest Romance." AL, 43 (1971), 323-35.

"There is no point in overlooking the numerous technical defects of the book. On the other hand, the structural unity of EDGAR HUNTLY appears to me greater than has usually been granted."

215. Sickles, Eleanor. "Shelley and Charles Brockden Brown." PMLA, 45
(1930), 1116-28.

> Argues that Brown influenced Shelley more than Solve be-
> lieves (see 217).

216. Snell, George. "Charles Brockden Brown." In THE SHAPERS OF AMER-
ICAN FICTION, 1798-1947. New York: E. P. Dutton, 1947; New
York: Cooper Square, 1961.

> Traces to Brown "an apocalyptic vision...which has been
> a preoccupation of the American imagination from WIELAND
> to ABSALOM, ABSALOM!"

217. Solve, Melvin T. "Shelley and the Novels of Brown." In FRED NEW-
TON SCOTT ANNIVERSARY PAPERS, ed. Clarence DeWitt Thorpe and
Charles E. Whitmore. Chicago, Ill.: University of Chicago Press, 1929.

> The author takes pains to prove that "it is impossible to say
> that [Shelley] was greatly indebted to the American novelist."
> See 215.

218. Tilton, Eleanor M. "The Sorrows of Charles Brockden Brown." PMLA,
69 (1954), 1304-8.

> A manuscript notebook which David Lee Clark and others
> assumed to contain sixteen actual letters from Brown to an
> unidentified paramour is really an "attempt to write an epis-
> tolary novel...in the manner of WERTHER."

219. Van Doren, Carl. "Minor Tales of Charles Brockden Brown, 1798-1800."
NATION, 100 (1915), 46-47.

> Identifies certain anonymous and pseudonymous writings as
> Brown's.

220. Vilas, Martin S. CHARLES BROCKDEN BROWN: A STUDY OF EARLY
AMERICAN FICTION. Burlington, Vt.: Free Press, 1904.

> First book to attempt a comprehensive treatment of Brown's
> fiction; far from definitive.

221. Warfel, Harry R. "Charles Brockden Brown's German Sources." MLQ,
1 (1940), 357-65.

> A persuasive attempt "to attenuate that claim of the English
> origin of Brown's fictional materials" by pointing out Brown's
> various German influences.

222. Ziff, Larzer. "A Reading of WIELAND." PMLA, 77 (1962), 51-57.

> WIELAND is an important novel because of the various "trans-
> formations" of attitude and viewpoint which take place.

WILLIAM HILL BROWN (1765-1793)

Principal Works

THE POWER OF SYMPATHY, 1789   Novel (usually considered the first
    American novel)
WEST POINT PRESERVED, 1797   Drama
IRA AND ISABELLA, 1807   Novel

Bibliography

223.   Ellis, Milton. "Bibliographical Note." In THE POWER OF SYMPATHY.
    New York: Columbia University Press, 1937.

> Deals with early editions of the novel and the mystery sur-
> rounding its authorship.

Critical Studies

224.   Byers, John R., Jr. "Further Verification of the Authorship of THE
    POWER OF SYMPATHY." AL, 43 (1971), 421-27.

> Letters and other documents (published here) substantiate
> Brown's authorship of the novel.

225.   Ellis, Milton. "The Author of the First American Novel." AL, 4
    (1933), 359-68.

> Evidence that Brown is the author of THE POWER OF SYM-
> PATHY.

226.   Haviland, Thomas P. See 199.

227.   McDowell, Tremaine. "The First American Novel." AmRev, 2 (1933),
    73-81.

> Deals with early attempts to suppress THE POWER OF SYM-
> PATHY.

228. Martin, Terence. "William Hill Brown's IRA AND ISABELLA." NEQ,
      32 (1959), 238-42.

      IRA AND ISABELLA is largely neglected, "yet in a surprising,
      adventitious, and clumsy way the novel addresses the problems
      of writing fiction in early America."

229. Pendleton, Emily and Milton Ellis. PHILENIA: THE LIFE AND WORKS
      OF MRS. SARAH WENTWORTH MORTON. Orono: University of Maine
      Studies, Second Series, No. 20, 1931. Pp. 38-39, 109-12.

      Until the presentation of the evidence discussed here, it was
      assumed that Mrs. Morton was the author of THE POWER OF
      SYMPATHY.

230. Walser, Richard. "More About the First American Novel." AL, 24
      (1952), 352-57.

      Two "peculiar dramatic pieces" shed light on THE POWER OF
      SYMPATHY: OCCURRENCES OF THE TIMES (which, according
      to Walser, was probably not by Brown) and THE BETTER SORT
      (which probably was).

GEORGE WASHINGTON CABLE (1844-1925)

Principal Works

OLD CREOLE DAYS, 1879	Stories	
THE GRANDISSIMES, 1880	Novel	
MADAME DELPHINE, 1881	Short Novel	
DR. SEVIER, 1885	Novel	
BONAVENTURE, 1888	Stories	
JOHN MARCH SOUTHERNER, 1894	Novel	
STRONG HEARTS, 1899	Stories	
THE CAVALIER, 1901	Novel	
BYLOW HILL, 1902	Novel	

Collected Works

231. THE WORKS OF GEORGE W. CABLE. Ed. Arlin Turner. New York: Garrett Press, 1970- .

    This edition, a reprint of the 1894 edition, is in progress.

232. THE NEGRO QUESTION: A SELECTION OF WRITINGS ON CIVIL RIGHTS IN THE SOUTH. Ed. Arlin Turner. Garden City, N.Y.: Doubleday, 1958.

    Essays from THE SILENT SOUTH (1889) and THE NEGRO QUESTION (1890) plus six essays published for the first time.

Letters

233. Butcher, Philip. "Cable to Boyesen on THE GRANDISSIMES." AL, 40 (1968), 391-94.

    A letter not included in 234.

234. Turner, Arlin. "A Novelist Discovers a Novelist: The Correspondence of H. H. Boyesen and George W. Cable." WHR, 5 (1951), 343-72.

    See 233.

235. _____. MARK TWAIN AND GEORGE W. CABLE: THE RECORD OF A LITERARY FRIENDSHIP. East Lansing: Michigan State University Press, 1960.

> Consists largely of the letters Cable wrote to his wife during the Twain–Cable reading tour of 1884–85. See 250.

236. See 240 and 250.

Bibliography

237. See 240, 241, and 243.

Checklist

238. Butcher, Philip. "George Washington Cable (1844-1925)." ALR, 1 (1967), 20-25.

> Lists and evaluates books about Cable and gives locations of books and memorabilia.

239. See 261.

Biography

240. Bikle, L. L. C. GEORGE W. CABLE: HIS LIFE AND LETTERS. New York: Charles Scribner's Sons, 1928.

> By Cable's daughter. Turner describes this book as "a volume of...letters connected by a thread of biography." Includes bibliography.

241. Butcher, Philip. GEORGE W. CABLE: THE NORTHAMPTON YEARS. New York: Columbia University Press, 1959.

> Primarily concerned with Cable as a social critic. Includes bibliography.

242. Ekstrom, Kjell. GEORGE WASHINGTON CABLE: A STUDY OF HIS EARLY LIFE AND WORK. Cambridge, Mass.: Harvard University Press, 1950.

> The critical sections are primarily concerned with Cable's treatment of the Creoles in his fiction.

243. Turner, Arlin. GEORGE W. CABLE: A BIOGRAPHY. Durham, N.C.: Duke University Press, 1956.

> The only thorough, scholarly biography of Cable. Includes bibliography.

Critical Studies

244. Arvin, Newton. "Introduction" to THE GRANDISSIMES. New York: Sagamore Press, 1957.

    Praises "the great qualities of THE GRANDISSIMES as a piece of social and historical realism."

245. Barrie, James M. "A Note on Mr. Cable's THE GRANDISSIMES." THE BOOKMAN, 7 (1898), 401-03.

    A highly subjective yet readable introduction to the novel.

246. Berthoff, Warner. "Bierce, Hearn, Cable, Kate Chopin." In THE FERMENT OF REALISM: AMERICAN LITERATURE, 1884-1919. New York: Free Press, 1965.

    Deals with Cable as a member of the New Orleans Renaissance of the 1870-90's and as a didactic writer.

247. Bowen, Edwin W. "George Washington Cable: An Appreciation." SAQ, 18 (1919), 145-55.

    A general and uncritical introduction.

248. Brooks, Van Wyck. "The South: Miss Murfree and Cable." In THE TIMES OF MELVILLE AND WHITMAN. New York: E. P. Dutton, 1947.

    A general essay on Cable's relations to the Creoles.

249. Butcher, Philip. GEORGE WASHINGTON CABLE. New York: Twayne, 1962.

    A study of "Cable's works set against the background of his life and times"; considers only the major literary work and not the essays on race, etc. Includes a useful "Selected Bibliography" of works by and about Cable.

250. Cardwell, Guy A. TWINS OF GENIUS. East Lansing: Michigan State College Press, 1953.

    A study of the Twain-Cable relationship. Includes letters. See 235.

251. Chase, Richard. "Cable's GRANDISSIMES." In THE AMERICAN NOVEL AND ITS TRADITION. Garden City, N.Y.: Doubleday, 1957.

    In THE GRANDISSIMES, Cable "transcended his usual limitations and wrote a minor masterpiece."

252. Coleman, Charles W., Jr. "The Recent Movement in Southern Literature." HARPER'S MAGAZINE, 74 (1887), 837-55.

    A contemporary attempt to establish a literary context for Cable's writings.

253. Cowie, Alexander. "George Washington Cable (1844-1925)." In THE RISE OF THE AMERICAN NOVEL. New York: American Book Co., 1951.

General commentary.

254. Dennis, Mary Cable. THE TAIL OF THE COMET. New York: E. P. Dutton, 1937.

A memoir by another of Cable's daughters; less useful than 240.

255. Eidson, John Olin. "George W. Cable's Philosophy of Progress." SWR, 21 (1936), 211-16.

Argues that Cable's philosophy of the New South "was the dominant influence upon his works."

256. Fulweiler, Howard W. "Of Time and the River: 'Ancestral Nonsense' vs. Inherited Guilt in Cable's 'Belles Demoiselles Plantation.'" MASJ, 7 (1966), 53-59.

Discusses the fusion of romantic theme and realistic technique in Cable's story.

257. Hearn, Lafcadio. "The Scenes of Cable's Romances." CENTURY MAGAZINE, 27 (1883), 40-7.

Evocative descriptions of locales where several of Cable's stories are set.

258. Johnson, Robert Underwood. "George Washington Cable." In COMMEMORATIVE TRIBUTES OF THE AMERICAN ACADEMY OF ARTS AND LETTERS, 1905-1941. Freeport, N.Y.: Books for Libraries Press, 1968.

A brief and impressionistic essay, notable for its statement that THE GRANDISSIMES "is not only the greatest American novel to date but...it stands in the front rank of the fiction of the world."

259. Martin, Jay. "George Washington Cable." In HARVESTS OF CHANGE: AMERICAN LITERATURE, 1865-1914. Englewood Cliffs, N.J.: Prentice-Hall, 1967.

Discusses mythic patterns in THE GRANDISSIMES.

260. Pattee, Fred Lewis. "The Era of Localized Romance." In THE DEVELOPMENT OF THE AMERICAN SHORT STORY. New York and London: Harper & Brothers, 1923.

Discusses Cable's several contributions to the development of the American short story.

261. Pugh, Griffith T. "George Washington Cable." MissQ, 20 (1967), 69-76.

A "re-evaluation" of Cable and a survey of Cable scholarship.

262. _____. GEORGE WASHINGTON CABLE: A BIOGRAPHICAL AND CRITICAL STUDY. Nashville, Tenn.: [private edition], 1947.

The critical sections give a balanced view of Cable's achievement as an artist.

263. _____. "George W. Cable as Historian." FLORIDA STATE UNIVERSITY STUDIES, 19 (1955), 29-38.

Examines Cable's historical writings as well as the relation of his concern with history to his fiction.

264. _____. "George W. Cable's Theory and Use of Folk Speech." SFQ, 24 (1960), 287-93.

Because of his greater fidelity to art than to nature, Cable felt that dialect should be " 'sketched rather than photographed.' "

265. Rubin, Louis D., Jr. "The Division of the Heart: Cable's THE GRANDISSIMES." SLJ, 1 (Spring 1969), 27-47.

The novel is "deeply flawed" because Cable was never able to reconcile the artistic impulse with that of the social critic. See 271.

266. _____. GEORGE W. CABLE: THE LIFE AND TIMES OF A SOUTHERN HERETIC. New York: Pegasus, 1969.

Concentrates on Cable and his works "in terms of their specific relationship to the Genteel Tradition in American literature and the long-range direction of Southern writing."

267. _____. "The Road to Yoknapatawpha: George W. Cable and JOHN MARCH, SOUTHERNER." In THE FARAWAY COUNTRY: WRITERS OF THE MODERN SOUTH. Seattle: University of Washington Press, 1963.

Despite critical opinion to the contrary, states Rubin, this novel is the most interesting and ambitious of Cable's works.

268. Stone, Edward. "Usher, Poquelin, and Miss Emily: The Progress of Southern Gothic." GaR, 14 (1960), 433-43.

Compares and contrasts three southern Gothic stories (including Cable's "Jean-ah Poquelin") to show how Faulkner goes beyond the conventional Gothic horror stories of Poe and Cable.

269. Tinker, Edward L. "Cable and the Creoles." AL, 5 (1934), 313-26.

An essay which is more factual, objective, and thoroughly researched than others similarly titled.

270. Turner, Arlin. GEORGE W. CABLE. Austin, Tex.: Steck-Vaughn, 1969.

A useful brief introduction. Includes a "Selected Bibliography."

271. _____. "George W. Cable, Novelist and Reformer." SAQ, 48 (1949), 539-45.

Counters the assertion that the reformer in Cable destroyed the artist; attempts "to relate the quality of his fiction to the varying intensity of his zeal for reform over a period of forty-five years." See 265.

272. _____. "Introduction" to CREOLES AND CAJUNS: STORIES OF OLD LOUISIANA BY GEORGE W. CABLE. Garden City, N.Y.: Doubleday, 1959; Gloucester, Mass.: Peter Smith, 1965.

A good introduction to Cable as a writer of short stories.

273. Wilson, Edmund. "Citizen of the Union." In THE SHORES OF LIGHT. New York: Farrar, Straus and Young, 1952.

A brief, insightful essay on Cable as "sociologist": though an admirer of Cable, Wilson finds little beauty in his writings.

274. _____. "Novelists of the Post-War South: Albion W. Tourgee, George W. Cable, Kate Chopin, Thomas Nelson Page." In PATRIOTIC GORE: STUDIES IN THE LITERATURE OF THE AMERICAN CIVIL WAR. New York: Oxford University Press, 1962.

An outline of Cable's career as well as evaluative comments on his works.

CHARLES W. CHESNUTT (1858-1932)

Chesnutt considered himself "the first man in the United States...to write serious fiction about the Negro."

Principal Works

THE CONJURE WOMAN, 1899	Stories	
FREDERICK DOUGLASS, 1899	Biography	
THE WIFE OF HIS YOUTH, 1899	Stories	
THE HOUSE BEHIND THE CEDARS, 1900	Novel	
THE MARROW OF TRADITION, 1901	Novel	
THE COLONEL'S DREAM, 1905	Novel	

Collected Works

275.   WORKS. New York: New York Public Library, 1969.

> Includes FREDERICK DOUGLASS, THE WIFE OF HIS YOUTH, THE CONJURE WOMAN, THE MARROW OF TRADITION, THE COLONEL'S DREAM, and essays by Chesnutt. Available on film.

Bibliography

276.   A LIST OF THE MANUSCRIPTS, PUBLISHED WORKS AND RELATED ITEMS IN THE CHARLES WADDELL CHESNUTT COLLECTION OF THE ERASTUS MILO CRAVATH MEMORIAL LIBRARY, FISK UNIVERSITY. Comps. Mildred Freeney and Mary T. Henry. Nashville, Tenn.: Fisk University Library, 1954.

Checklist

277.   Keller, Dean H. "Charles Waddell Chesnutt (1858-1932)." ALR, 1 (1968), 1-4.

A brief overview of the current status of Chesnutt scholarship; concludes with suggestions for further study.

278. See 33.

Biography

279. Chesnutt, Helen M. CHARLES WADDELL CHESNUTT: PIONEER OF THE COLOR LINE. Chapel Hill: University of North Carolina Press, 1952.

A sensitive appraisal of Chesnutt by his daughter; relies largely on his letters.

Critical Studies

280. Ames, Russell. "Social Realism in Charles W. Chesnutt." PHYLON, 14 (1953), 199-206.

Chesnutt's significance as a social commentator.

281. Baldwin, Richard E. "The Art of THE CONJURE WOMAN." AL, 43 (1971), 385-98.

Through subtleties of technique, Chesnutt solved in these stories "the major artistic problems faced by early black writers."

282. Chamberlain, John. "The Negro as Writer." THE BOOKMAN, 70 (1930), 603-11.

A general introduction to black American literature, beginning with Chesnutt.

283. Chesnutt, Charles W. "Post-Bellum--Pre-Harlem." THE COLOPHON, Part 5 (1931), [unnumbered].

A revealing commentary on his own works and the role of the Negro writer.

284. Farnsworth, Robert M. "Charles Chesnutt and the Color Line." In MINOR AMERICAN NOVELISTS, ed. Charles Alva Hoyt. Carbondale: Southern Illinois University Press, 1971.

"A contemporary review of [Chesnutt's] achievement."

285. _____. "Introduction" to THE MARROW OF TRADITION. Ann Arbor: University of Michigan Press, 1969.

A general discussion of the novel ("the most comprehensively realistic picture of the black man's dilemma in the South yet to be published in American fiction") and of Chesnutt's career as a whole.

286. Gartner, Carol B. "Charles W. Chesnutt: Novelist of a Cause." MarkR, 3 (1968), 5-12.

Deals with Chesnutt as a champion of Negro rights.

287. Gloster, Hugh M. "Charles W. Chesnutt." In NEGRO VOICES IN AMERICAN FICTION. Chapel Hill: University of North Carolina Press, 1948; New York: Russell & Russell, 1965.

An adequate general introduction to Chesnutt which places him within the context of black American literature.

288. Howells, William Dean. "A Psychological Counter-Current in Recent Fiction." NAR, 173 (1901), 881-83.

On THE MARROW OF TRADITION. Though it is "of the same strong material as his earlier books, it is less simple throughout, and therefore less excellent in manner."

289. _____. "Mr. Charles W. Chesnutt's Stories." ATLANTIC, 85 (1900), 699-701.

On THE CONJURE WOMAN and THE WIFE OF HIS YOUTH. Howells cites certain weaknesses but includes Chesnutt in "the good school."

290. Loggins, Vernon. In THE NEGRO AUTHOR. New York: Columbia University Press, 1931; Port Washington, N.Y.: Kennikat Press, 1964.

Comments on various works by Chesnutt.

291. Mason, Julian D., Jr. "Charles W. Chesnutt as Southern Author." MissQ, 20 (1967), 77-89.

Chesnutt is seldom treated as a Southern writer, an error which this essay seeks to correct.

292. Render, Sylvia Lyons. "Tar Heelia in Chesnutt." CLAJ, 9 (1965), 39-50.

Chesnutt's work was heavily influenced by dialects, settings, people, and events of North Carolina.

293. Smith, Robert A. "A Note on the Folktales of Charles W. Chesnutt." CLAJ, 5 (1962), 229-32.

A general commentary on Chesnutt's short stories.

294. Socken, June. "Charles Waddell Chesnutt and the Solution to the Race Problem." NALF, 3 (1969) 52-56.

Discusses Chesnutt's "dominant theme," miscegenation.

KATE CHOPIN (1851-1904)

Principal Works

AT FAULT, 1890   Novel
BAYOU FOLK, 1894   Stories
A NIGHT IN ACADIE, 1897   Stories
THE AWAKENING, 1899   Novel

Collected Works

295.   THE COMPLETE WORKS OF KATE CHOPIN. Ed. Per Seyersted. 2 vols. Baton Rouge: Louisiana State University Press, 1969.

Bibliography

296. See 300.

Checklist

297.   Potter, Richard H. "Kate Chopin and Her Critics: An Annotated Checklist." MHSB, 26 (1970), 306-17.

Covers 125 books, articles, theses, dissertations.

298.   Seyersted, Per. "Kate Chopin (1851-1904)." ALR, 3 (1970), 151-59.

A brief overview of the current status of Chopin scholarship; includes suggestions for further study.

Biography

299.   Rankin, Daniel S. KATE CHOPIN AND HER CREOLE STORIES. Philadelphia: University of Pennsylvania Press, 1932.

The only full-scale treatment prior to Seyersted. Divided into two parts: "Kate Chopin" and "Short Stories" (the latter concentrates on regional aspects of her writing).

300. Seyersted, Per. KATE CHOPIN: A CRITICAL BIOGRAPHY. Baton Rouge: Louisiana State University Press, 1969.

The only thorough examination of her life and works. Unlike other appraisals which approach Chopin solely as a regionalist, this one discusses her significance as a literary realist. Includes bibliography.

Critical Studies

301. Arms, George. "Kate Chopin's THE AWAKENING in the Perspective of Her Literary Career." In ESSAYS ON AMERICAN LITERATURE IN HONOR OF JAY B. HUBBELL, ed. Clarence Gohdes. Durham, N.C.: Duke University Press, 1967.

A comprehensive if not particularly penetrating survey of Chopin's work (except AT FAULT).

302. Arnavon, Cyrille. "Introduction" to Chopin's EDNA. Paris: Club du Bibliophile de France, 1953.

This valuable discussion of THE AWAKENING (issued as EDNA in France) is at least partly responsible for the recent revival of interest in Chopin.

303. Arner, Robert D. "Kate Chopin's Realism: 'At the 'Cadian Ball' and 'The Storm.' " MarkR, 2 (1970), 1-4.

Chopin's development from "local color sentimentalism" toward "genuine realism" may be seen by comparing the earlier story to its sequel.

304. Berthoff, Warner. "Bierce, Hearn, Cable, Kate Chopin." In THE FERMENT OF REALISM: AMERICAN LITERATURE 1884-1919. New York: Free Press, 1965.

A brief discussion of THE AWAKENING.

305. Eble, Kenneth. "A Forgotten Novel: Kate Chopin's THE AWAKENING." WHR, 10 (1956), 261-69.

A rescue operation; unlike other such essays, however, this one is scholarly and objective.

306. Leary, Lewis. "Introduction" to THE AWAKENING AND OTHER STORIES. New York: Holt, Rinehart and Winston, 1970.

A good introduction to Chopin and her work; useful comments on imagery in THE AWAKENING.

307. _____. "Kate Chopin's Other Novel." SLJ, 1 (December 1968), 60-74.

Examines AT FAULT as an artistic experiment.

308. May, John R. "Local Color in THE AWAKENING." SoR, 6 (1970), 1031-40.

Analyzes "the integral relationship between local color in the novel and the development of its theme as well as...Chopin's use of related symbolism."

309. Pattee, Fred Lewis. In THE DEVELOPMENT OF THE AMERICAN SHORT STORY. New York and London: Harper & Brothers, 1923.

In light of recent reappraisals of Chopin, Pattee's remarks must be seen as something of an undervaluation.

310. Quinn, Arthur Hobson. In AMERICAN FICTION: AN HISTORICAL AND CRITICAL SURVEY. New York: Appleton-Century-Crofts, 1936.

THE AWAKENING "belongs rather among studies of morbid psychology than local color."

311. Reilly, Joseph J. "Stories by Kate Chopin." COMMONWEAL, 25 (1937), 606-07.

Chopin is "incomparably the greatest American short story writer of her sex."

312. Spangler, George. "Kate Chopin's THE AWAKENING: A Partial Dissent." NOVEL, 3 (1970), 249-55.

"This essay would call in question the conclusion of THE AWAKENING, a conclusion which undercuts the otherwise superb characterization of the protagonist and thus prevents a very good novel from being the masterpiece its discoverers claim that it is."

313. Wilson, Edmund. "Novelists of the Post-War South: Albion W. Tourgee, George W. Cable, Kate Chopin, Thomas Nelson Page." In PATRIOTIC GORE: STUDIES IN THE LITERATURE OF THE AMERICAN CIVIL WAR. New York: Oxford University Press, 1962.

A brief commentary, chiefly devoted to Chopin's fiction.

314. Ziff, Larzer. "An Abyss of Inequality: Sarah Orne Jewett, Mary Wilkins Freeman, Kate Chopin." In THE AMERICAN 1890s: LIFE AND TIMES OF A LOST GENERATION. New York: Viking, 1966.

A general introduction to Chopin; concentrates on THE AWAKENING.

315. Zlotnick, Joan. "A Woman's Will: Kate Chopin on Selfhood, Wifehood, and Motherhood." MarkR, 1 (1968), 1-5.

An analysis of the ways in which Chopin questions traditional female roles.

SAMUEL L. CLEMENS (1835-1910)

Although the pseudonym "Mark Twain" is generally preferred in writings about the author and his works, "Samuel Clemens" is used more widely in bibliographies, catalogs, and reference books.

Principal Works

THE CELEBRATED JUMPING FROG OF CALAVERAS COUNTY, AND OTHER SKETCHES, 1867
THE INNOCENTS ABROAD, 1869   Travel Narrative
ROUGHING IT, 1872   Travel Narrative
THE GILDED AGE, 1873   Novel (with Charles Dudley Warner)
THE ADVENTURES OF TOM SAWYER, 1876   Novel
A TRAMP ABROAD, 1880   Travel Narrative
THE PRINCE AND THE PAUPER, 1882   Novel
THE STOLEN WHITE ELEPHANT, 1882   Sketches
LIFE ON THE MISSISSIPPI, 1883   Autobiographical Narrative
THE ADVENTURES OF HUCKLEBERRY FINN, 1885   Novel
A CONNECTICUT YANKEE IN KING ARTHUR'S COURT, 1889   Novel
THE AMERICAN CLAIMANT, 1892   Stories
THE £1,000,000 BANK-NOTE, 1893   Stories
TOM SAWYER ABROAD, 1894   Novel
THE TRAGEDY OF PUDD'NHEAD WILSON, 1894   Novel
PERSONAL RECOLLECTIONS OF JOAN OF ARC, 1896   Fictional Biography
TOM SAWYER ABROAD. TOM SAWYER, DETECTIVE AND OTHER STORIES, 1896
FOLLOWING THE EQUATOR, 1897   Travel Narrative
THE MAN THAT CORRUPTED HADLEYBURG AND OTHER STORIES AND ESSAYS, 1900
A DOUBLE BARRELLED DETECTIVE STORY, 1902   Novel
WHAT IS MAN?, 1906   Essay
THE $30,000 BEQUEST, 1906   Stories
EVE'S DIARY, 1906   Fictional Diary
CHRISTIAN SCIENCE, 1907   Essay
IS SHAKESPEARE DEAD?, 1909   Essay
EXTRACT FROM CAPTAIN STORMFIELD'S VISIT TO HEAVEN, 1909   Novel
THE MYSTERIOUS STRANGER, 1916   Novel

Collected Works

316. THE WRITINGS OF MARK TWAIN. Ed. A. B. Paine. 37 vols. New York: Harper & Brothers, 1922-25.

316a. MARK TWAIN PAPERS. Ed. Frederick Anderson et al. 14 vols. projected. Berkeley: University of California Press, 1967- .

In progress.

316b. IOWA-CALIFORNIA EDITION OF THE WORKS OF MARK TWAIN. Ed. John C. Gerber et al. 24 vols. projected. Berkeley: University of California Press, 1969- .

In progress.

316c. There are numerous collections of Twain's ephemerae; see 336 for a partial listing.

Letters

These four are the most important collections of Twain's letters, although there are numerous others; see 336 for a partial listing.

317. THE LOVE LETTERS OF MARK TWAIN. Ed. Dixon Wecter. New York: Harper and Brothers, 1949.

318. MARK TWAIN-HOWELLS LETTERS...1872-1910. Ed. Henry Nash Smith and William M. Gibson. 2 vols. Cambridge, Mass.: Harvard University Press, 1960.

319. MARK TWAIN'S LETTERS. Ed. A. B. Paine. 2 vols. New York: Harper & Brothers, 1917.

320. TWINS OF GENIUS. Ed. Guy A. Cardwell. East Lansing: Michigan State College Press, 1953.

Twain's correspondence with G. W. Cable.

Bibliography

321. Johnson, Merle. A BIBLIOGRAPHY OF THE WORKS OF MARK TWAIN. Rev. ed. New York: Harper & Brothers, 1935.

Checklist

322. Asselineau, Roger. THE LITERARY REPUTATION OF MARK TWAIN FROM 1910-1950. Paris: Didier, 1954.

Consists of two parts: an essay describing "the evolution of Mark Twain criticism in the United States since [his] death" and an annotated bibliography of Twain criticism in the United States and abroad.

323. Beebe, Maurice and John Feaster. "Criticism of Mark Twain: A Selected Checklist." MFS, 14 (1968), 93-139.

Like all the MFS checklists, this one is useful because it includes not only general studies but also specific discussions of Twain's individual writings (listed under the titles of the works themselves).

324. Branch, Edgar M. "Mark Twain Scholarship: Two Decades." In THE ADVENTURES OF HUCKLEBERRY FINN, ed. James K. Bowen and Richard VanDerBeets. Glenview, Ill.: Scott, Foresman, 1970.

325. Long, E. Hudson. MARK TWAIN HANDBOOK. New York: Hendricks House, 1957.

Summarizes and evaluates contributions to scholarship in various areas of Twain studies (biography, background studies, works, etc.).

326. See 399.

Journals

327. MARK TWAIN JOURNAL. 1936- .

Published 1936-1954 as MARK TWAIN QUARTERLY. Current address: Kirkwood, Mo. 63122.

328. THE TWAINIAN. 1939-41; new series, 1942- .

Published bimonthly by the Mark Twain Research Foundation, Perry, Mo. 63462.

Biography

There are numerous other biographical and semibiographical volumes on Clemens; see 336 for a partial listing. Several of these are included under "Critical Studies," below, not because of their biographical· value but for the critical insights they provide.

329. THE AUTOBIOGRAPHY OF MARK TWAIN. Ed. Charles Nieder. New York: Harper & Brothers, 1959.

Rearranged by Nieder so that the sections are organized chronologically. While more useful than the Paine edition (see 332), the result is still less than the ideal autobiography.

330. Ferguson, DeLancey. MARK TWAIN: MAN AND LEGEND. Indianapolis, Ind.: Bobbs-Merrill, 1943.

The best complete biography to date, though far from definitive.

331. Kaplan, Justin. MR. CLEMENS AND MARK TWAIN, A BIOGRAPHY. New York: Simon & Schuster, 1966.

Superior to Paine (see 332) in its treatment of the later years.

332. Paine, A. B. MARK TWAIN: A BIOGRAPHY. 3 vols. New York: Harper & Brothers, 1912.

Twain's autobiographical recollections, dictated and recorded nonsequentially. See 329.

333. Wecter, Dixon. SAM CLEMENS OF HANNIBAL. Ed. Elizabeth Wecter. Boston, Mass.: Houghton Mifflin, 1952.

Fullest account of Clemens's early life.

Critical Studies

Note: A number of the following essays originally appeared in periodicals and are reprinted in the various collections; several appear in more than one collection and, rather than allow the references to proliferate, only the original appearance is noted in each case.

334. Adams, Richard P. "The Unity and Coherence of HUCKLEBERRY FINN." TSE, 6 (1956), 87-103.

Following a useful summary of the major interpretations of the novel, Adams examines its "thematic, structural, and symbolic workings" to demonstrate "a remarkably high degree consistency, coherence, and unity."

335. Baetzhold, Howard G. MARK TWAIN AND JOHN BULL: THE BRITISH CONNECTION. Bloomington: Indiana University Press, 1970.

Discusses English influences on Twain's work.

336. Baldanza, Frank. MARK TWAIN: AN INTRODUCTION AND INTERPRETATION. New York: Holt, Rinehart and Winston, 1961.

A useful introduction for the nonspecialist. Includes bibliography.

337. Bellamy, Gladys Carmen. MARK TWAIN AS A LITERARY ARTIST. Norman: University of Oklahoma Press, 1950.

Considered one of the best general books on Twain.

338. Blair, Walter. MARK TWAIN AND HUCK FINN. Berkeley and Los Angeles: University of California Press, 1960.

A full account of the genesis of HUCKLEBERRY FINN; one of the best books on Twain.

339. Branch, Edgar M. THE LITERARY APPRENTICESHIP OF MARK TWAIN. Urbana: University of Illinois Press, 1950.

A study of Twain's writings to 1867 with an appended essay on HUCKLEBERRY FINN.

340. Brashear, Minnie. MARK TWAIN, SON OF MISSOURI. Chapel Hill: University of North Carolina Press, 1934.

Superseded by 333 in many ways, this book still provides certain insights, e.g., in the chapter on Twain's readings.

341. Brooks, Van Wyck. THE ORDEAL OF MARK TWAIN. Rev. ed. New York: E. P. Dutton, 1933.

A psychological study with numerous defects which was nonetheless important enough to trigger a debate which continues, to some extent, to the present day. See 351 and 366.

342. Budd, Louis J. MARK TWAIN: SOCIAL PHILOSOPHER. Bloomington: Indiana University Press, 1962.

Traces the development of Twain's social and political thinking, including his economic conservatism and his racial attitudes (which ameliorated over the years).

343. Canby, Henry Seidel. TURN WEST, TURN EAST. Boston, Mass.: Houghton Mifflin, 1951.

A useful study which, while adding no new material, discusses the differences and (more importantly) the similarities between Twain and Henry James.

344. Cardwell, Guy A., ed. DISCUSSIONS OF MARK TWAIN. Boston, Mass.: D. C. Heath, 1963.

Eighteen essays by authors from Harte and Howells to the present.

345. Colwell, James L. "Huckleberries and Humans: On the Naming of Huckleberry Finn." PMLA, 86 (1971), 70-76.

A delightful piece of scholarship which thoroughly explores "the significance of...a famous and unusual name."

346. Covici, Pascal, Jr. MARK TWAIN'S HUMOR, THE IMAGE OF A WORLD. Dallas, Tex.: Southern Methodist University Press, 1962.

Twain's use of various comic devices in HUCKLEBERRY FINN, "The Man Who Corrupted Hadleyburg," and THE MYSTERIOUS STRANGER.

347. Cox, James M. MARK TWAIN: THE FATE OF HUMOR. Princeton, N.J.: Princeton University Press, 1966.

A valuable discussion of humor in Twain and other matters.

348. _____. "Remarks on the Sad Initiation of Huckleberry Finn." SR, 62 (1954), 389–405.

> A perceptive essay which compares and contrasts the characters of Tom and Huck and refers to the ending of HUCKLEBERRY FINN as "a stylistic rather than a structural flaw, a failure in taste rather than in conception."

349. Cummings, Sherwood. "Science and Mark Twain's Theory of Fiction." PQ, 37 (1958), 26–33.

> Documents Twain's familiarity with the theories of Darwin and Taine.

350. De Voto, Bernard. MARK TWAIN AT WORK. Cambridge, Mass.: Harvard University Press, 1942.

> Perceptive analysis of the composition of TOM SAWYER, HUCKLEBERRY FINN, and THE MYSTERIOUS STRANGER. Includes hitherto unpublished MSS. See 356.

351. _____. MARK TWAIN'S AMERICA. Boston, Mass.: Little, Brown, 1932.

> A rebuttal of Brooks's argument and a discussion of the effect of the frontier on Twain's writing. See 341 and 366.

352. Eliot, T. S. "Introduction" to THE ADVENTURES OF HUCKLEBERRY FINN. New York: Chanticleer Press, 1950.

> Along with Trilling's, one of the first essays to defend the ending of the novel. See 374 and 395.

353. Fiedler, Leslie. "Come Back to the Raft Ag'in Huck Honey!" In AN END TO INNOCENCE. Boston, Mass.: Beacon Press, 1955.

> A provocative essay on homoerotic possibilities in HUCKLE-BERRY FINN and other American novels.

354. Gerber, John C., comp. THE MERRILL STUDIES IN HUCKLEBERRY FINN. Columbus, Ohio: Charles E. Merrill, 1971.

> Contemporary reviews as well as more recent critical opinion.

355. _____. "The Relations Between Point of View and Style in the Works of Mark Twain." In STYLE IN PROSE FICTION: ENGLISH INSTITUTE ESSAYS, ed. H. C. Martin. New York: Columbia University Press, 1959.

> An extremely useful analysis of the effect of point of view on Twain's style as studied in seven major works.

356. Gibson, William. "Introduction" to MARK TWAIN'S MYSTERIOUS STRANGER MANUSCRIPTS. Berkeley: University of California Press, 1969.

> The standard version of THE MYSTERIOUS STRANGER (on

which De Voto wrote; see 350) is proved to be a hybrid of
two different versions put together by Twain's editors.

357. Goold, Edgar H., Jr. "Mark Twain on the Writing of Fiction." AL,
26 (1954), 141-53

Develops a Twainian theory of realistic fiction out of notebook references, letters, etc.

358. Gullason, Thomas A. "The 'Fatal' Ending of HUCKLEBERRY FINN."
AL, 29 (1957), 86-91.

Twain's "primary objective" [sic] in the final chapters of the
novel is to ridicule "the romantic tradition as exemplified by
Tom Sawyer" and "win final sympathy for the realistic tradition and its hero, Huck."

359. Hemminghaus, Edgar H. MARK TWAIN IN GERMANY. New York:
Columbia University Press, 1939.

Seeks to trace "the development of German interest in the
works of Mark Twain from 1874 to the present."

360. Hill, Hamlin L. "The Composition and the Structure of TOM SAWYER."
AL, 32 (1961), 379-92.

A more exacting study than De Voto's (see 350); corroborates
the assertion that the novel is carefully structured.

361. Hoffman, Daniel G. FORM AND FABLE IN AMERICAN FICTION.
New York: Oxford University Press, 1961.

Devotes two chapters to the concept of Huckleberry Finn as
metamorphic folk hero.

362. Jones, Alexander E. "Mark Twain and Sexuality." PMLA, 71 (1956),
595-616.

A well-documented psychoanalytic study of sex and guilt in
Twain's writings.

363. Kaplan, Justin, ed. MARK TWAIN: A PROFILE. New York: Hill
and Wang, 1967.

Essays by various hands.

364. Krause, Sidney J. MARK TWAIN AS CRITIC. Baltimore, Md.: Johns
Hopkins University Press, 1967.

Examines the different masks that Twain used in his role as
literary critic.

365. Lane, Lauriat, Jr. "Why HUCKLEBERRY FINN is a Great World Novel."
CE, 17 (1955), 1-5.

Praises and evaluates the novel largely in terms of its affinities with other literary genres (epic poem, allegory). See 376.

366. Leary, Lewis, ed. A CASEBOOK ON MARK TWAIN'S WOUND. New York: Thomas Y. Crowell, 1962.

Focuses on the Brooks-De Voto debate; reprints sections of 341 and 351 as well as other essays which argue the degree to which Twain's genius may or may not have been hampered by environment and other factors.

367. _____. MARK TWAIN. Minneapolis: University of Minnesota Press, 1960.

A useful short introduction.

368. _____. SOUTHERN EXCURSIONS: ESSAYS ON MARK TWAIN AND OTHERS. Baton Rouge: Louisiana State University Press, 1971.

Five important essays on Twain, two on Kate Chopin, and others (all previously published).

369. Lynn, Kenneth S. MARK TWAIN AND SOUTHWESTERN HUMOR. Boston, Mass.: Little, Brown, 1960.

Places Twain in relation to the southern and southwestern humorists who preceded him.

370. MacDonald, Dwight. "Mark Twain." In AGAINST THE AMERICAN GRAIN: ESSAYS ON THE EFFECTS OF MASS CULTURE. New York: Random House, 1962.

Comments on the bulk of Twain's work and his "peculiar inability to speak in his own voice."

371. MARK TWAIN ISSUE. AQ, 16 (1964).

Notes and articles by various hands.

372. MARK TWAIN ISSUE. MFS, 14 (1968).

Essays by various hands plus the most useful checklist of secondary comment (see 323).

373. Marks, Barry A., ed. MARK TWAIN'S HUCKLEBERRY FINN. Boston, Mass.: D. C. Heath, 1959.

A useful collection which gathers together much of the best criticism of the novel, including essays by Trilling, Marx, Cox, Adams, Lane, and others.

374. Marx, Leo. "Mr. Eliot, Mr. Trilling, and HUCKLEBERRY FINN." ASch, 22 (1953), 423-40.

Refutes the two critics' contention that the ending of HUCKLEBERRY FINN is more or less satisfactory (see 352 and 395).

375. Moore, Olin Harris. "Mark Twain and Don Quixote." PMLA, 37 (1922), 324-46.

This article reminds the reader that our "most American" author was highly influenced by Cervantes and other Europeans.

376. O'Connor, William Van. "Why HUCKLEBERRY FINN Is Not the Great American Novel." CE, 17 (1955), 6-10.

Criticizes the novel because of Huck's limited usefulness as a symbol. Between this essay and Lane's (see 365), most of the major virtues and shortcomings of the novel are covered.

377. Regan, Robert. UNPROMISING HEROES: MARK TWAIN AND HIS CHARACTERS. Berkeley and Los Angeles: University of California Press, 1966.

Concerned with the effect on Twain's writing of a body of folktales that center on the Unpromising Hero.

378. Rogers, Franklin P. MARK TWAIN'S BURLESQUE PATTERNS AS SEEN IN THE NOVELS AND NARRATIVES, 1855-1885. Dallas, Tex.: Southern Methodist University Press, 1960.

Twain's major works take the form of a "narrative-plank" (to use his term) with equally spaced holes into which comic and serious plugs can be put. (The evidence for this thesis is sometimes sketchy.)

379. Rubin, Louis D., Jr. " 'The Begum of Bengal': Mark Twain and the South." In INDIVIDUAL AND COMMUNITY: VARIATIONS ON A THEME IN AMERICAN FICTION, ed. Kenneth H. Baldwin and David K. Kirby. Durham, N.C.: Duke University Press, 1975.

Twain's art is rooted in his ambivalent attitudes toward the South; he felt attracted to and yet separate from its ideals and way of life. See 397.

380. _____. "Mark Twain: THE ADVENTURES OF TOM SAWYER." In LANDMARKS OF AMERICAN WRITING, ed. Hennig Cohen. New York: Basic Books, 1969.

A readable essay which approaches the novel largely as a story about the passage of time.

381. Salomon, Roger B. MARK TWAIN AND THE IMAGE OF HISTORY. New Haven, Conn.: Yale University Press, 1961.

Traces the changes that Twain's ideas about history underwent and the effects of those ideas on his fiction.

382. Scott, Arthur L. MARK TWAIN AT LARGE. Chicago, Ill.: Henry Regnery, 1969.

Deals with Twain's travels and his opinions of other countries.

383. _____, ed. MARK TWAIN, SELECTED CRITICISM. Rev. ed. Dallas,

Tex.: Southern Methodist University Press, 1967.

Of the various collections this one features the best selection of early criticism; in all, it includes thirty-four separate items.

384. Seelye, John. THE TRUE ADVENTURES OF HUCKLEBERRY FINN. Evanston, Ill.: Northwestern University Press, 1970.

A rewriting intended to satisfy all critical objections. In this version, Huck smokes hemp and masturbates, Jim drowns, and Tom hardly appears at all.

385. Shrell, Darwin H. "Twain's Owl and His Bluejays." In ESSAYS IN HONOR OF ESMOND LINWORTH MARILLA, ed. Thomas A. Kirby and William J. Olive. Baton Rouge: Louisiana State University Press, 1971.

"Baker's Bluejay Yarn" depicts a "confrontation of two different sets of literary values."

386. Simpson, Claude M., ed. TWENTIETH CENTURY INTERPRETATIONS OF THE ADVENTURES OF HUCKLEBERRY FINN. Englewood Cliffs, N.J.: Prentice-Hall, 1968.

Essays by various hands.

387. Smith, Henry Nash. "Introduction" to THE ADVENTURES OF HUCKLEBERRY FINN. Boston, Mass.: Houghton Mifflin, 1958.

One of the best essays on the novel; particularly valuable for its comments on structure.

388. _____, ed. MARK TWAIN; A COLLECTION OF CRITICAL ESSAYS. Englewood Cliffs, N.J.: Prentice-Hall, 1963.

Twelve essays (most of which appeared after 1950) by various hands.

389. _____. MARK TWAIN, THE DEVELOPMENT OF A WRITER. Cambridge, Mass.: Harvard University Press, 1962.

A major study of Twain's craftsmanship and its development through the writing of nine major works.

390. Spengemann, William C. MARK TWAIN AND THE BACKWOODS ANGEL: THE MATTER OF INNOCENCE IN THE WORKS OF SAMUEL L. CLEMENS. Kent, Ohio: Kent State University Press, 1966.

Twain's major writings document his equivocal attitudes toward innocence.

391. Stone, Albert E., Jr. THE INNOCENT EYE, CHILDHOOD IN MARK TWAIN'S IMAGINATION. New Haven, Conn.: Yale University Press, 1961.

Analyzes Twain's use of the theme of childhood throughout his career as a tool to explore American life; contrasts Twain with other contemporary writers about children.

392. Tanner, Tony. "The Literary Children of James and Clemens." NCF, 16 (1961), 205-18.

 A useful addition to studies comparing and contrasting the two artists; James thought gain of maturity was worth loss of innocence, but Clemens did not.

393. Taylor, Walter Fuller. "Mark Twain." In THE ECONOMIC NOVEL IN AMERICA. Chapel Hill: University of North Carolina Press, 1942.

 A well-documented study which focuses largely on THE GILDED AGE and CONNECTICUT YANKEE.

394. Towers, Tom H. "Mark Twain's CONNECTICUT YANKEE: The Trouble in Camelot." In CHALLENGES IN AMERICAN CULTURE, ed. Ray B. Browne, Larry N. Landrum, and William K. Bottorff. Bowling Green, Ohio: Bowling Green University Popular Press, 1971.

 In Twain's novel, it is the absence of human love and community, not merely technology gone awry, that destroys all hope for mankind.

395. Trilling, Lionel. "Introduction" to THE ADVENTURES OF HUCKLE-BERRY FINN. New York: Holt, Rinehart and Winston, 1948.

 Along with Eliot's essay, this is one of the first attempts to justify the conclusion of the novel. See 352 and 374.

396. Tuckey, John S., ed. MARK TWAIN'S "THE MYSTERIOUS STRANGER" AND THE CRITICS. Belmont, Calif.: Wadsworth Publishing Co., 1968.

 The text of the story plus thirteen important critical essays (most of which were previously published elsewhere).

397. Turner, Arlin. "Mark Twain and the South: An Affair of Love and Anger." SoR, 4 (1968), 493-519.

 A thorough analysis of Twain's changing moods about the South. See 379.

398. Wagenknecht, Edward. "The Lincoln of Our Literature." In CAVAL-CADE OF THE AMERICAN NOVEL. New York: Henry Holt and Co., 1952.

 Useful mainly for the brief opinions on each of the major works.

399. _____. MARK TWAIN: THE MAN AND HIS WORK. 3rd ed. Norman: University of Oklahoma Press, 1967.

 A still useful "psychograph" of Twain which was originally published in 1935 but largely rewritten for later editions. Includes appendix on Twain scholarship since 1960.

400. Wiggins, Robert A. MARK TWAIN: JACKLEG NOVELIST. Seattle:

University of Washington Press, 1964.

A sympathetic treatment of Twain as "jackleg" (incompetent workman) except in the writing of HUCKLEBERRY FINN.

JAMES FENIMORE COOPER (1789-1851)

Principal Works

PRECAUTION, 1820   Novel
THE SPY, 1821   Novel
THE PIONEERS, 1823   Novel
THE PILOT, 1823   Novel
LIONEL LINCOLN, 1825   Novel
THE LAST OF THE MOHICANS, 1826   Novel
THE PRAIRIE, 1827   Novel
THE RED ROVER, 1827   Novel
NOTIONS OF THE AMERICANS, 1828   Fictional Letters
THE WEPT OF WISH TON-WISH, 1829   Novel
THE WATER-WITCH, 1831   Novel
THE BRAVO, 1831   Novel (this and the following two books form a
      trilogy.)
THE HEIDENMAUER, 1832   Novel
THE HEADSMAN, 1833   Novel
A LETTER TO HIS COUNTRYMEN, 1834   Essay
THE MONIKINS, 1835   Satire
GLEANINGS IN EUROPE, 1837-38   Travel Essays and Social Criticism
THE AMERICAN DEMOCRAT, 1838   Essay
HOMEWARD BOUND, 1838   Novel
HOME AS FOUND, 1838   Novel (sequel to HOMEWARD BOUND)
HISTORY OF THE NAVY OF THE UNITED STATES, 1839
THE PATHFINDER, 1840   Novel
MERCEDES OF CASTILE, 1840   Novel
THE DEERSLAYER, 1841   Novel
THE TWO ADMIRALS, 1842   Novel
THE WING-AND-WING, 1842   Novel
NED MYERS, 1843   Fictional Biography
WYANDOTTE, 1843   Novel
LE MOUCHOIR, 1843   Novel (retitled AUTOBIOGRAPHY OF A POCKET
      HANDKERCHIEF)
AFLOAT AND ASHORE, 1844   Novel
MILES WALLINGFORD, 1844   Novel (sequel to AFLOAT AND ASHORE)
SATANSTOE, 1845   Novel (this and the following two books form a
      trilogy known as the "Littlepage Manuscripts.")
THE CHAINBEARER, 1845   Novel

THE REDSKINS, 1846   Novel
LIVES OF DISTINGUISHED AMERICAN NAVAL OFFICERS, 1846   (supplements HISTORY OF THE NAVY OF THE UNITED STATES)
THE CRATER, 1847   Novel
JACK TIER, 1848   Novel
THE OAK OPENINGS, 1848   Novel
THE SEA LIONS, 1849   Novel
THE WAYS OF THE HOUR, 1850   Novel

Note: The Leather-Stocking (often "Leatherstocking") Tales are, in order of composition, THE PIONEERS, THE LAST OF THE MOHICANS, THE PRAIRIE, THE PATHFINDER, and THE DEERSLAYER. Their sequence in terms of plot chronology is THE DEERSLAYER, THE LAST OF THE MOHICANS, THE PATHFINDER, THE PIONEERS, and THE PRAIRIE.

Collected Works

401.   COOPER'S NOVELS. 32 vols. New York: W. A. Townsend, 1859-61.

    The most nearly definitive edition.

402.   J. FENIMORE COOPER'S WORKS. Household Edition, with introductions by Susan Fenimore Cooper. 32 vols. New York and Cambridge, Mass.: Hurd and Houghton, 1876, 1881-84.

403.   THE WORKS OF JAMES FENIMORE COOPER. Mohawk Edition. 33 vols. New York: G. P. Putnam's Sons, 1895-96.

Letters

404.   CORRESPONDENCE OF JAMES FENIMORE COOPER. Ed. James Fenimore Cooper. 2 vols. New Haven, Conn.: Yale University Press, 1922.

    Edited by Cooper's grandson.

405.   THE LETTERS AND JOURNALS OF JAMES FENIMORE COOPER. Ed. James F. Beard. 6 vols. Cambridge, Mass.: Harvard University Press, 1960-68.

    Contains letters not in 404. See also 447.

Bibliography

406.   Spiller, Robert E. and Philip C. Blackburn. A DESCRIPTIVE BIBLIOGRAPHY OF THE WRITINGS OF JAMES FENIMORE COOPER. New York: Bowker, 1934.

Checklist

407. Beard, James Franklin. "James Fenimore Cooper." In FIFTEEN AMERI-
     CAN AUTHORS BEFORE 1900, ed. Robert A. Rees and Earl N. Harbert.
     Madison: University of Wisconsin Press, 1971.

     A comprehensive essay on Cooper criticism (as well as other
     aspects of Cooper bibliography).

408. Walker, Warren S. "Selected Bibliography." In JAMES FENIMORE
     COOPER: AN INTRODUCTION AND INTERPRETATION. New York:
     Holt, Rinehart and Winston, 1962.

     Particularly useful for the listing of articles on individual
     works.

Biography

409. Boynton, Henry W. JAMES FENIMORE COOPER. New York: Apple-
     ton-Century-Crofts, 1931.

     A somewhat superficial portrait.

410. Clavel, Marcel. FENIMORE COOPER: SA VIE ET SON OEUVRE, LA
     JEUNESSE, 1789-1826. Aix-en-Provence, France: Imprimerie Univer-
     sitaire de Provence, 1938.

     Beard (see 407) describes this as "the weightiest and most
     methodic biographical study," one that is "encyclopedic" if
     not definitive.

411. Clymer, W. Shubrick. JAMES FENIMORE COOPER. Boston, Mass.:
     Small, Maynard, 1900.

     Relies to a great extent on letters from Cooper to Clymer's
     grandfather.

412. Grossman, James. JAMES FENIMORE COOPER. New York: Sloan,
     1949.

     Beard (see 407) refers to this book as "possibly the best one-
     volume introduction to Cooper."

413. Lounsbury, Thomas R. JAMES FENIMORE COOPER. Boston, Mass.:
     Houghton Mifflin, 1882.

     A readable book which suffers from Lounsbury's lack of access
     to important source materials.

414. Phillips, Mary E. JAMES FENIMORE COOPER. New York: Lane,
     1913.

     Phillips's portrait of Cooper, like Clymer's (see 411), is some-
     what more rounded than that of Lounsbury.

415. Spiller, Robert E. FENIMORE COOPER: CRITIC OF HIS TIMES. New York: Minton, Balch, 1931.

    A scholarly study which compensates for many of Lounsbury's inadequacies.

Critical Studies

416. Anderson, Charles. "Cooper's Sea Novels Spurned in the Maintop." MLN, 66 (1951), 388-91.

    Despite a traditional belief in the authenticity of Cooper's sea novels, they were rejected by ordinary seamen. See also 429.

417. Baym, Nina. "The Women of Cooper's Leatherstocking Tales." AQ, 23 (1971), 696-709.

    "In the Leatherstocking Tales, order is achieved only at the cost of a social submission that falls with particular complete- ness and severity on the women."

418. Becker, George J. "James Fenimore Cooper and American Democracy." CE, 17 (1956), 325-34.

    Criticizes Cooper's rigid views on democracy.

419. Bewley, Marius. "Form in Fenimore Cooper's Novels." In THE ECCEN- TRIC DESIGN. New York: Columbia University Press, 1959.

    A significant analysis of THE DEERSLAYER (THE BRAVO and THE HEIDENMAUER are treated in an earlier chapter).

420. Bonner, William H. "Cooper and Captain Kidd." MLN, 61 (1946), 21-27.

    Cooper drew on the legend of Captain Kidd in THE RED ROVER, THE DEERSLAYER, THE SEA LIONS, and THE WATER-WITCH.

421. Brady, Charles A. "Mythmaker and Christian Romancer." In AMERICAN CLASSICS RECONSIDERED: A CHRISTIAN REAPPRAISAL, ed. Harold C. Gardiner, S. J. New York: Charles Scribner's Sons, 1958.

    A discussion of the mythic and epic aspects of the Leather- stocking series.

422. Brownell, William C. "Cooper." In AMERICAN PROSE MASTERS. New York: Charles Scribner's Sons, 1909.

    A still useful appraisal of Cooper's work.

423. Chase, Richard. "The Significance of Cooper." In THE AMERICAN NOVEL AND ITS TRADITION. Garden City, N.Y.: Doubleday, 1957.

    SATANSTOE and THE PRAIRIE treat the problem of the indi- vidual versus traditional society.

424. Clavel, Marcel. FENIMORE COOPER AND HIS CRITICS. Aix-en-Provence, France: Imprimerie Universitaire de Provence, 1938.

Deals with (1) Cooper's early literary reputation in general and (2) the evolution of critical opinion concerning each of his early novels.

425. Collins, Frank M. "Cooper and the American Dream." PMLA, 71 (1966), 79-94.

A discussion of Cooper's lifelong concern with morality and the effect of society on man.

426. Cowie, Alexander. "James Fenimore Cooper and the Historical Romance." In THE RISE OF THE AMERICAN NOVEL. New York: American Book Co., 1951.

A sensible essay; largely celebratory, it does not overlook Cooper's major defect--his style. See 452 and 457.

427. Cunningham, Mary, ed. JAMES FENIMORE COOPER: A REAPPRAISAL. Cooperstown: New York State Historical Association, 1954.

Twelve essays read at the Cooper Centennial Celebration at Cooperstown in 1951.

428. Dekker, George. JAMES FENIMORE COOPER: THE AMERICAN SCOTT. New York: Barnes & Noble, 1967.

Primarily an analysis of the individual novels, this book also discusses Cooper's politics as well as his "assimilation and development of the historical novel as first perfected by Sir Walter Scott."

429. Flanagan, John T. "The Authenticity of Cooper's THE PRAIRIE." MLQ, 2 (1941), 99-104.

Though Cooper made frequent errors in topography, botany, geography, and ethnology, his only Western novel has "verisimilitude," if not "authenticity." See 416.

430. Frederick, John T. "Cooper's Eloquent Indians." PMLA, 71 (1956), 1004-17.

Disputes "the recurring charge that Cooper idealized and falsified" the speech of his Indian characters.

431. Frisch, Morton J. "Cooper's NOTIONS OF THE AMERICANS: A Commentary on Democracy." ETHICS, 71 (1961), 114-20.

An analysis of Cooper's understanding of democracy as expressed in this volume of fictional letters.

432. Gates, W. B. "Cooper's Indebtedness to Shakespeare." PMLA, 67 (1952), 716-31.

A discussion of the considerable influence exerted on Cooper by Shakespeare in terms of incident, plot, and character.

433. Hastings, George E. "How Cooper Became a Novelist." AL, 12 (1940), 20-51.

An interesting if overextended commentary on the various novels that may have prompted Cooper to write PRECAUTION.

434. House, Kay Seymour. COOPER'S AMERICANS. Columbus: Ohio State University Press, 1965.

A study of Cooper's "communities" of characters: women, Indians, Negroes, the Dutch, the gentry, Yankees, seamen.

435. Howard, David. "James Fenimore Cooper's LEATHERSTOCKING TALES: 'without a cross.' " In TRADITION AND TOLERANCE IN NINETEENTH-CENTURY FICTION, ed. David Howard, et al. New York: Barnes & Noble, 1967.

Considers all the tales, although the emphasis is on THE LAST OF THE MOHICANS and its "controlling ironic vision which is also a celebration of life."

436. Jones, Howard Mumford. "Prose and Pictures: James Fenimore Cooper." TSE, 3 (1952), 133-54.

Discusses "some of the ways in which Cooper as a moralist is involved in the aesthetic and philosophic currents of his age." In particular, notes Jones, "the relation of landscape painting by the Hudson River School to Cooper's fictional technique and to his view of life is matter of considerable import."

437. Kaul, A. N. "James Fenimore Cooper: The History and the Myth of American Civilization." In THE AMERICAN VISION: ACTUAL AND IDEAL SOCIETY IN NINETEENTH-CENTURY FICTION. New Haven, Conn., and London: Yale University Press, 1963.

While the Littlepage trilogy suggests the impossibility of moral perfection in society as it exists, the Leatherstocking Tales look ahead to a new society, a "dream beyond democracy" (D. H. Lawrence's phrase).

438. Kirk, Russell. "Cooper and the European Puzzle." CE, 7 (1946), 198-207.

Analyzes THE BRAVO, THE HEIDENMAUER, and THE HEADS-MAN in terms of the political criticism they contain.

439. Krause, Sidney J. "Cooper's Literary Offenses: Mark Twain in Wonderland." NEQ, 38 (1965), 291-311.

Discusses the literary devices employed by Twain to deceive scholars who accept his essay on Cooper as serious criticism.

440. Lawrence, D. H. STUDIES IN CLASSIC AMERICAN LITERATURE. New York: Viking, 1961.

Includes two impressionistic but occasionally insightful essays on Cooper.

441. McAleer, John J. "Biblical Analogy in the Leatherstocking Tales." NCF, 17 (1962), 217-35.

Cooper uses Biblical analogies to focus on American materialism, particularly in THE PRAIRIE.

442. Martin, Terence. "From the Ruins of History: THE LAST OF THE MOHICANS." NOVEL, 2 (1969), 221-29.

An engaging discussion of the relation that Cooper establishes between fictional characters and historical events.

443. Parrington, Vernon L. "James Fenimore Cooper: Critic." In MAIN CURRENTS IN AMERICAN THOUGHT, vol. 2. New York: Harcourt, Brace, 1930.

A discussion of Cooper's political and social thought.

444. Pearce, Roy Harvey. "The Leatherstocking Tales Re-examined." SAQ, 46 (1947), 524-36.

An analysis of the aesthetic shortcomings of the Tales.

445. Philbrick, Thomas. JAMES FENIMORE COOPER AND THE DEVELOPMENT OF AMERICAN SEA FICTION. Cambridge, Mass.: Harvard University Press, 1961.

A significant book; first full-length treatment of Cooper's sea novels.

446. Ringe, Donald A. JAMES FENIMORE COOPER. New York: Twayne, 1962.

Less strictly biographical than many of the Twayne studies, this book unabashedly treats Cooper as "a major American artist." Includes a useful "Selected Bibliography" of works by and about Cooper.

447. _____. "James Fenimore Cooper: An American Democrat." PLL, 6 (1970), 420-31.

A review essay on Beard's edition of the LETTERS AND JOURNALS (see 405); judiciously uses quotations from that edition in order to shed new light on various aspects of Cooper's career.

448. Rose, John F. THE SOCIAL CRITICISM OF FENIMORE COOPER. Berkeley: University of California Press, 1933.

Cooper represents "not only American self-criticism but also individualism thwarted by conflict with the herd."

449. Scudder, Harold H. "Cooper and the Barbary Coast." PMLA, 62 (1947),

784-92.

An account of the genesis of HOMEWARD BOUND.

450. Shulenberger, Arvid. COOPER'S THEORY OF FICTION: HIS PREFACES AND THEIR RELATION TO HIS NOVELS. Lawrence: University of Kansas Press, 1955.

"The purpose of this study is twofold: to present Cooper's views on fiction in some detail for the first time, and to provide a connected description of his novels in relation to his theory."

451. Smith, Henry Nash. VIRGIN LAND. New York: Alfred A. Knopf, 1957.

Includes important commentary on the Leatherstocking series.

452. Spiller, Robert E. "Cooper's Notes on Language." AMERICAN SPEECH, 4 (1929), 294-300.

Refers largely to GLEANINGS IN EUROPE for Cooper's attitudes toward language and style. See 426 and 457.

453. _____. JAMES FENIMORE COOPER. Minneapolis: University of Minnesota Press, 1965.

A general introduction to Cooper's works. The selected bibliography, though useful, is shorter than Walker's (see 408).

454. Walker, Warren S. JAMES FENIMORE COOPER: AN INTRODUCTION AND INTERPRETATION. New York: Holt, Rinehart and Winston, 1962.

A brief but useful overview. Includes selected bibliography.

455. _____, ed. LEATHERSTOCKING AND THE CRITICS. Chicago, Ill.: Scott, Foresman, 1965.

Selected criticism of the Leatherstocking Tales, both favorable and unfavorable, from the 1820's to the present.

456. Waples, Dorothy. THE WHIG MYTH OF FENIMORE COOPER. New Haven, Conn.: Yale University Press, 1938.

Traces to his Whig rivals many of the persistent misinterpretations of Cooper the Democrat.

457. Winters, Yvor. "Fenimore Cooper, or the Ruins of Time." In MAULE'S CURSE. Norfolk, Conn.: New Directions, 1938.

A perceptive commentary on Cooper's literary style and other matters. See 426 and 452.

458. Zoellner, Robert H. "Conceptual Ambivalence in Cooper's Leatherstocking." AL, 31 (1960), 397-420.

Cooper's concept of Leatherstocking's character becomes more ambivalent as the series progresses.

459. _____. "Fenimore Cooper: Alienated American." AQ, 13 (1961), 55-66.

Cooper's sense of alienation may be traced throughout his work, and is particularly apparent in the Littlepage trilogy.

STEPHEN CRANE (1871-1900)

Principal Works

MAGGIE   A GIRL OF THE STREETS, 1893   Novel
THE RED BADGE OF COURAGE, 1895   Novel
THE BLACK RIDERS, 1895   Verse
THE LITTLE REGIMENT, 1896   Stories
GEORGE'S MOTHER, 1896   Novel
THE THIRD VIOLET, 1897   Novel
THE OPEN BOAT, 1898   Stories
ACTIVE SERVICE, 1899   Novel
THE MONSTER, 1899   Stories
WAR IS KIND, 1899   Verse
WOUNDS IN THE RAIN, 1900   Sketches and Stories
WHILOMVILLE STORIES, 1900
GREAT BATTLES OF THE WORLD, 1901   History
LAST WORDS, 1902   Sketches and Stories
THE O'RUDDY, 1903   Novel (unfinished; completed by Robert Barr)
THE NOTEBOOK OF STEPHEN CRANE, 1969

Collected Works

460. COLLECTED POEMS. Ed. Wilson Follett. New York: Alfred A. Knopf, 1930.

461. COMPLETE SHORT STORIES AND SKETCHES. Ed. Thomas A. Gullason. Garden City, N.Y.: Doubleday, 1963.

462. COMPLETE NOVELS. Ed. Thomas A. Gullason. Garden City, N.Y.: Doubleday, 1967.

463. THE POEMS OF STEPHEN CRANE. Ed. Joseph Katz. New York: Cooper Square Publishers, 1966.

464. STEPHEN CRANE: UNCOLLECTED WRITINGS. Ed. Olov W. Fryckstedt. Uppsala, Sweden: University of Uppsala Press, 1963.

465. THE WORK OF STEPHEN CRANE. Ed. Wilson Follett. 12 vols. New York: Alfred A. Knopf, 1925–26. Reissued by Russell & Russell, 1963.

466. THE WORKS OF STEPHEN CRANE. Ed. Fredson Bowers et al. 10 vols. projected. Charlottesville: University Press of Virginia, 1969– .

   In progress.

Letters

467. LOVE LETTERS TO NELLIE CROUSE. Ed. Edwin H. Cady and Lester G. Wells. Syracuse, N.Y.: Syracuse University Press, 1954.

468. STEPHEN CRANE: LETTERS. Ed. R. W. Stallman and Lillian Gilkes. New York: New York University Press, 1960.

Bibliography

469. Stallman, R. W. STEPHEN CRANE: A CRITICAL BIBLIOGRAPHY. Ames: Iowa State University Press, 1972.

   Comprehensive, annotated, definitive, and massive (642 pp.), this book should serve as a model for other bibliographies. Also includes works about Crane.

470. Williams, Ames W. and Vincent Starrett. STEPHEN CRANE: A BIBLI-OGRAPHY. Glendale, Calif.: J. Valentine, 1948.

Checklist

471. Beebe, Maurice and Thomas A. Gullason. "Criticism of Stephen Crane." MFS, 5 (1959), 282–91.

472. Katz, Joseph. THE MERRILL CHECKLIST OF STEPHEN CRANE. Columbus, Ohio: Charles E. Merrill, 1969.

   Major publications, editions, letters, bibliographies and check-lists, biographies, scholarship, and criticism.

473. Pizer, Donald. "Stephen Crane." In FIFTEEN AMERICAN AUTHORS BEFORE 1900, ed. Robert A. Rees and Earl N. Harbert. Madison: University of Wisconsin Press, 1971.

   Manuscripts, bibliography, editions, texts, reprints, biography, and criticism.

474. Wertheim, Stanley. "Stephen Crane." In HAWTHORNE, MELVILLE, STEPHEN CRANE: A CRITICAL BIBLIOGRAPHY, by Theodore L. Gross and Stanley Wertheim. New York: Free Press, 1971.

   Editions, other primary materials, biographies, and an indi-spensable selected bibliography of critical studies (all of which are abstracted at length).

475.   THE STEPHEN CRANE NEWSLETTER publishes a quarterly checklist, and
the magazine THOTH publishes an annual bibliography of Crane scholarship. See also 469.

Journals

476.   STEPHEN CRANE NEWSLETTER. 1966- .

Address: Department of English, University of South Carolina,
Columbia, S.C. 29208. A quarterly.

Biography

477.   Beer, Thomas. STEPHEN CRANE. New York: Alfred A. Knopf, 1923.

A nonscholarly but still useful biography; largely based on
interviews and correspondence with Crane's intimates as well
as such literati as Joseph Conrad and Hamlin Garland.

478.   Berryman, John. STEPHEN CRANE. New York: William Sloane, 1950;
Cleveland, Ohio: Meridian Books, 1962.

While some of the psychoanalytic speculation is dubious, the
comments on Crane's writings are sound.

479.   Gilkes, Lillian. CORA CRANE. Bloomington: Indiana University Press,
1960.

Although the emphasis is on his wife, new information is
supplied concerning Crane's life in England. See also Gilkes,
"Stephen Crane and the Biographical Fallacy: The Cora Influence" in MFS, 16 (1970), 441-61.

480.   Raymond, Thomas L. STEPHEN CRANE. Newark, N.J.: Carteret Book
Club, 1923.

The first biography of Crane.

481.   Stallman, R. W. STEPHEN CRANE. New York: Braziller, 1968.

The definitive biography to date, though frequently criticized
for its inaccuracies.

Critical Studies

482.   Adams, Richard P. "Naturalistic Fiction: 'The Open Boat.'" TSE,
4 (1954), 137-46.

Discusses thematic inconsistency in the story.

483. Ahnebrink, Lars. THE BEGINNINGS OF NATURALISM IN AMERICAN FICTION. New York: Russell & Russell, 1961.

Several chapters are devoted to Crane and deal with the influence of Zola and Tolstoy on Crane and other matters.

484. Albrecht, Robert C. "Content and Style in THE RED BADGE OF COURAGE." CE, 27 (1966), 487-92.

Crane's style changes throughout the novel in conjunction with changes in content.

485. Bassan, Maurice, ed. STEPHEN CRANE; A COLLECTION OF CRITICAL ESSAYS. Englewood Cliffs, N.J.: Prentice-Hall, 1967.

Essays by various hands: "portraits" of Crane, general discussions, studies of individual works.

486. Berthoff, Warner. "Frank Norris, Stephen Crane." In THE FERMENT OF REALISM: AMERICAN LITERATURE 1884-1919. New York: Free Press, 1965.

A succinct and perceptive commentary on the mechanics of Crane's writing, his style, and his "motive."

487. Brennan, Joseph X. "Ironic and Symbolic Structure in Crane's MAGGIE." NCF, 16 (1962), 303-15.

The first closely analytical study of MAGGIE.

488. _____. "Stephen Crane and the Limits of Irony." CRITICISM, 11 (1969), 183-200.

A persuasive study of Crane's "abuse of the ironic mode" in several works, notably "The Open Boat."

489. Cady, Edwin H. STEPHEN CRANE. New York: Twayne, 1962.

An important contribution to Crane studies. There are two chapters on his life, but most of the major emphasis is on Crane's ideas and his writings. Includes a useful "Selected Bibliography" of works by and about Crane.

490. Cazemajou, Jean. STEPHEN CRANE. Minneapolis: University of Minnesota Press, 1969.

A brief introduction; divided into biographical and critical sketches.

491. Colvert, James B. "The Origins of Stephen Crane's Literary Creed." TEXAS STUDIES IN ENGLISH, 34 (1955), 179-88.

Argues that Kipling's THE LIGHT THAT FAILED influenced Crane more than the French and Russian naturalists who are usually cited.

492.   _____. "Structure and Theme in Stephen Crane's Fiction." MFS, 5 (1959), 199-208.

There is a double perspective in Crane's work: that of the self-deluded characters and that of the more knowledgeable narrator. (This essay is the basis for a number of other commentaries that consider this double perspective.)

493.   _____. "Style and Meaning in Stephen Crane: THE OPEN BOAT." TEXAS STUDIES IN ENGLISH, 37 (1958), 34-45.

Crane's method is one of indirection and ambiguity; thus nature may be seen to have different and even contradictory attributes throughout the story, none of which necessarily excludes any of the others. It is futile, then, to classify Crane as a realist, naturalist, etc.

494.   Cox, James T. "The Imagery of THE RED BADGE OF COURAGE." MFS, 5 (1959), 209-19.

A close examination of the various interacting patterns of imagery.

495.   Cunliffe, Marcus. "Stephen Crane and the American Background of MAGGIE." AQ, 7 (1955), 31-44.

A well-documented argument that MAGGIE may have been influenced as much by popular American social literature as by Zola's L'ASSOMMOIR.

496.   Ellison, Ralph. "Stephen Crane and the Mainstream of American Fiction." In THE RED BADGE OF COURAGE AND FOUR GREAT STORIES BY STEPHEN CRANE. New York: Dell, 1960; reprinted in SHADOW AND ACT (New York: Random House, 1964).

Most useful for its treatment of the social and cultural context of RED BADGE and for its discussion of Negro characters in Crane's writings.

497.   Fitelson, David. "Stephen Crane's MAGGIE and Darwinism." AQ, 16 (1964), 182-94.

"The Naturalism of MAGGIE [can] be identified as a rigorous, Darwinistic determinism."

498.   Frohock, W. M. "THE RED BADGE and the Limits of Parody." SoR, 6 (1970), 137-48.

In contrast to Solomon's argument (see 529) that "Crane's craft consisted of a capacity for turning established stereotypes and cliches inside out," Frohock argues that RED BADGE succeeds by foregoing parody.

499.   Fryckstedt, Olov W. "Henry Fleming's Tuppenny Fury: Cosmic Pessimism in Stephen Crane's THE RED BADGE OF COURAGE." SN, 33

(1961), 265-81.

> An illuminating comparison of the final version of RED BADGE with the manuscript.

500. Geismar, Maxwell. "Stephen Crane: Halfway House." In REBELS AND ANCESTORS: THE AMERICAN NOVEL, 1890-1915. Boston, Mass.: Houghton Mifflin, 1953.

> A stimulating essay, if somewhat unyielding in its insistence on the "oedipal drama" as central to Crane's writings.

501. Gibson, Donald. THE FICTION OF STEPHEN CRANE. Carbondale: Southern Illinois University Press, 1968.

> Ordinarily, books of limited usefulness are excluded from the present work; since, however, Gibson's is the only full-length study of Crane's fiction and is therefore liable to be widely consulted, it should be noted that almost every commentator finds it deficient in one respect or another.

502. _____. " 'The Blue Hotel' and the Ideal of Human Courage." TSLL, 6 (1964), 388-97.

> A perceptive reading which sees in "The Blue Hotel" the unfulfilled possibility of man's capacity to thwart evil.

503. Gleckner, Robert F. "Stephen Crane and the Wonder of Man's Conceit." MFS, 5 (1959), 271-81.

> A significant interpretation of "The Blue Hotel."

504. Greenfield, Stanley B. "The Unmistakable Stephen Crane." PMLA, 73 (1958), 562-72.

> Reviews the criticism of RED BADGE and suggests that the "duality of view" that is the key to the novel is best revealed if RED BADGE is examined in conjunction with "The Open Boat" and "The Blue Hotel."

505. Griffith, Clark. "Stephen Crane and the Ironic Last Word." PQ, 47 (1968), 83-91.

> Crane's heroes only appear to learn from experience; in reality, they end up as far from the truth as ever.

506. Gullason, Thomas A., ed. STEPHEN CRANE'S CAREER: PERSPECTIVES AND EVALUATIONS. New York: New York University Press, 1972.

> An invaluable collection of more than fifty studies of every aspect of Crane's life and works. Includes a checklist of further studies.

507. _____. "Stephen Crane's Private War on Yellow Journalism." HLQ, 22 (1959), 201-8.

> Quotes from the fiction and poetry as well as the newspaper

sketches to show Crane's contempt for irresponsible journalism.

508. _____. "Thematic Patterns in Stephen Crane's Early Novels." NCF, 16 (1961), 59-67.

Sees MAGGIE, GEORGE'S MOTHER, and RED BADGE as a "painstaking trilogy."

509. Hoffman, Daniel G. THE POETRY OF STEPHEN CRANE. New York: Columbia University Press, 1957.

A thorough analysis of Crane's major themes, his poetics, and his place in the poetic tradition; based on the Crane collection at Columbia University and other manuscript sources.

510. Holton, Milne. "The Sparrow's Fall and the Sparrow's Eye: Crane's MAGGIE." SN, 41 (1969), 115-29.

This article begins with a useful summary of the critical debate over MAGGIE and then offers a new interpretation which reconciles the naturalistic elements of the novel with Maggie's own incapacity of vision.

511. Hungerford, Harold R. " 'That Was at Chancellorsville': The Factual Framework of THE RED BADGE OF COURAGE." AL, 34 (1963), 520-31.

An interesting account of the factual basis of RED BADGE and its aesthetic implications.

512. Johnson, George W. "Stephen Crane's Metaphor of Decorum." PMLA, 78 (1963), 250-56.

Deals with Crane's protagonists and their unsuccessful attempts to reconcile their own self-concepts with conventional roles.

513. Katz, Joseph. " 'The Blue Batallions' and the Uses of Experience." SN, 38 (1966), 107-16.

An important essay on one of Crane's most problematic poems. "The Blue Batallions" is also discussed in 509 and 521.

514. _____, ed. STEPHEN CRANE IN TRANSITION: CENTENARY ESSAYS. DeKalb: Northern Illinois University Press, 1972.

Essays written expressly for this collection by leading Crane scholars. Especially valuable for the afterword, "Resources for the Study of Stephen Crane."

515. Klotz, Marvin. "Stephen Crane: Tragedian or Comedian: 'The Blue Hotel.' " UKCR, 27 (1961), 170-74.

Reads the story as "a deliberate burlesque of literary naturalism."

516. LaFrance, Marston. A READING OF STEPHEN CRANE. London:

Clarendon Press, Oxford, 1971.

> An important and, for the most part, persuasive reading of almost all of Crane's writings in terms of a recurrent pattern of psychological growth which "implicitly rejects naturalism."

517. Lytle, Andrew. "'The Open Boat': A Pagan Tale." In THE HERO WITH THE PRIVATE PARTS. Baton Rouge: Louisiana State University Press, 1966.

> Although Lytle hedges on the story's conclusion, his charting of the characters' progress from a pagan view of the universe toward a Christian one is useful.

518. McDermott, John J. "Symbolism and Psychological Realism in THE RED BADGE OF COURAGE." NCF, 23 (1968), 324-31.

> Crane's central symbol, the red badge, "is the perfect vehicle to convey gracefully the complexities and ironies of his limited character's psychological development."

519. Marcus, Mordecai. "The Unity of THE RED BADGE OF COURAGE." In THE RED BADGE OF COURAGE: TEXT AND CRITICISM, ed. Richard Lettis, et al. New York: Harcourt, Brace, 1960.

> Crane excised passages from the manuscript of the novel. Now available to scholars, these passages reveal much about Crane's attitude toward the resolution of the novel.

520. Martin, Jay. "The Great American Novel: Stephen Crane." In HARVESTS OF CHANGE: AMERICAN LITERATURE, 1865-1914. Englewood Cliffs, N.J.: Prentice-Hall, 1967.

> A concise discussion of Crane's fiction which still manages to focus on the details of his major works.

521. Nelson, Harland S. "Stephen Crane's Achievement as a Poet." TSLL, 4 (1963), 564-82.

> Whereas Hoffman (see 509) praises the Crane poems that frequently appear to be the most modern in terms of symbolism and complexity, Nelson argues the case for "the bare unadorned parables."

522. Osborn, Neal J. "The Riddle in 'The Clan': A Key to Crane's Major Fiction?" BNYPL, 69 (1965), 247-58.

> Crane's story "The Clan of No-Name" contains a verse riddle which asserts a humanitarian and Christian metaphysic that transcends the naturalistic bias of Crane's major fiction.

523. Pizer, Donald. "Crane Reports Garland on Howells." MLN, 70 (1955), 37-39.

> Crane was greatly influenced by a lecture in which Hamlin Garland discussed William Dean Howells (and emphasized

"personal honesty and vision").

524. _____. "Stephen Crane's MAGGIE and American Naturalism." CRITI-CISM, 7 (1965), 168-75.

Though Crane is a naturalistic writer, a study of MAGGIE reveals that "his primary concern is not a dispassionate, pessimistic tracing of inevitable forces but a satiric assault on weaknesses in social morality."

525. Rogers, Rodney O. "Stephen Crane and Impressionism." NCF, 24 (1969), 292-304.

Crane's precise debt to the French Impressionists is difficult to establish, although his "careful control of point of view" suggests an implicit debt.

526. Schneider, Robert W. "Stephen Crane." In FIVE NOVELISTS OF THE PROGRESSIVE ERA. New York and London: Columbia University Press, 1965.

A useful introduction; Schneider quotes freely from the letters, poems, and fiction.

527. Shroeder, John W. "Stephen Crane Embattled." UKCR, 17 (1950), 119-29.

Most of Crane's "artistic shortcomings" are due to Naturalism, and his best work represents "an effort to get beyond it."

528. Solomon, Eric. "Another Analogue for THE RED BADGE OF COURAGE." NCF, 13 (1958), 63-67.

Plot similarities between Kirkland's THE CAPTAIN OF COMPANY K and Crane's novel. Alexander R. Tamke (in ESSAYS IN HONOR OF ESMOND LINWORTH MARILLA, ed. Thomas A. Kirby and William J. Olive, Baton Rouge: Louisiana State University Press, 1971) treats the same subject and sees Kirkland's novel as the principal source of Crane's.

529. _____. STEPHEN CRANE: FROM PARODY TO REALISM. Cambridge, Mass.: Harvard University Press, 1966.

"Crane's major fiction most often commences in parody and concludes in creativity.... In his best work parody and realism become one." See also 498.

530. _____. "Stephen Crane's War Stories." TSLL, 3 (1961), 67-80.

A study of Crane's changing attitudes toward war as indicated by stories written in three distinct periods of his life.

531. _____. "The Structure of THE RED BADGE OF COURAGE." MFS, 5 (1959), 220-34.

Argues that the ending of RED BADGE is not ironic and that

Henry Fleming emerges as a mature person.

532. Stallman, R. W. "Crane's MAGGIE: A Reassessment." MFS, 5 (1959), 251-59.

"His plot is less impressive than his theme, and the theme less impressive than the style.... His plot is a sentimental melodrama, like Norris's McTEAGUE, but in style MAGGIE is not sentimentalized."

533. _____. "Fiction and Its Critics: A Reply to Mr. Rahv." KR, 19 (1957), 290-99.

A rejoinder to Philip Rahv's article in KR, 18 (1956), 276-99, part of which is an attack on Stallman's New Critical approach to RED BADGE.

534. _____. "Stephen Crane's Revision of MAGGIE: A GIRL OF THE STREETS." AL, 26 (1955), 528-36.

A comparison of the 1893 and 1896 versions of MAGGIE reveals important differences, including a "leering fat man" who appears in Chapter 17 of the earlier edition but not the later, on which most modern versions are based. (See pp. 265-66 of Wertheim [474] for a further discussion of the two different versions.)

535. Stein, William Bysshe. "Stephen Crane's Homo Absurdus." BuR, 8 (1959), 168-88.

A cogent study of the implications of the metaphor of Crane's sensibility, "the night of the jungle." For Crane, as for Kierkegaard and Kafka, it means that he finds absurdity everywhere; for his characters, it means "bafflement and frustration crowned by an oath."

536. STEPHEN CRANE NUMBER. MFS, 5 (1959).

Essays by various hands, most of which are mentioned in the present study; also includes a useful selective bibliography.

537. Stone, Edward. "The Many Suns of THE RED BADGE OF COURAGE." AL, 29 (1957), 322-26.

The six instances in which the sun is used symbolically in RED BADGE are intricately related to the "interior action" of the story.

538. Walcutt, Charles Child. "Stephen Crane: Naturalist and Impressionist." In AMERICAN LITERARY NATURALISM, A DIVIDED STREAM. Minneapolis: University of Minnesota Press, 1956.

Analyzes Crane's major works to show that they constitute "one of the few perfect and successful embodiments of the theory [of Naturalism] in the American novel."

539.   Weimer, David R. "Landscape of Hysteria: Stephen Crane." In THE
        CITY AS METAPHOR. New York: Random House, 1966.

        Comments on MAGGIE and GEORGE'S MOTHER; compares
        Crane's writings to those of Howells and Kafka.

540.   Weisenberger, Bernard. "THE RED BADGE OF COURAGE." In TWELVE
        ORIGINAL ESSAYS ON GREAT AMERICAN NOVELS, ed. Charles Sha-
        piro. Detroit, Mich.: Wayne State University Press, 1958.

        A useful essay on various aspects of the book; the main
        emphasis is on RED BADGE as a novel of self-discovery and
        anti-religious redemption.

541.   Weiss, Daniel. "THE RED BADGE OF COURAGE." PSYCHOANALYTIC
        REVIEW, 52 (1965), 176-95, 461-84.

        This two-part analysis of RED BADGE finds in the novel "a
        medically valid depiction of the psychology of fear."

542.   Wertheim, Stanley, ed. THE MERRILL STUDIES IN MAGGIE AND
        GEORGE'S MOTHER. Columbus, Ohio: Charles E. Merrill, 1970.

        This collection is intended to suggest "the development and
        variety of approaches to MAGGIE and GEORGE'S MOTHER...
        from the time of their first publication to the present."

543.   West, Ray B., Jr. "Stephen Crane: Author in Transition." AL, 34
        (1962), 215-28.

        Suggests that Crane refined both his attitudes and techniques
        throughout his career and that he occupies a sort of middle
        ground between the naturalists and Henry James.

544.   Westbrook, Max. "Stephen Crane's Poetry: Perspective and Arrogance."
        BuR, 11 (December 1963), 24-34.

        A study of the two dominant and sometimes seemingly arbitrary
        voices in Crane's poetry reveals that both contribute to an
        "essential unity."

545.   _____. "Stephen Crane's Social Ethic." AQ, 14 (1962), 587-96.

        An important analysis of MAGGIE and "The Blue Hotel" which
        finds in Crane a synthesis between determinism and individual
        responsibility.

546.   Ziff, Larzer. "Outstripping the Event: Stephen Crane." In THE AMER-
        ICAN 1890s: LIFE AND TIMES OF A LOST GENERATION. New York:
        Viking, 1966.

        Uses biographical data and the evidence of his writings to
        account for Crane's personality and his attitudes toward society.

JOHN WILLIAM DE FOREST (1826-1906)

De Forest is frequently described as the first American realist.

Principal Works

HISTORY OF THE INDIANS OF CONNECTICUT, 1851
ORIENTAL ACQUAINTANCE, 1856   Travel Sketches
EUROPEAN ACQUAINTANCE, 1858   Travel Sketches
SEACLIFF OR THE MYSTERY OF THE WESTERVELTS, 1859   Novel
MISS RAVENEL'S CONVERSION FROM SECESSION TO LOYALTY, 1867
     Novel (the first realistic Civil War novel)
OVERLAND, 1871   Novel
KATE BEAUMONT, 1872   Novel
THE WETHEREL AFFAIR, 1873   Novel
HONEST JOHN VANE, 1875   Novel
PLAYING THE MISCHIEF, 1875   Novel
JUSTINE'S LOVERS, 1878   Novel
IRENE THE MISSIONARY, 1879   Novel
THE BLOODY CHASM, 1881   Novel
A LOVER'S REVOLT, 1898   Novel
THE DE FORESTS OF AVESNES, 1900   Genealogy
THE DOWNING LEGENDS, 1901   Verse Tales
POEMS MEDLEY AND PALESTINA, 1902
A VOLUNTEER'S ADVENTURES, 1946   War Memoirs
A UNION OFFICER IN THE RECONSTRUCTION, 1948   (sequel to A
     VOLUNTEER'S ADVENTURES)

Bibliography

547.   Hagemann, E. R. "A Checklist of the Writings of John William De
     Forest (1826-1906)." SB, 8 (1956), 185-94.

Checklist

548.   "John William De Forest (1826-1906): A Critical Bibliography of Secon-
     dary Comment." ALR, 1 (1968), 1-56.

An indispensable annotated listing of books and essays about De Forest and his writings. See 549.

549. Hagemann, E. R. "A John William De Forest Supplement, 1970." ALR, 3 (1970), 148-52.

A supplement to the preceding item.

Biography

550. Light, James F. JOHN WILLIAM DE FOREST. New York: Twayne, 1965.

Accurately described by its author as "a relatively comprehensive study of De Forest's life, mind, and art." Includes a useful "Selected Bibliography" of works by and about De Forest.

Critical Studies

551. Cecil, L. Moffitt. "MISS RAVENEL'S CONVERSION and PILGRIM'S PROGRESS." CE, 23 (1962), 352-57.

Argues that the two works share distinct similarities and that De Forest was consciously influenced by Bunyan.

552. Croushore, James H. and David M. Potter. "Introduction" to A UNION OFFICER IN THE RECONSTRUCTION. New Haven, Conn.: Yale University Press, 1948.

Discussion of De Forest's work in and writings about the Freedman's Bureau.

553. Falk, Robert P. "John W. De Forest: The Panoramic Novel of Realism." In THE VICTORIAN MODE IN AMERICAN FICTION: 1865-1885. East Lansing: Michigan State University Press, 1965.

A realistic appraisal of De Forest's career.

554. Gargano, James W. "A De Forest Interview." AL, 29 (1957), 320-22.

In an interview in the NEW YORK TIMES of December 17, 1898, De Forest made revealing remarks about his own work.

555. _____. "John W. De Forest and the Critics." ALR, 1 (1968), 57-64.

De Forest's contemporaries, like most modern critics, preferred his earlier novels to the later ones.

556. Hagemann, E. R. "John William De Forest's 'Great American Novel.' " In MINOR AMERICAN NOVELISTS, ed. Charles Alva Hoyt. Carbondale: Southern Illinois University Press, 1971.

Actually a study of a pentology of novels written between

1857 and 1875: WITCHING TIMES (which was published serially but not as a book), KATE BEAUMONT, MISS RAVENEL'S CONVERSION, HONEST JOHN VANE, and PLAYING THE MISCHIEF.

557. Haight, Gordon S. "Introduction" to MISS RAVENEL'S CONVERSION FROM SECESSION TO LOYALTY. New York: Harper & Brothers, 1939.

Brief but perceptive discussion of the novel's realistic characterization.

558. _____. "The John William De Forest Collection." YULG, 14 (1939), 41-46.

Descriptions of De Forest manuscripts at Yale.

559. Howells, William Dean. "The Heroine of KATE BEAUMONT." In HEROINES OF FICTION, vol. 2. New York and London: Harper & Brothers, 1901.

A sprightly commentary on what Howells considered the "shapeliest" of De Forest's novels.

560. Levy, Leo B. "Naturalism in the Making: De Forest's HONEST JOHN VANE." NEQ, 37 (1964), 89-98.

Treats the novel as a transitional work between realism and naturalism.

561. Mariani, Umberto. "Il realismo di John W. De Forest." SA, 7 (1961), 77-103.

Comments on the lack of a definite critical assessment of De Forest's achievement as a writer and points out that MISS RAVENEL'S CONVERSION is similar in several ways to Manzoni's I PROMESSI SPOSI.

562. O'Donnell, Thomas F. "De Forest, Van Petten, and Stephen Crane." AL, 27 (1956), 578-80.

Suggests De Forest's influence on Crane by way of their mutual acquaintance Van Petten.

563. Rubin, Joseph Jay. "Introduction" to HONEST JOHN VANE. State College, Pa.: Bald Eagle Press, 1960.

A comprehensive essay on the various contexts of the novel, social and historical as well as literary.

564. _____. "Introduction" to KATE BEAUMONT. State College, Pa.: Bald Eagle Press, 1963.

A useful though somewhat clumsy overview of De Forest's life and works in relation to KATE BEAUMONT.

565. _____. "Introduction" to PLAYING THE MISCHIEF. State College,

Pa.: Bald Eagle Press, 1961.

Useful if somewhat incoherent discussion of the novel's Washington background and other matters.

566. Simpson, Claude M., Jr. "John W. De Forest, MISS RAVENEL'S CONVERSION." In THE AMERICAN NOVEL FROM JAMES FENIMORE COOPER TO WILLIAM FAULKNER, ed. Wallace Stegner. New York and London: Basic Books, 1965.

Discusses characterization and the novel's literary and historical context.

567. Stone, Albert E., Jr. "Reading, Writing, and History: Best Novel of the Civil War." AH, 13 (June 1962), 84-88.

Discusses the realistic portrayal of the war in MISS RAVENEL'S CONVERSION.

568. Williams, Stanley T. "Introduction" to A VOLUNTEER'S ADVENTURES. New Haven, Conn.: Yale University Press, 1946.

A perceptive discussion of De Forest's realism.

569. Wilson, Edmund. "The Chastening of American Prose Style; John William De Forest." In PATRIOTIC GORE: STUDIES IN THE LITERATURE OF THE AMERICAN CIVIL WAR. New York: Oxford University Press, 1962.

A lengthy (due, in part, to extended quotations) and perceptive essay.

EDWARD EGGLESTON (1837-1902)

Principal Works

THE HOOSIER SCHOOL-MASTER, 1871   Novel
THE END OF THE WORLD, 1872   Novel
THE MYSTERY OF METROPOLISVILLE, 1873   Novel
THE CIRCUIT RIDER, 1874   Novel
ROXY, 1878   Novel
THE HOOSIER SCHOOL-BOY, 1883   Novel
THE GRAYSONS, 1888   Novel
THE FAITH DOCTOR, 1891   Novel

Eggleston also wrote several books of juvenile fiction, biography, and history.

Bibliography

570.   See 573.

Checklist

571.   Randel, William Peirce. "Edward Eggleston (1837-1902)." ALR, 1
(1967), 36-38.

Biography

572.   Eggleston, George Cary. THE FIRST OF THE HOOSIERS. Philadelphia,
Pa.: D. Biddle, 1903.

>   The first full-length biography; by Eggleston's brother. Some-
>   what overwritten.

573.   Randel, William Peirce. EDWARD EGGLESTON: AUTHOR OF "THE
HOOSIER SCHOOL-MASTER." New York: King Crown Press, 1946.

>   A competent scholarly biography. Includes bibliography of
>   Eggleston's works.

Critical Studies

574. Ahnebrink, Lars. "Edward Eggleston, Edgar Watson Howe, and Joseph Kirkland." In THE BEGINNINGS OF NATURALISM IN AMERICAN FICTION. New York: Russell & Russell, 1961.

Describes Eggleston as a realist whose work is marred by a strain of sentimentality.

575. Cowie, Alexander. "Edward Eggleston (1837-1902)." In THE RISE OF THE AMERICAN NOVEL. New York: American Book Co., 1951.

General commentary.

576. Flanagan, John T. "The Novels of Edward Eggleston." CE, 5 (1944), 250-54.

A general introduction to Eggleston's work.

577. Hamilton, Holman. "Introduction" to THE CIRCUIT RIDER: A TALE OF THE HEROIC AGE. Lexington: The University Press of Kentucky, 1970.

General commentary on both Eggleston and THE CIRCUIT RIDER.

578. Randel, William Peirce. EDWARD EGGLESTON. New York: Twayne, 1963.

Devotes more space to criticism of the works than does Randel's earlier biography (see 573).

579. _____. "Introduction" to THE CIRCUIT RIDER. New Haven, Conn.: College and University Press, 1966.

A succinct yet fairly comprehensive introduction to both novel and novelist; deals with the critical reception of both.

580. Schlesinger, Arthur M. "Evolution of A Historian." Introduction to THE TRANSIT OF CIVILIZATION FROM ENGLAND TO AMERICA IN THE SEVENTEENTH CENTURY. Boston, Mass.: Beacon Press, 1959.

Although the main emphasis is on Eggleston as historian, some space is given to the relation between his imaginative and historical writings.

581. Wilson, Jack H. "Eggleston's Indebtedness to George Eliot in ROXY." AL, 42 (1970), 38-49.

The novel was significantly influenced by Eliot's ROMOLA and MIDDLEMARCH.

HAROLD FREDERIC (1856-1898)

Principal Works

SETH'S BROTHER'S WIFE, 1887   Novel
THE LAWTON GIRL, 1890   Novel
IN THE VALLEY, 1890   Novel
THE RETURN OF THE O'MAHONY, 1892   Novel
THE COPPERHEAD, 1893   Novel
MARSENA AND OTHER STORIES, 1894
THE DAMNATION OF THERON WARE, 1896   Novel
MARCH HARES, 1896   Novel
GLORIA MUNDI, 1898   Novel
THE MARKET-PLACE, 1899   Novel

Collected Works

582.   HAROLD FREDERIC'S STORIES OF YORK STATE.   Ed. Thomas O'Donnell;
       introduction by Edmund Wilson.   Syracuse, N.Y.:   Syracuse University
       Press, 1966.

583.   THE MAJOR WORKS.   5 vols.   New York: Greenwood Press, 1969.

584.   WORKS BY HAROLD FREDERIC.   5 vols.   New York: Charles Scribner's
       Sons, 1897.

Bibliography

585.   Woodward, Robert H.   "Harold Frederic: A Bibliography."   SB, 13
       (1960), 247-57.

586.   Woodward, Robert H. and Stanton Garner.   "Frederic's Short Fiction:
       A Checklist."   ALR, 1 (1968), 73-76.

Checklist

587.   "Harold Frederic (1856-1898): A Critical Bibliography of Secondary

Comment." ALR, 1 (1968), 1-72.

An indispensable annotated listing of books and essays about Frederic and his work. See also 589.

588. O'Donnell, Thomas F. CHECKLIST OF HAROLD FREDERIC. Columbus, Ohio: Charles E. Merrill, 1969.

Includes primary as well as secondary items.

589. Woodward, Robert H. "Harold Frederic: Supplemental Critical Bibliography of Secondary Comment." ALR, 3 (1970), 94-147.

Supplement to 587.

News Letter

590. THE FREDERIC HERALD. 1967- .

Published at Utica College, Utica, N.Y.

Biography

591. Haines, Paul. "Harold Frederic." New York University, 1945 (Ph.D. dissertation).

Still the standard biography.

Critical Studies

592. Blackall, Jean F. "Perspectives on Harold Frederic's MARKET-PLACE." PMLA, 86 (1971), 388-405.

A discussion of Joel Thorpe (the hero), a character whose complexity stems from Frederic's "dualistic concepts of his nature."

593. Briggs, Austin, Jr. THE NOVELS OF HAROLD FREDERIC. Ithaca, N.Y.: Cornell University Press, 1969.

A perceptive study which argues that Frederic is an ironist as well as a realist.

594. Carter, Everett. "Introduction" to THE DAMNATION OF THERON WARE. Cambridge, Mass.: Harvard University Press, 1960.

The relation of this novel to the realistic movement.

595. Crane, Stephen. "Harold Frederic." THE CHAP-BOOK, 8 (March 15, 1898), 358-59.

Praises Frederic for "the perfect evenness of [his] craft" and attacks his critics.

596. Davies, Horton. "Divines in Doubt." In A MIRROR OF THE MINISTRY IN MODERN NOVELS. New York: Oxford University Press, 1959.

THE DAMNATION OF THERON WARE is not an argument for the new theology; indeed, the "older generation in religion" is treated sympathetically.

597. Earnest, Ernest. "The Flamboyant American: Harold Frederic." In EXPATRIATES AND PATRIOTS. Durham, N.C.: Duke University Press, 1968.

Earnest comments on most of Frederic's major novels, contrasts him with Henry James, and ultimately views him as "a wide-ranging social critic of considerable stature."

598. Eichelberger, Clayton L. "Philanthropy in Frederic's THE MARKET PLACE." AQ, 20 (1968), 111-16.

Like many others of his day, Frederic was skeptical of philanthropy, as a close reading of THE MARKET-PLACE indicates.

599. Garner, Stanton. HAROLD FREDERIC. Minneapolis: University of Minnesota Press, 1969.

A brief but perceptive commentary which treats Frederic as a descendant of Melville and Hawthorne rather than a regionalist or realist.

600. Johnson, George W. "Harold Frederic's Young Goodman Ware: The Ambiguities of a Realistic Romance." MFS, 8 (1963), 361-74.

This flawed but admirable novel combines Howellsian social realism with the Hawthornian "melodrama of solitary man making his anguished and impossible choice of good and evil."

601. Kane, Patricia. " 'Lest Darkness Come Upon You': An Interpretation of THE DAMNATION OF THERON WARE." IOWA ENGLISH YEAR-BOOK, 10 (1965), 55-59.

Discusses the consistent use of Biblical symbols and images in the novel.

602. Lovett, Robert Morss. "Introduction" to THE DAMNATION OF THERON WARE. New York: Boni, 1924.

An insightful discussion of the various characters of the novel.

603. O'Donnell, Thomas F. "Editor's Foreword" to HAROLD FREDERIC'S STORIES OF YORK STATE. Syracuse, N.Y.: Syracuse University Press, 1966.

A brief account of the literary background of the stories in this volume: "The Copperhead," "The Deserter," "Marsena," "A Day in the Wilderness," "The War Widow," "The Eve of the Fourth," and "My Aunt Susan." See also 611.

604. O'Donnell, Thomas F. and Hoyt C. Franchere. HAROLD FREDERIC. New York: Twayne, 1961.

First full-length study of Frederic; corrects many of the earlier misinterpretations of his work. Includes a useful "Selected Bibliography" of works by and about Frederic.

605. Quinn, Arthur Hobson. In AMERICAN FICTION: AN HISTORICAL AND CRITICAL SURVEY. New York: Appleton-Century-Crofts, 1936.

A highly favorable commentary on a "realist who began under the influence of Howells but changed somewhat in method toward the end of his career."

606. Raleigh, John Henry. "THE DAMNATION OF THERON WARE." AL, 30 (1958), 210-27.

A comprehensive reading of its "three historical and cultural levels."

607. Suderman, Elmer F. "THE DAMNATION OF THERON WARE as a Criticism of American Religious Thought." HLQ, 33 (1969), 61-75.

Frederic's novel is based on a fictional convention--the conversion of a skeptic by a female evangelist--which Frederic modifies and uses to criticize premises implicit in the convention.

608. Towers, Tom H. "The Problem of Determinism in Frederic's First Novel." CE, 26 (1965), 361-66.

On SETH'S BROTHER'S WIFE. Rejects the interpretations of Walcutt and O'Donnell and Franchere (see 610 and 604) in favor of one which "comprehends the whole novel."

609. Vanderfleets, Richard. "The Ending of THE DAMNATION OF THERON WARE." AL, 36 (1964), 358-59.

Manuscripts in the Library of Congress indicate that Frederic originally planned a tragic ending to the novel.

610. Walcutt, Charles Child. "Adumbrations: Harold Frederic and Hamlin Garland." In AMERICAN LITERARY NATURALISM, A DIVIDED STREAM. Minneapolis: University of Minnesota Press, 1956.

Examines SETH'S BROTHER'S WIFE and THE DAMNATION OF THERON WARE as proto-naturalistic novels.

611. Wilson, Edmund. "Introduction" to HAROLD FREDERIC'S STORIES OF YORK STATE. Syracuse, N.Y.: Syracuse University Press, 1966.

The historical background of "The Copperhead" and other stories in this collection. See 603.

612. Woodward, Robert H. "The Political Background of Harold Frederic's Novel SETH'S BROTHER'S WIFE." NYH, 43 (1962), 239-48.

How Frederic's admiration of Grover Cleveland (and others) affected the writing of this novel.

613. _____ "Some Sources for Harold Frederic's THE DAMNATION OF THERON WARE." AL, 33 (1961), 46-51.

Frederic conscientiously studied Greek civilization, Biblical criticism, and philosophy so that he could make the conversation of his "intellectual" characters ring true.

614. Ziff, Larzer. "Overcivilization: Harold Frederic, the Roosevelt-Adams Outlook, Owen Wister." In THE AMERICAN 1890s: LIFE AND TIMES OF A LOST GENERATION. New York: Viking, 1966.

Frederic's protagonist Theron Ware was, in contrast to the manly Rooseveltian temper of the times, "overcivilized."

MARY E. WILKINS FREEMAN (1852-1930)

Freeman is referred to occasionally as "Wilkins," since a number of her early works appeared under her maiden name.

Principal Works

DECORATIVE PLAQUES, 1883   Poems
A HUMBLE ROMANCE, 1887   Stories
A NEW ENGLAND NUN AND OTHER STORIES, 1891
JANE FIELD, 1893   Novel
GILES COREY, YEOMAN, 1893   Play
PEMBROKE, 1894   Novel
JEROME, A POOR MAN, 1897   Novel
THE HEART'S HIGHWAY, 1900   Novel
THE PORTION OF LABOR, 1901   Novel
THE WIND IN THE ROSE-BUSH, 1903   Stories
EDGEWATER PEOPLE, 1918   Stories

Bibliography

615. See 617.

Checklist

616. Westbrook, Perry D.   "Mary E. Wilkins Freeman (1852-1930)." ALR, 2 (1969), 139-42.

> A brief overview of the current status of Freeman scholarship; includes suggestions for further study.

Biography

617. Foster, Edward. MARY E. WILKINS FREEMAN. New York: Hendricks House, 1956.

The only full-length biography. Includes the best bibliography to date of her writings.

Critical Studies

618. Brooks, Van Wyck. "Country Pictures." In NEW ENGLAND: INDIAN SUMMER. New York: E. P. Dutton, 1940.

   Freeman "revealed the desolation of the Yankee ebb-tide. But, better than anyone else, she also pictured the powers of last resistance in the Yankee soul."

619. Gallagher, Edward J. "Freeman's 'The Revolt of Mother.' " EXPLICA-TOR, 27 (June 1969), item 48.

   How careful selection of characters' names enriched the story.

620. Hirsch, David H. "Subdued Meaning in 'A New England Nun.' " SSF, 2 (1965), 124-36.

   A thorough, scholarly discussion of one of Freeman's short masterpieces.

621. [Howells, William Dean.] "Editor's Study." HARPER'S NEW MONTHLY, 74 (1887), 482-86.

   An important discussion of Freeman as part of the realist tradition at large.

622. Matthiessen, F. O. "New England Stories." In AMERICAN WRITERS ON AMERICAN LITERATURE, ed. John Macy. New York: Horace Liveright, 1931.

   Draws contrasts between Freeman's work and that of Stowe and Jewett.

623. Pattee, Fred Lewis. "On the Terminal Moraine of New England Puritan-ism." In SIDE-LIGHTS ON AMERICAN LITERATURE. New York: Cen-tury Co., 1922.

   A biographical-critical treatment which concludes that Free-man's "kinship is with Hawthorne rather than with the realists."

624. _____. "Recorders of New England Decline." In A HISTORY OF AMERICAN LITERATURE SINCE 1870. New York: Century Co., 1915.

   Like most critics, Pattee prefers the earlier Freeman and her tales of "repression" to the later, "sophisticated and self-conscious" tales.

625. Quina, James H., Jr. "Character Types in the Fiction of Mary Wilkins Freeman." CLQ, 9 (1971), 432-39.

   Freeman achieves thematic unity in her fiction through the interaction of four character types: those in control, the ascetics, the activists, and the moderators.

626. Toth, Susan A. "Mary Wilkins Freeman's Parable of Wasted Life." AL, 42 (1971), 564-67.

> Freeman's "The Three Old Sisters and the Old Beau" is a harsh commentary on late nineteenth-century New England life.

627. [Unsigned.] "New England in the Short Story." ATLANTIC, 67 (1891), 845-50.

> An insightful early study of Freeman which finds her fiction superior to that of other writers in its accurate portrayal of the loneliness of rural New England life.

628. Warner, Sylvia Townsend. "Item, One Empty House." NY, 42 (March 26, 1966), 131-38.

> A cogent, nonscholarly causerie on the enduring spirit of Freeman's New England.

629. Westbrook, Perry D. "The Anatomy of the Will: Mary Wilkins Freeman." In ACRES OF FLINT: WRITERS OF RURAL NEW ENGLAND, 1870-1900. Washington, D.C.: Scarecrow, 1951.

> Artistically inferior to Hawthorne, Dickinson, and E. A. Robinson, Freeman partially compensates by bringing to her work an objectivity superior to theirs.

630. _____. MARY WILKINS FREEMAN. New York: Twayne, 1967.

> "Mrs. Freeman's greatest strength lies in her insights into the post-Calvinist psyche as it existed in the back-country of New England at the end of the nineteenth century." This study includes a useful "Selected Bibliography" of works by and about Freeman.

HENRY B. FULLER (1857-1929)

Principal Works

THE CHEVALIER OF PENSIERI-VANI, 1890   Novel (published under the pseudonym of Stanton Page)
THE CHATELAINE OF LA TRINITE, 1892   Novel
THE CLIFF-DWELLERS, 1893   Novel
WITH THE PROCESSION, 1895   Novel
FROM THE OTHER SIDE, 1898   Stories
THE LAST REFUGE, 1900   Novel
UNDER THE SKYLIGHTS, 1901   Stories
WALDO TRENCH AND OTHERS, 1908   Stories
ON THE STAIRS, 1918   Novel
BERTRAM COPE'S YEAR, 1919   Novel
GARDENS OF THIS WORLD, 1929   Novel
NOT ON THE SCREEN, 1930   Novel

Bibliography

631. See 633.

Checklist

632. Williams, Kenny Jackson. "Henry Blake Fuller (1857-1929)." ALR, 1 (1968), 9-13.

> A brief overview of the current status of Fuller scholarship; includes suggestions for further study.

Biography

633. Griffin, Constance Magee. HENRY BLAKE FULLER: A CRITICAL BIOG-RAPHY. Philadelphia: University of Pennsylvania Press, 1939.

> A brief biographical sketch along with two previously un-published works: THE RED CARPET (play) and "Carl Carlsen's Progress" (story). Includes bibliography of Fuller's works.

634. Pilkington, John. HENRY BLAKE FULLER. New York: Twayne, 1970.

The only study of Fuller since Griffin. Surveys the life and
major literary works and includes a useful "Selected Bibliography" of works by and about Fuller.

Critical Studies

635. Abel, Darrel. "Expatriation and Realism in American Fiction in the
1880's: Henry Blake Fuller." ALR, 3 (1970), 245-57.

First publication and discussion of a Fuller essay which treats
"the present state and prospects of American literary realism"
and "the risks and rewards of foreign travel and residence for
American writers."

636. Duffey, Bernard. "Henry Fuller." In THE CHICAGO RENAISSANCE
IN AMERICAN LETTERS: A CRITICAL HISTORY. East Lansing: Michigan State College Press, 1954.

A realistic appraisal of Fuller's development as an author.

637. Harris, Mark. "Fuller and the American Procession." Introduction to
WITH THE PROCESSION. Chicago, Ill.: University of Chicago Press,
1965.

An awkwardly written essay with a superficial sociological
viewpoint; contains some valid insights nonetheless.

638. Morgan, Anna, ed. TRIBUTES TO HENRY B. Chicago, Ill.: Ralph
Fletcher Seymour, 1929.

An important collection of more than seventy tributes to and
evaluations of Fuller.

639. Murray, Donald M. "Henry B. Fuller: Friend of Howells." SAQ, 52
(1953), 431-44.

A useful essay; puts Fuller's career in the proper perspective
by comparing it to that of Howells.

640. Wilson, Edmund. "Two Neglected Novelists: I--Henry B. Fuller: The
Art of Making It Flat." NY, 46 (May 23, 1970), 112-39.

A highly favorable review of Fuller's career.

HAMLIN GARLAND (1860-1940)

Principal Works

MAIN-TRAVELLED ROADS, 1891   Stories
JASON EDWARDS AN AVERAGE MAN, 1892   Novel
A SPOIL OF OFFICE, 1892   Novel
A MEMBER OF THE THIRD HOUSE, 1892   Novel
A LITTLE NORSK, 1892   Novel
PRAIRIE FOLKS, 1893   Stories
CRUMBLING IDOLS, 1894   Essays
ROSE OF DUTCHER'S COOLLY, 1895   Novel
WAYSIDE COURTSHIPS, 1897   Stories
BOY LIFE ON THE PRAIRIE, 1899   Stories
THE CAPTAIN OF THE GRAY-HORSE TROOP, 1902   Novel
CAVANAGH FOREST RANGER, 1910   Novel
OTHER MAIN-TRAVELLED ROADS, 1910   Stories   (collected from PRAIRIE
     FOLKS and WAYSIDE COURTSHIPS)
A SON OF THE MIDDLE BORDER, 1917   Autobiography
A DAUGHTER OF THE MIDDLE BORDER, 1921   Autobiography
TRAIL-MAKERS OF THE MIDDLE BORDER, 1926   Autobiography
BACK-TRAILERS FROM THE MIDDLE BORDER, 1928   Autobiography
ROADSIDE MEETINGS, 1930   Memoirs
COMPANIONS ON THE TRAIL, 1931   Memoirs
MY FRIENDLY CONTEMPORARIES, 1932   Memoirs
AFTERNOON NEIGHBORS, 1934   Memoirs

Collected Works

641.   THE WORKS OF HAMLIN GARLAND. Border Edition. 12 vols. New
       York: Harper & Brothers, 1922.

642.   HAMLIN GARLAND'S DIARIES. Ed. Donald Pizer. San Marino, Calif.:
       Huntington Library, 1968.

Letters

643. Flanagan, John T. "Hamlin Garland Writes to His Chicago Publishers." AL, 23 (1952), 447-57.

Nine letters from Garland to Herbert Stone.

Bibliography

644. CENTENNIAL TRIBUTES AND A CHECKLIST OF THE HAMLIN GARLAND PAPERS IN THE UNIVERSITY OF SOUTHERN CALIFORNIA LIBRARY. Ed. Lloyd A. Arvidson. Los Angeles: University of Southern California Library Bulletin No. 9, 1962.

645. Pizer, Donald. "Hamlin Garland: A Bibliography of Newspaper and Periodical Publications (1885-1895)." BB, 22 (1957), 41-44.

646. See also 650.

Checklist

647. Bryer, Jackson R. and Eugene Harding. "Hamlin Garland (1860-1940): A Bibliography of Secondary Comment." ALR, 3 (1970), 290-387.

An indispensable annotated listing of book and periodical references to Garland. See next item.

648. Bryer, Jackson R. and Eugene Harding, with the assistance of Robert A. Rees. "Hamlin Garland: Reviews and Notices of His Work." ALR, 4 (1971), 103-56.

A supplement to the preceding item.

649. Pizer, Donald. "A Bibliography of Hamlin Garland." ALR, 1 (1967), 45-51.

All major contributions to Garland scholarship since 1950 are mentioned.

Biography

650. Holloway, Jean. HAMLIN GARLAND: A BIOGRAPHY. Austin: University of Texas Press, 1960.

A useful book, though not intended to serve as the definitive biography. Treats sympathetically the question of Garland's "selling out." Includes bibliography.

651. Mane, Robert. HAMLIN GARLAND: L'HOMME ET L'OEUVRE. Paris: Didier, 1968.

The most extensive biographical-critical volume on Garland

to date.

652. Pizer, Donald. HAMLIN GARLAND'S EARLY WORKS AND CAREER.
      Berkeley: University of California Press, 1960.

      A thorough discussion of Garland's career during the years
      1884-1895.

Critical Studies

653. Ahnebrink, Lars. THE BEGINNINGS OF NATURALISM IN AMERICAN
      FICTION. New York: Russell & Russell, 1961.

      A standard work on Garland and others.

654. _____ . "Garland and Dreiser: An Abortive Friendship." MJ, 7 (1955-
      56), 285-92.

      Though Garland liked SISTER CARRIE, "differences in tempera-
      ment and ideals" kept him from becoming Dreiser's friend.

655. Bledsoe, T. A. "Introduction" to MAIN-TRAVELLED ROADS: SIX
      MISSISSIPPI VALLEY STORIES. New York: Rinehart, 1954.

      This essay not only discusses the merits of the individual stories
      but also describes a thematic interrelationship which unifies
      the collection. See 675 and 681.

656. Browne, R. B. " 'Popular' & Folk Songs: Unifying Force in Garland's
      Autobiographical Works." SEQ, 25 (1961), 153-66.

      The themes of Middle Border songs that shaped Garland's life
      lend unity to his four autobiographical volumes.

657. Christman, H. M. "Introduction" to A SON OF THE MIDDLE BORDER.
      New York: Macmillan, 1962.

      A discussion of the social, economic, and political back-
      ground of Garland's work.

658. Daly, J. P., S. J. "Hamlin Garland's ROSE OF DUTCHER'S COOLLY."
      ENGLISH LANGUAGE & LITERATURE (Korea), 11 (1962), 51-65.

      Discusses the effect of the novel's unfavorable critical recep-
      tion on the rest of Garland's career.

659. Duffey, Bernard. "Hamlin Garland." In THE CHICAGO RENAISSANCE
      IN AMERICAN LETTERS: A CRITICAL HISTORY. East Lansing: Mich-
      igan State College Press, 1954.

      A general account of the conflicting forces that determined
      Garland's career.

660. _____ . "Hamlin Garland's 'Decline' from Realism." AL, 25 (1953),
      69-74.

A succinct and well-documented account of Garland's Boston years (1884-93) and the extent to which even his realistic writings appear to be compromises with "the vagaries of editorial taste." See 665.

661. Harrison, Stanley R. "Hamlin Garland and the Double Vision of Naturalism." SSF, 6 (1969), 548-56.

"It is strange that the compelling fascination of literary naturalism resides in its somber tone and its non-exit circumstance when, in fact, it is excitation of hope and the potential for escape that create the naturalistic vibration."

662. Henson, Clyde E. "Joseph Kirkland's Influence on Hamlin Garland." AL, 23 (1952), 458-63.

Kirkland's letters to Garland demonstrate the extent of the latter's debt to the former.

663. Howells, W. D. "Mr. Garland's Books." NAR, 196 (1912), 523-28.

A succinct discussion of Garland's writings as native American literature; heavy with praise.

664. Johnson, Jane. "Introduction" to CRUMBLING IDOLS. Cambridge, Mass.: Harvard University Press, 1960.

An analysis of the major themes in this important collection of essays.

665. Koerner, J. D. "Comment on 'Hamlin Garland's "Decline" from Realism.' " AL, 26 (1954), 427-32.

Counters Duffey's assertion that Garland was a "complete literary opportunist" (Koerner's phrase). See 660.

666. Lazenby, W. "Idealistic Realist on the Platform: Hamlin Garland." QJS, 49 (1963), 138-45.

An account of Garland's activities on behalf of Henry George's economic theories.

667. McElderry, B. R., Jr. "Hamlin Garland and Henry James." AL, 23 (1952), 433-46.

Quotes James's letters and other documents to demonstrate that, "slight as it was, the acquaintance of Garland and James testifies to much stronger kinship than might be suspected."

668. _____. "Introduction" to BOY LIFE ON THE PRAIRIE. Lincoln: University of Nebraska Press, 1961.

A favorable reading of BOY LIFE (stories based on Garland's life) which contrasts it with similar reminiscences by other authors as well as with Garland's other works.

669. Mencken, H. L. "Six Members of the Institute: A Stranger on Parnassus." In PREJUDICES: FIRST SERIES. New York: Alfred A. Knopf, 1919.

A largely negative treatment of Garland (though A SON OF THE MIDDLE BORDER is grudgingly called "an honest book").

670. Miller, C. T. "Hamlin Garland's Retreat from Realism." WAL, 1 (1966), 119-29.

For economic reasons, Garland abandoned realism and wrote in a stereotyped romantic style between 1900 and 1916.

671. Morgan, H. Wayne. "Hamlin Garland: The Rebel as Escapist." In AMERICAN WRITERS IN REBELLION FROM TWAIN TO DREISER. New York: Hill and Wang, 1965.

A generally satisfactory introduction (with a certain tendency toward cliche) to Garland.

672. Pizer, Donald. "Hamlin Garland in the STANDARD." AL, 26 (1954), 401-15.

The uncollected writings of Garland for the STANDARD reveal much about his thinking during the period of his most intense literary and political activity.

673. _____. "Hamlin Garland's A SON OF THE MIDDLE BORDER: An Appreciation." SAQ, 65 (1966), 448-59.

Garland's autobiography develops several important themes and ultimately transcends its narrow generic confines.

674. _____. "Hamlin Garland's A SON OF THE MIDDLE BORDER: Autobiography as Art." In ESSAYS IN AMERICAN LITERATURE PRESENTED TO BRUCE McELDERRY, JR., ed. Max F. Schultz, et al. Athens: Ohio University Press, 1968.

A close examination of the work primarily in terms of its themes and form (rather than as a cultural document).

675. _____. "Introduction" to MAIN-TRAVELLED ROADS. Columbus, Ohio: Charles E. Merrill, 1970.

Despite weaknesses in some of the stories, this collection is "artful and moving" as a whole and is unified by certain images which are employed throughout. See 655 and 681.

676. _____. "Introduction" to ROSE OF DUTCHER'S COOLLY. Lincoln: University of Nebraska Press, 1969.

A perceptive analysis of ROSE which compares it to other comtemporary works (by Hardy, Ibsen, Dreiser, etc.) that deal with the effects of sexual knowledge and experience.

677. _____. In REALISM AND NATURALISM IN NINETEENTH-CENTURY AMERICAN LITERATURE. Carbondale and Edwardsville: Southern Illinois

University Press, 1966.

Includes two chapters on Garland and Crane: one on their
literary affinities and another on their friendship.

678. _____. "Romantic Individualism in Garland, Norris, and Crane." AQ,
10 (1958), 463-75.

In CRUMBLING IDOLS, Garland's romantic individualism is
indicated by his belief in the superiority of the artist's per-
ceptions to literary convention.

679. Raw, Ruth M. "Hamlin Garland, the Romanticist." SR, 36 (1928),
202-10.

Realistic in point of view and technique, Garland is nonetheless a romantic in his attitude toward life.

680. Reamer, O. J. "Garland and the Indians." NMQ, 34 (1964), 257-80.

An account of Garland's "Indian period," between 1895 and
1905, when he wrote most of the stories later collected in
THE BOOK OF THE AMERICAN INDIAN.

681. Schorer, Mark. "Afterword" to MAIN-TRAVELLED ROADS. New York:
New American Library, 1962.

Deals with themes that the stories have in common ("the return to his rural past" and "the irrelevance of romantic love").
See 655 and 675.

682. Simpson, Claude M., Jr. "Hamlin Garland's Decline," SWR, 26 (1941),
223-34.

A general overview of Garland's career predicated on the fact
that Garland "ceased to grow almost with the first appearance
of real success."

683. Stronks, James B. "A Realist Experiments with Impressionism: Hamlin
Garland's 'Chicago Studies.' " AL, 36 (1964), 38-52.

Garland abandoned realism in 1892-93 to experiment with
impressionism. Six impressionistic "Chicago Studies," previously unpublished, are printed here.

684. Taylor, Walter Fuller. "Hamlin Garland." In THE ECONOMIC NOVEL
IN AMERICA. Chapel Hill: University of North Carolina Press, 1942.

A comprehensive study of Garland's economic and social
writing and thought.

685. Walcutt, Charles Child. "Adumbrations: Harold Frederic and Hamlin
Garland." In AMERICAN LITERARY NATURALISM, A DIVIDED STREAM.
Minneapolis: University of Minnesota Press, 1956.

Interesting comments on Garland's "incoherent" fictional
structures.

686.   Whitford, Kathryn. "Crusader Without a Cause: An Examination of
       Hamlin Garland's Middle Border." MASJ, 6 (1965), 61-72.

       Accounts for Garland's abandonment of the Middle Border as
       a subject.

687.   _____. "Patterns of Observation: A Study of Hamlin Garland's Middle
       Border Landscape." TWA, 50 (1961), 331-38.

       An appraisal of Garland's talent for accurate description of
       the environment.

JOEL CHANDLER HARRIS (1848-1908)

Principal Works

UNCLE REMUS HIS SONGS AND SAYINGS, 1881   Stories
NIGHTS WITH UNCLE REMUS, 1883   Stories
MINGO AND OTHER SKETCHES IN BLACK AND WHITE, 1884   Stories
FREE JOE, 1887   Stories
UNCLE REMUS AND HIS FRIENDS, 1892   Stories
MR. RABBIT AT HOME, 1895   Stories
SISTER JANE HER FRIENDS AND ACQUAINTANCES, 1896   Novel
TALES OF THE HOME FOLKS IN PEACE AND WAR, 1898   Stories
GABRIEL TOLLIVER, 1902   Novel
THE MAKING OF A STATESMAN, 1902   Stories
THE TAR-BABY AND OTHER RHYMES OF UNCLE REMUS, 1904
TOLD BY UNCLE REMUS, 1905   Stories
UNCLE REMUS AND BRER RABBIT, 1906   Stories
UNCLE REMUS AND THE LITTLE BOY, 1910   Stories

Collected Works

688. Chase, Richard, comp. THE COMPLETE TALES OF UNCLE REMUS. Boston, Mass.: Houghton Mifflin, 1955.

689. JOEL CHANDLER HARRIS: EDITOR AND ESSAYIST. Ed. Julia Collier Harris. Chapel Hill: University of North Carolina Press, 1931.

   Representative writings from the ATLANTA CONSTITUTION and other contemporary newspapers and periodicals.

Letters

690. See 695.

Bibliography

691. See 693, 695, and 697.

Checklist

692. Turner, Arlin. "Joel Chandler Harris." ALR, 1 (1968), 18-23.

> A brief overview of the current status of Harris scholarship;
> concludes with suggestions for further study.

Biography

693. Cousins, Paul M. JOEL CHANDLER HARRIS. Baton Rouge: Louisiana
State University Press, 1968.

> A much-needed scholarly biography which cites hitherto un-
> published material. Includes bibliography of books by and
> studies of Harris.

694. Harlow, Alvin F. JOEL CHANDLER HARRIS: PLANTATION STORY
TELLER. New York: Julian Messner, 1941.

> A popular, nonscholarly biography.

695.) Harris, Julia Collier. THE LIFE AND LETTERS OF JOEL CHANDLER
HARRIS. Boston, Mass.: Houghton Mifflin, 1918.

> By Harris's daughter-in-law. Includes a number of letters as
> well as a bibliography of Harris's books and periodical ap-
> pearances.

696. Wiggins, Robert L. THE LIFE OF JOEL CHANDLER HARRIS. Nashville,
Tenn.: M. E. Church, South, 1918.

> A detailed treatment of Harris's early life.

Critical Studies

697. Brookes, Stella Brewer. JOEL CHANDLER HARRIS: FOLKLORIST.
Athens: University of Georgia Press, 1950.

> "An account of [Harris's] own idea of folklore and an analy-
> sis of his tales, proverbs, and songs by types" (trickster tales,
> myths, etc.). Includes bibliography of Harris's books and
> of writings about him.

698. Brown, Sterling. THE NEGRO IN AMERICAN FICTION. Washington,
D.C.: Associates in Negro Folk Education, 1937.

> "With all of his value as a realist, Harris never came fully
> to grips with the reality of the South or of Negro experience."

699. Buck, Paul. THE ROAD TO REUNION, 1865-1900. Boston, Mass.:
Little, Brown, 1947; New York: Vintage, 1959.

> The role of Harris and other writers in restoring the Union.

700. Dauner, Louise. "Myth and Humor in the Uncle Remus Fables." AL, 20 (1948), 129-43.

   The mythic and comic implications of Harris's fables give them "an imaginative and dramatic vitality" that other Southern local-color writings lack.

701. English, Thomas H., ed. MARK TWAIN TO UNCLE REMUS. Atlanta, Ga.: Emory University Library, 1953.

   A brief account of the friendship of the two authors, with letters from Twain to Harris.

702. Glazier, Lyle. "The Uncle Remus Stories: Two Portraits of American Negroes." JGE, 22 (1970), 71-79.

   Deals with the ironic discrepancy between the actual weakness of Uncle Remus and the seeming weakness of Brer Rabbit.

703. Harris, Julia Collier. "Joel Chandler Harris: Constructive Realist." In SOUTHERN PIONEERS IN SOCIAL INTERPRETATION, ed. H. W. Odum. Chapel Hill: University of North Carolina Press, 1925; Freeport, N.Y.: Books for Libraries Press, 1967.

   A not altogether unbiased presentation of Harris's social thought.

704. Ives, Sumner. THE PHONOLOGY OF THE UNCLE REMUS STORIES. Gainesville, Fla.: The American Dialect Society, 1954.

   The phonology of the stories is consistent and "clearly based on accurate observation of a genuine folk speech."

705. Stafford, John. "Patterns of Meaning in NIGHTS WITH UNCLE REMUS." AL, 18 (1946), 89-108.

   An analysis of the four levels of meaning in this book indicates that Harris, usually studied as a folklorist, dialectician, or social historian, is a complex literary strategist as well.

706. Turner, Darwin T. "Daddy Joel Harris and His Old-Time Darkies." SLJ, 1 (Autumn 1968), 20-41.

   A useful essay in that it examines closely Harris's treatment of Negro characters other than Uncle Remus.

BRET HARTE (1836-1902)

Principal Works

THE LOST GALLEON AND OTHER TALES, 1867   Poems
CONDENSED NOVELS, 1867   Parodies
THE LUCK OF ROARING CAMP, AND OTHER SKETCHES, 1870   Stories
MRS. SKAGGS'S HUSBANDS, AND OTHER SKETCHES, 1873
TALES OF THE ARGONAUTS, 1875   Stories
GABRIEL CONROY, 1876   Novel
TWO MEN OF SANDY BAR, 1876   Play
AN HEIRESS OF RED DOG AND OTHER TALES, 1879
JEFF BRIGGS'S LOVE STORY AND OTHER SKETCHES, 1880
A SAPPHO OF GREEN SPRINGS, 1891   Stories
COLONEL STARBOTTLE'S CLIENT, 1892   Stories

Collected Works

707.   THE WRITINGS OF BRET HARTE. Standard Library Edition. 20 vols. Boston, Mass. and New York: Houghton Mifflin, 1896-1914.

Letters

708.   Booth, Bradford A. "Bret Harte Goes East: Some Unpublished Letters." AL, 19 (1948), 318-35.

        Thirteen letters to Lowell, Longfellow, Bierce, Howells, and others.

709.   THE LETTERS OF BRET HARTE. Ed. Geoffrey Bret Harte. Boston, Mass. and New York: Houghton Mifflin, 1926.

Bibliography

710.   Gaer, Joseph, ed. BRET HARTE: BIBLIOGRAPHY AND BIOGRAPHICAL DATA. New York: Burt Franklin, 1968.

711.   Stewart, G. R. A BIBLIOGRAPHY OF THE WRITINGS OF BRET HARTE IN THE MAGAZINES AND NEWSPAPERS OF CALIFORNIA, 1857-1871. UCPES, 3 (1933), 119-70.

Checklist

712.   Morrow, Patrick. "Bret Harte (1836-1902)." ALR, 3 (1970), 167-77.

> An overview of the current state of Harte scholarship; includes suggestions for further study.

Biography

713.   O'Connor, Richard. BRET HARTE, A BIOGRAPHY. Boston, Mass.: Little, Brown, 1966.

> A readable book which adds little to Stewart's account.

714.   Stewart, George R., Jr. BRET HARTE: ARGONAUT AND EXILE. Boston, Mass.: Houghton Mifflin, 1931.

> The definitive biography to date.

Critical Studies

715.   Boggan, J. R. "The Regeneration of 'Roaring Camp.' " NCF, 22 (1967), 271-80.

> Argues against the Christian interpretation of the story in which the men of Roaring Camp are regenerated.

716.   Duckett, Margaret. MARK TWAIN AND BRET HARTE. Norman: University of Oklahoma Press, 1964.

> A study of the rift between the two writers, for which Twain receives most of the blame.

717.   Harrison, Joseph B., ed. "Introduction" to BRET HARTE: REPRESENTATIVE SELECTIONS. New York: American Book Co., 1941.

> A comprehensive introduction to Harte's life and works.

718.   Howells, William Dean. "Mr. Bret Harte's Miggles, and Mr. T. B. Aldrich's Marjorie Daw." In HEROINES OF FICTION, vol. 2. New York and London: Harper & Brothers, 1901.

> Harte's "Magdalenes of the mining community" are more interesting than his "politer ladies."

719.   Stegner, Wallace. "Introduction" to HARTE'S "THE OUTCASTS OF POKER FLAT" AND OTHER TALES. New York and Toronto: New American Library, 1961.

A useful commentary on Harte's strengths and weaknesses as a writer.

NATHANIEL HAWTHORNE (1804-1864)

Principal Works

FANSHAWE, 1828   Novel
TWICE-TOLD TALES, 1837
GRANDFATHER'S CHAIR, 1841   Children's Stories
MOSSES FROM AN OLD MANSE, 1846   Stories
THE SCARLET LETTER, 1850   Novel
THE HOUSE OF THE SEVEN GABLES, 1851   Novel
THE SNOW-IMAGE, AND OTHER TWICE-TOLD TALES, 1851
THE BLITHEDALE ROMANCE, 1852   Novel
LIFE OF FRANKLIN PIERCE, 1852   Biography
A WONDER-BOOK FOR GIRLS AND BOYS, 1852   Greek myths retold
TANGLEWOOD TALES, FOR GIRLS AND BOYS, 1853   Greek myths retold
THE MARBLE FAUN, 1860   Novel
OUR OLD HOME, 1863   Sketches
PASSAGES FROM THE AMERICAN NOTE-BOOKS, 1868
PASSAGES FROM THE ENGLISH NOTE-BOOKS, 1870
PASSAGES FROM THE FRENCH AND ITALIAN NOTE-BOOKS, 1872
SEPTIMIUS FELTON; OR THE ELIXIR OF LIFE, 1872   Unfinished Novel
THE DOLLIVER ROMANCE, 1876   Unfinished Novel
DOCTOR GRIMSHAWE'S SECRET, 1883   Unfinished Novel
THE AMERICAN NOTEBOOKS, 1932
HAWTHORNE AS EDITOR   SELECTIONS FROM HIS WRITINGS IN THE
        AMERICAN MAGAZINE OF USEFUL AND ENTERTAINING KNOWLEDGE,
        1941
THE ENGLISH NOTEBOOKS, 1941

Collected Works

720.   THE COMPLETE WORKS OF NATHANIEL HAWTHORNE. Riverside
        Edition. 12 vols. Boston, Mass.: Houghton Mifflin, 1883.

        This is the standard edition, although it will be superseded
        by the following item.

721.   THE CENTENARY EDITION OF THE WORKS OF NATHANIEL HAW-
        THORNE. Ed. William Charvat, et al. 14 vols. projected. Columbus:

Ohio State University Press, 1962–

In progress. See 720.

Letters

722. LETTERS OF NATHANIEL HAWTHORNE TO WILLIAM D. TICKNOR, 1851–64. Newark, N.J.: Carteret Book Club, 1910.

723. LOVE LETTERS OF NATHANIEL HAWTHORNE, 1839–41 AND 1841–63. Chicago, Ill.: Society of the Dofobs, 1907.

Journals

724. THE NATHANIEL HAWTHORNE JOURNAL. 1971– . Published by NCR Microcards, Washington, D.C.

Bibliography

725. Browne, Nina E. A BIBLIOGRAPHY OF NATHANIEL HAWTHORNE. Boston, Mass.: Houghton Mifflin, 1905.

Includes early criticism, poems about Hawthorne, etc., in addition to his own publications.

726. Cathcart, Wallace H. BIBLIOGRAPHY OF THE WORKS OF NATHANIEL HAWTHORNE. Cleveland, Ohio: Rowfant Club, 1905.

727. FIRST EDITIONS OF THE WORKS OF NATHANIEL HAWTHORNE TO-GETHER WITH SOME MANUSCRIPTS, LETTERS, AND PORTRAITS. New York: The Grolier Club, 1904.

728. Ricks, Beatrice, et al. NATHANIEL HAWTHORNE: A REFERENCE BIBLIOGRAPHY. Boston, Mass.: G. K. Hall, 1972.

Includes items by and about Hawthorne.

Checklist

729. Beebe, Maurice and Jack Hardie. "Criticism of Nathaniel Hawthorne: A Selected Checklist." SNNTS, 2 (1970), 519–87.

Particularly useful because discussions of individual works are grouped under the titles of the works (which are listed alphabetically).

730. Cady, Edwin H. " 'The Wizard Hand': Hawthorne, 1864–1900." In THE LIGHT OF COMMON DAY: REALISM IN AMERICAN FICTION. Bloomington: Indiana University Press, 1971.

The critical treatment of Hawthorne during these years is important because "Hawthorne's became the first unquestionably major American fictional reputation."

731. Clark, C. E. Frazer, Jr. THE MERRILL CHECKLIST OF NATHANIEL HAWTHORNE. Columbus, Ohio: Charles E. Merrill, 1970.

Hawthorne's books and separate publications, editions, letters, bibliographies and checklists, biographies and memoirs, scholarship and criticism.

732. Gross, Theodore L. "Nathaniel Hawthorne." In HAWTHORNE, MELVILLE, STEPHEN CRANE: A CRITICAL BIBLIOGRAPHY, by Theodore L. Gross and Stanley Wertheim. New York: Free Press, 1971.

Editions, primary materials, bibliographies, biographies and critical biographies, plus an indispensable listing of 170 critical items, each of which is abstracted at length.

733. Jones, Buford. A CHECKLIST OF HAWTHORNE CRITICISM, 1951-1966. Hartford, Conn.: Transcendental Books, 1967.

Bibliographies, critical introductions, books, monographs, essays, dissertations, foreign criticism. Annotated. This book may be used in conjunction with Kenneth W. Cameron's HAWTHORNE INDEX TO THEMES, MOTIFS...AND KEY WORDS DEALT WITH IN RECENT CRITICISM, Hartford, Conn.: Transcendental Books, 1968. Cameron's book is somewhat baffling in that it also includes portraits of twenty-nine American authors as well as some Emerson miscellanea in addition to the Hawthorne index.

734. See 728.

Biography

Note: there are a number of additional biographies and critical biographies. See 731, 732, and 809.

735. Arvin, Newton. HAWTHORNE. Boston, Mass.: Little, Brown, 1929.

One of the important biographies in the history of modern Hawthorne scholarship, though occasionally inaccurate.

736. Conway, Moncure D. LIFE OF NATHANIEL HAWTHORNE. New York: Scribner and Welford, 1890.

A perceptive early study.

737. Hawthorne, Julian. NATHANIEL HAWTHORNE AND HIS WIFE. 2 vols. Boston, Mass.: Houghton Mifflin, 1884.

A reminiscence by Hawthorne's son. No critical treatment of the works.

738. Lathrop, George Parsons. A STUDY OF HAWTHORNE. Boston, Mass.: J. R. Osgood, 1876.

   First full-length study; by Hawthorne's son-in-law.

739. Loggins, Vernon. THE HAWTHORNES, THE STORY OF SEVEN GENER-ATIONS OF AN AMERICAN FAMILY. New York: Columbia University Press, 1951.

   The history of the Hawthorne family·from the fifteenth century to the mid-twentieth century.

740. Stewart, Randall. NATHANIEL HAWTHORNE, A BIOGRAPHY. New Haven, Conn.: Yale University Press, 1948.

   The most reliable biography, if not definitive.

741. Wagenknecht, Edward. NATHANIEL HAWTHORNE: MAN AND WRITER. New York: Oxford University Press, 1961.

   A critical biography.

742. Woodberry, George E. NATHANIEL HAWTHORNE. Boston, Mass.: Houghton Mifflin, 1902.

   First scholarly biography.

Critical Studies

743. Abel, Darrel. "Giving Lustre to Gray Shadows: Hawthorne's Potent Art." AL, 41 (1969), 373-88.

   A careful examination of Hawthorne's fictional methods.

744. _____. "Hawthorne's House of Tradition." SAQ, 52 (1953), 561-78.

   Approaches THE HOUSE OF THE SEVEN GABLES as "a kind of prose symphony organized in five stages or movements."

745. _____. "A Masque of Love and Death." UTQ, 23 (1953), 9-25.

   A perceptive study of the symbolic values of the characters in THE MARBLE FAUN.

746. Adams, Richard P. "Hawthorne: The Old Manse Period." TSE, 8 (1958), 115-51.

   An overview of the twenty pieces Hawthorne wrote between 1842 and 1845. They fall into three categories of subject matter: "satire, the life and work of the artist, and what he called 'Allegories of the Heart' " (this last group includes "Rappacini's Daughter").

747. Asselineau, Roger, comp. THE MERRILL STUDIES IN THE HOUSE OF THE SEVEN GABLES. Columbus, Ohio: Charles E. Merrill, 1970.

The essays are divided into three sections: contemporaneous reactions; "A Grudging Admirer: Henry James" (an excerpt from James's HAWTHORNE; see 782); and twentieth-century interpretations.

748. Baym, Nina. "THE MARBLE FAUN: Hawthorne's Elegy for Art." NEQ, 44 (1971), 355-76.

The "conventional moral ending" of THE MARBLE FAUN may be seen as "a gesture of heartsickness and despair, of hopes denied, effort repudiated." The novel itself is deliberately defaced by its author, is "discolored, disfigured, and shattered by his prudence, his conscience, his fatigue, his sense of futility."

749. _____. "Passion and Authority in THE SCARLET LETTER." NEQ, 43 (1970), 209-30.

A provocative discussion of the world view which infuses the novel and which is decidedly not Puritanical but Romantic in nature.

750. Bell, Millicent. HAWTHORNE'S VIEW OF THE ARTIST. New York: State University of New York, 1962.

A discussion of Hawthorne's ambivalent attitude toward art, his "negative Romanticism," and his suspicion of "the morality of self-absorbed artistic activity."

751. Bewley, Marius. THE COMPLEX FATE: HAWTHORNE, HENRY JAMES AND SOME OTHER AMERICAN WRITERS. London: Chatto and Windus, 1952.

The three essays relevant to students of Hawthorne deal with (1) Hawthorne, James, and the American novel; (2) THE BLITHEDALE ROMANCE and THE BOSTONIANS; and (3) THE MARBLE FAUN and THE WINGS OF THE DOVE.

752. Chase, Richard. "Hawthorne and the Limits of Romance." In THE AMERICAN NOVEL AND ITS TRADITION. Garden City, N.Y.: Doubleday, 1957.

Discussions of THE SCARLET LETTER and THE BLITHEDALE ROMANCE.

753. Cifelli, Edward. "Hawthorne and the Italian." SA, 14 (1968), 87-96.

Hawthorne came gradually to dislike Italians, as indicated by evidence in THE HOUSE OF THE SEVEN GABLES and THE MARBLE FAUN.

754. Cohen, B. Bernard. THE MERRILL GUIDE TO NATHANIEL HAWTHORNE. Columbus, Ohio: Charles E. Merrill, 1970.

A brief general commentary for the nonexpert.

755.   _____,ed. THE RECOGNITION OF NATHANIEL HAWTHORNE: SELECT-
ED CRITICISM SINCE 1828. Ann Arbor: University of Michigan Press, 1969.

Includes more than forty critical items as well as a preface
which traces the growth of Hawthorne's reputation.

756.   Cowley, Malcolm. "Five Acts of THE SCARLET LETTER." In TWELVE
ORIGINAL ESSAYS ON GREAT AMERICAN NOVELS, ed. Charles
Shapiro. Detroit, Mich.: Wayne State University Press, 1958.

The novel may be read in terms of the traditional five acts
of Greek tragedy.

757.   Crews, Frederick C. "A New Reading of THE BLITHEDALE ROMANCE."
AL, 29 (1957), 147-70.

Previously considered an artistic failure, the novel is successful if read as "a parable of the modern mind" (i.e., Cover-
dale's). See William L. Hedges, NCF, 14 (1960), 303-16,
for a refutation of Crews.

758.   _____. THE SINS OF THE FATHERS: HAWTHORNE'S PSYCHOLOGI-
CAL THEMES. New York: Oxford University Press, 1966.

A study of Hawthorne's ambiguity and of the similarity of his
plots in terms of their ambiguous psychological patterns.

759.   Crowley, Joseph Donald, ed. HAWTHORNE: THE CRITICAL HERITAGE.
New York: Barnes & Noble, 1970.

Includes 142 items, mostly reviews and notices of Hawthorne's
book publications; prefaced by a useful essay on the development of Hawthorne's critical reputation. The reader will find
this collection more useful than a similar though less well-
organized book, Kenneth W. Cameron's HAWTHORNE AMONG
HIS CONTEMPORARIES (Hartford, Conn.: Transcendental
Books, 1968).

760.   Davidson, Edward H. HAWTHORNE'S LAST PHASE. New Haven, Conn.:
Yale University Press, 1949.

The definitive work on Hawthorne's life and works, 1858-64.

761.   Donohue, Agnes McNeill, ed. A CASEBOOK ON THE HAWTHORNE
QUESTION. New York: Thomas Y. Crowell, 1963.

Sketches and tales, essays on the tales, classic studies of
Hawthorne (Poe through Q. D. Leavis), appendices.

762.   Doubleday, Neal. "Hawthorne's Criticism of New England Life." CE,
2 (1941), 639-53.

Readings of THE BLITHEDALE ROMANCE and THE HOUSE OF
THE SEVEN GABLES in terms of their social criticism.

763.   Dryden, Edgar A. "Hawthorne's Castle in the Air: Form and Theme in

THE HOUSE OF THE SEVEN GABLES." ELH, 38 (1971), 294-317.

> A "sense of homelessness" is "the original impulse or basic theme of Hawthornian Romance," as THE HOUSE OF THE SEVEN GABLES suggests. "To read Hawthorne's books is to encounter a sense of the ephemeral, to feel that the story is about to end at any moment."

764. _____. "The Limits of Romance: A Reading of THE MARBLE FAUN." In INDIVIDUAL AND COMMUNITY: VARIATIONS ON A THEME IN AMERICAN FICTION, ed. Kenneth H. Baldwin and David K. Kirby. Durham, N.C.: Duke University Press, 1975.

> In this novel, Hawthorne explores the various alternatives to isolation: culture, nature, religion, love.

765. Durr, Robert Allen. "Hawthorne's Ironic Mode." NEQ, 30 (1957), 486-95.

> Although limited mainly to his lesser tales, this essay serves as a corrective to the notion that Hawthorne was always grimly serious.

766. Elder, Marjorie J. NATHANIEL HAWTHORNE: TRANSCENDENTAL SYMBOLIST. Athens, Ohio: Ohio University Press, 1969.

> Hawthorne's relationship to the Transcendentalists and the development of his own theories from the Transcendental aesthetic.

767. Feidelson, Charles, Jr. "Four American Symbolists." In SYMBOLISM AND AMERICAN LITERATURE. Chicago, Ill.: University of Chicago Press, 1953.

> The section that deals with Hawthorne is largely a discussion of the relation of "The Custom House" to THE SCARLET LETTER.

768. Fiedler, Leslie A. "Clarissa in America: Toward Marjorie Morningstar." In LOVE AND DEATH IN THE AMERICAN NOVEL. Rev. ed. New York: Stein and Day, 1966.

> In the section that treats THE SCARLET LETTER, Fiedler sees in the story of Hester and Dimmesdale "a paradigm of the fall of love in the New World."

769. Fogle, Richard Harter. HAWTHORNE'S FICTION: THE LIGHT AND THE DARK. Norman: University of Oklahoma Press, 1952.

> Separate chapters on each of six tales and the four major novels. For a refutation of Fogle's New Critical method, see Leon Howard, NCF, 7 (1953), 237-50.

770. _____. HAWTHORNE'S IMAGERY: THE "PROPER LIGHT AND SHADOW" IN THE MAJOR ROMANCES. Norman: University of Oklahoma Press, 1969.

A "narrower and more intensive" supplement to 769.

771. Fussell, Edwin. "Hawthorne, James, and 'The Common Doom.' " AQ, 10 (1958), 438-54.

> The "richest aspect" of the literary relationship of the two men is their quite similar counterpointing of two opposed themes: isolation and withdrawal versus participation in the common bond of humanity.

772. Gale, Robert L. PLOTS AND CHARACTERS IN THE FICTION AND SKETCHES OF NATHANIEL HAWTHORNE. Hamden, Conn.: Archon Books, 1968.

> A useful "dictionary" of short plot summaries and character sketches.

773. Gerber, John C., ed. TWENTIETH CENTURY INTERPRETATIONS OF THE SCARLET LETTER. Englewood Cliffs, N.J.: Prentice-Hall, 1968.

> Essays by various hands; divided into four sections: Background, Form, Technique, Interpretations.

774. Green, Martin. "The Hawthorne Myth: A Protest." In RE-APPRAISALS: SOME COMMONSENSE READINGS IN AMERICAN LITERATURE. New York: W. W. Norton, 1965.

> A discussion of Hawthorne's aesthetic deficiencies.

775. Gross, Seymour L. "Hawthorne Versus Melville." BuR, 14 (December 1966), 89-109.

> A discussion of the authors' differences and affinities (the two works by Hawthorne dealt with at greatest length are "My Kinsman, Major Molineux" and "Young Goodman Brown.")

776. _____, ed. A SCARLET LETTER HANDBOOK. San Francisco, Calif.: Wadsworth, 1960.

> The essays collected here fall into four categories: theme, character, symbolism, and structure.

777. Hall, Lawrence Sargent. HAWTHORNE, CRITIC OF SOCIETY. New Haven, Conn.: Yale University Press, 1944.

> This study of Hawthorne's social thought is a useful corrective to what was for years the stereotyped view of Hawthorne as a "reticent spook."

778. Hoeltje, Hubert H. INWARD SKY: THE MIND AND HEART OF NA-THANIEL HAWTHORNE. Durham, N.C.: Duke University Press, 1962.

> A "spiritual portrait" based on the whole range of Hawthorne's writings.

779. Hoffman, Daniel G. FORM AND FABLE IN AMERICAN FICTION.

New York: Oxford University Press, 1961.

> About one-third of this book is devoted to the relation of folklore and myth to THE HOUSE OF THE SEVEN GABLES, THE SCARLET LETTER, THE BLITHEDALE ROMANCE, and three of Hawthorne's tales.

780. Howe, Irving. "Hawthorne: Pastoral and Politics." In POLITICS AND THE NOVEL. New York: Horizon Press, 1957.

> A discussion of the "failure" of THE BLITHEDALE ROMANCE.

781. Jacobson, Richard J. HAWTHORNE'S CONCEPTION OF THE CREATIVE PROCESS. Cambridge, Mass.: Harvard University Press, 1965.

> A brief study of Hawthorne's eclectically-formed attitudes on the workings of the creative processes.

782. James, Henry. HAWTHORNE. London: Macmillan, 1879; Ithaca, N. Y.: Cornell University Press, 1956.

> This essay may be more useful to students of James than of Hawthorne, although some of the critical comments are still noteworthy.

783. Kaul, A. N. "Character and Motive in THE SCARLET LETTER." CritQ, 10 (1968), 373-84.

> Instead of addressing the usual problems of background, theme, allegory, and symbolism, Kaul attempts to answer certain questions about Hester's mysterious behavior.

784. _____, ed. HAWTHORNE: A COLLECTION OF CRITICAL ESSAYS. Englewood Cliffs, N.J.: Prentice-Hall, 1966.

> Essays by various hands.

785. Kesselring, Marion L. HAWTHORNE'S READING, 1828-1850. New York: New York Public Library, 1949. Reprinted from NYPLB, 53 (1949), 55-71, 121-38, 173-94.

> This is a reprint of the records of the Salem Athenaeum which show what books Hawthorne read during the years mentioned. A useful introduction mentions definite patterns in Hawthorne's reading.

786. Kesterson, David B., comp. THE MERRILL STUDIES IN THE MARBLE FAUN. Columbus, Ohio: Charles E. Merrill, 1971.

> Essays by various hands, including early reviews and criticism as well as twentieth-century views.

787. Lawrence, D. H. STUDIES IN CLASSIC AMERICAN LITERATURE. New York: Viking, 1964.

> Includes essays on THE SCARLET LETTER and THE BLITHEDALE ROMANCE. As a critic, Lawrence is idiosyncratic and im-

pressionistic; his insights, though occasional, are truly perceptive.

788. Levin, Harry. THE POWER OF BLACKNESS: HAWTHORNE, POE, AND
MELVILLE. New York: Alfred A. Knopf, 1958.

Levin's thesis is that "our most perceptive minds have distinguished themselves from our popular spokesmen by concentrating on the dark other half of the situation."

789. Levy, Leo B. "The Landscape Modes of THE SCARLET LETTER." NCF,
23 (1969), 377-92.

A study of "the impact of the traditions of the sublime and
the picturesque on THE SCARLET LETTER."

790. _____. "THE MARBLE FAUN: Hawthorne's Landscape of the Fall."
AL, 42 (1970), 139-56.

A detailed examination of the novel's setting and its implications in terms of "the ambivalence of Hawthorne's responses
to the idea of progress."

791. Lewis, R. W. B. "The Return into Time: Hawthorne." In THE AMERI-
CAN ADAM: INNOCENCE, TRAGEDY, AND TRADITION IN THE
NINETEENTH CENTURY. Chicago, III.: University of Chicago Press,
1955.

A consideration of the idea of the American as Adam ("before and during and after the Fall") as well as other aspects
of Hawthorne.

792. Liebman, Sheldon W. "The Design of THE MARBLE FAUN." NEQ, 40
(1967), 61-78.

A well-documented delineation of the recurring structural
pattern which unifies the novel.

793. McCarthy, Harold T. "Hawthorne's Dialogue with Rome: THE MARBLE
FAUN." SA, 14 (1968), 97-112.

The novel's characters speak Hawthorne's thoughts as he recorded them in his notebook, even when they contradict each
other.

794. McPherson, Hugo. HAWTHORNE AS MYTH-MAKER: A STUDY IN
IMAGINATION. Toronto: University of Toronto Press, 1969.

Attempts to define that "inward vision or drama of which his
works are the particular if partial formulations."

795. Male, Roy R. HAWTHORNE'S TRAGIC VISION. Austin: University
of Texas Press, 1957.

Interpretations of the major works in terms of Hawthorne's
view of tragedy, which is always equated (in Hawthorne's

mind) with the Biblical fall.

796. Martin, Terence. NATHANIEL HAWTHORNE. New York: Twayne, 1965.

An excellent introduction to Hawthorne.

797. Matthiessen, F. O. AMERICAN RENAISSANCE: ART AND EXPRESSION IN THE AGE OF EMERSON AND WHITMAN. London: Oxford University Press, 1941.

A landmark in Hawthorne studies. The nearly 200 pages on Hawthorne are especially useful for those seeking a study of Hawthorne in the context of his time.

798. Mills, Barriss. "Hawthorne and Puritanism." NEQ, 21 (1948), 78-102.

A useful discussion of the aspects of Puritanism which Hawthorne accepted as well as those he rejected.

799. Moss, Sidney P. "The Symbolism of the Italian Background in THE MARBLE FAUN." NCF, 23 (1968), 332-36.

The history of Rome mirrors the history of Donatello: both pass through stages of innocence, decadence, and Christian redemption.

800. NATHANIEL HAWTHORNE SPECIAL NUMBER. SNNTS, 2 (1970), 389-587.

Essays by various hands and a selected checklist of Hawthorne criticism.

801. Normand, Jean. NATHANIEL HAWTHORNE: AN APPROACH TO AN ANALYSIS OF ARTISTIC CREATION, trans. Derek Coltman. Cleveland, Ohio: Press of Case Western Reserve University, 1970.

A weighty, provocative psychological study of Hawthorne's creative processes, his "spiritual arabesques."

802. O'Connor, Evangeline Maria. AN ANALYTICAL INDEX TO THE WORKS OF NATHANIEL HAWTHORNE. Boston, Mass.: Houghton Mifflin, 1882; Detroit, Mich.: Gale Research Co., 1967.

Includes topics (mountains, opium-dreams, etc.) as well as characters and place names.

803. Orians, G. Harrison. "Hawthorne and Puritan Punishments." CE, 13 (1952), 424-32.

This article, most of which is devoted to the scarlet A, is of slight critical value, although it is useful for background information.

804. Paulits, Walter J. "Ambivalence in 'Young Goodman Brown.'" AL, 41 (1970), 577-84.

Sees the story as an allegory of ambivalence in which the
protagonist has only partial knowledge and chooses wrongly,
whether knowingly or not.

805.   Pearce, Roy Harvey. "Day-Dream and Fact: The Import of THE BLITHE-
DALE ROMANCE." In INDIVIDUAL AND COMMUNITY: VARIATIONS
ON A THEME IN AMERICAN FICTION, ed. Kenneth H. Baldwin and
David K. Kirby. Durham, N.C.: Duke University Press, 1975.

Hawthorne's fictional community fails because the characters
ultimately act "like children, trying to reduce or return life
to terms impossible for adults."

806.   _____, ed. HAWTHORNE CENTENARY ESSAYS. Columbus: Ohio
State University Press, 1964.

Eighteen important studies by various hands.

807.   Rohrberger, Mary. HAWTHORNE AND THE MODERN SHORT STORY.
The Hague and Paris: Mouton, 1966.

"Beginning with an examination of Hawthorne's literary theory
and noticing the clear relationship between what Hawthorne
thought literature should be and what his stories were, then
moving to the literary theory and a selection of stories by
representative modern masters of the form, I find similarities
which seem to me to be useful."

808.   Stubbs, John C. THE PURSUIT OF FORM: A STUDY OF HAWTHORNE
AND THE ROMANCE. Urbana: University of Illinois Press, 1970.

Considerations of Hawthorne's concept of the romance as well
as analyses of the tales and the four major romances themselves.

809.   Turner, Arlin. NATHANIEL HAWTHORNE, AN INTRODUCTION AND
INTERPRETATION. New York: Holt, Rinehart and Winston, 1961.

A useful "brief history of his mind."

810.   _____, ed. THE MERRILL STUDIES IN THE SCARLET LETTER. Columbus, Ohio: Charles E. Merrill, 1970.

Essays by various hands on the writing of the novel; contemporary reviews; reviews by the later realists (James, Trollope,
Howells); modern interpretations.

811.   Van Doren, Mark. NATHANIEL HAWTHORNE. New York: William
Sloane Associates, 1949.

A reliable critical biography more useful for its treatment of
the works than the life.

812.   Waggoner, Hyatt. HAWTHORNE, A CRITICAL STUDY. Rev. ed.
Cambridge, Mass.: Harvard University Press, 1963.

Close and perceptive readings of Hawthorne's tales and romances. Waggoner has also written a useful brief introductory work, NATHANIEL HAWTHORNE (Minneapolis: University of Minnesota Press, 1962).

813. Walcutt, Charles C. "THE SCARLET LETTER and Its Modern Critics." NCF, 7 (1953), 251–64.

Identifies five dominant readings of the novel.

814. Warren, Austin. "Nathaniel Hawthorne." In RAGE FOR ORDER, ESSAYS IN CRITICISM. Chicago, Ill.: University of Chicago Press, 1948.

Perceptive general commentary.

815. Winters, Yvor. "Maule's Curse, or Hawthorne and the Problem of Allegory." In IN DEFENSE OF REASON. Denver, Col.: Alan Swallow, 1947. (Reprinted from MAULE'S CURSE, Norfolk, Conn.: New Directions, 1938).

Sees THE SCARLET LETTER as Hawthorne's one perfect allegory and the other major works as "impure novels, or novels with unassimilated allegorical elements."

816. Wright, Nathalia. "The Language of Art: Hawthorne." In AMERICAN NOVELISTS IN ITALY; THE DISCOVERERS: ALLSTON TO JAMES Philadelphia: University of Pennsylvania Press, 1965.

Includes an illuminating analysis of THE MARBLE FAUN

E. W. HOWE (1853-1937)

Principal Works

THE STORY OF A COUNTRY TOWN, 1883   Novel
THE MYSTERY OF THE LOCKS, 1885   Novel
A MOONLIGHT BOY, 1887   Novel
THE CONFESSION OF JOHN WHITLOCK, 1891   Novel
COUNTRY TOWN SAYINGS, 1911   Observations
VENTURES IN COMMON SENSE, 1919   Observations
PLAIN PEOPLE, 1929   Autobiography
THE INDIGNATIONS OF E. W. HOWE, 1933   Observations

Bibliography

817. See 821.

Checklist

818. Eichelberger, Clayton L. "Edgar Watson Howe and Joseph Kirkland: More Critical Comment." ALR, 4 (1971), 279-90.

    Mainly incidental items which supplement the following checklist.

819. Eichelberger, Clayton L. and Frank L. Stallings, Jr. "Edgar Watson Howe (1853-1937): A Critical Bibliography of Secondary Comment." ALR, 2 (1969), 1-49.

    An indispensable annotated listing of books and articles about Howe and his writings.

820. See 821.

Biography

821.   Pickett, Calder M.   ED HOWE: COUNTRY TOWN PHILOSOPHER.
Lawrence: University Press of Kansas, 1968.

A definitive biography which relies heavily on Howe's journalistic and other writings.   Includes bibliography and checklist.

Critical Studies

822.   Pickett, Calder M.   "Edgar Watson Howe and the Kansas Scene."
KANQ, 2 (Spring 1970), 39-45.

An attempt to counter the prevalent belief in Howe's "supposed
hatred for the small town and the agrarian tradition."

823.   Quinn, Arthur Hobson.   In AMERICAN FICTION: AN HISTORICAL
AND CRITICAL SURVEY.   New York: Appleton-Century-Crofts, 1936.

"The book [THE STORY OF A COUNTRY TOWN] would not
be worthy of much notice except that it illustrates the critical
stupidity which praises a sordid picture of life as necessarily
true."

824.   Schorer, C. E.   "Growing Up With the Country."   MJ, 6 (1954),
12-26.

Defends THE STORY OF A COUNTRY TOWN against Carl
Van Doren's criticism of it (see 81) and relates Howe's work
to that of other American novelists.   See 825.

825.   Simpson, Claude M., Jr.   "Introduction" to THE STORY OF A COUNTRY
TOWN.   Cambridge, Mass.:   Harvard University Press, 1961.

Deals with the relationship of Howe's work to Twain, Dickens,
and other authors; see 824.

826.   Stronks, James B.   "William Dean Howells, Ed Howe, and THE STORY
OF A COUNTRY TOWN."   AL, 29 (1958), 473-83.

How Howells promoted the reputation of the novel while making
use of it "in his own campaign for the new realism."

827.   "The University of California Collection, Howe's COUNTRY TOWN."
TWAINIAN, 27 (January-February 1968, 4, and March-April 1968,
1-2).

Reprints and comments on a letter from Twain to Howe in which
he praises and criticizes THE STORY OF A COUNTRY TOWN.
The same letter appears in AL, 27 (1955), 109-12.

828.   Wasserstrom, William.   "The Lily and the Prairie Flower."   AQ, 9

(1957), 398-411.

An analysis of midwestern literary heroines, including those
in THE STORY OF A COUNTRY TOWN.

WILLIAM DEAN HOWELLS (1837-1920)

Principal Works

VENETIAN LIFE, 1866   Travel Essays
SUBURBAN SKETCHES, 1871
THEIR WEDDING JOURNEY, 1872   Novel
A CHANCE ACQUAINTANCE, 1873   Novel
A FOREGONE CONCLUSION, 1875   Novel
THE LADY OF THE AROOSTOOK, 1879   Novel
THE UNDISCOVERED COUNTRY, 1880   Novel
DOCTOR BREEN'S PRACTICE, 1881   Novel
A FEARFUL RESPONSIBILITY AND OTHER STORIES, 1881
A DAY'S PLEASURE, AND OTHER SKETCHES, 1881
A MODERN INSTANCE, 1882   Novel
A WOMAN'S REASON, 1883   Novel
THE RISE OF SILAS LAPHAM, 1885   Novel
INDIAN SUMMER, 1886   Novel
THE MINISTER'S CHARGE, 1887   Novel
APRIL HOPES, 1888   Novel
ANNIE KILBURN, 1889   Novel
A HAZARD OF NEW FORTUNES, 1889   Novel
A BOY'S TOWN, 1890   Autobiography
THE SHADOW OF A DREAM, 1890   Novel
CRITICISM AND FICTION, 1891   Essays
AN IMPERATIVE DUTY, 1891   Novel
THE QUALITY OF MERCY, 1892   Novel
THE WORLD OF CHANCE, 1893   Novel
THE COAST OF BOHEMIA, 1893   Novel
A TRAVELER FROM ALTRURIA, 1894   Novel
STOPS OF VARIOUS QUILLS, 1895   Poems
THE DAY OF THEIR WEDDING, 1896   Novel
A PARTING AND A MEETING, 1896   Stories
THE LANDLORD AT LION'S HEAD, 1897   Novel
AN OPEN-EYED CONSPIRACY, 1897   Novel
THE STORY OF A PLAY, 1898   Novel
RAGGED LADY, 1899   Novel
THEIR SILVER WEDDING JOURNEY, 1899   Novel
LITERARY FRIENDS AND ACQUAINTANCE, 1900   Memoirs

A PAIR OF PATIENT LOVERS, 1901   Stories
THE KENTONS, 1902   Novel
LETTERS HOME, 1903   Novel
QUESTIONABLE SHAPES, 1903   Stories
THE SON OF ROYAL LANGBRITH, 1904   Novel
MISS BELLARD'S INSPIRATION, 1905   Novel
THROUGH THE EYE OF THE NEEDLE, 1907   Novel
BETWEEN THE DARK AND THE DAYLIGHT, 1907   Stories
FENNEL AND RUE, 1908   Novel
MY MARK TWAIN, 1910   Memoir
THE LEATHERWOOD GOD, 1916   Novel
YEARS OF MY YOUTH, 1916   Autobiography
THE DAUGHTER OF THE STORAGE AND OTHER THINGS IN PROSE AND
    VERSE, 1916
THE VACATION OF THE KELWYNS, 1920   Novel
MRS. FARRELL, 1921   Novel

Collected Works

829.   A SELECTED EDITION OF W. D. HOWELLS. 40 vols. projected. Ed.
Edwin H. Cady, et al. Bloomington: Indiana University Press, 1968- .

    In progress.

830.   THE WRITINGS OF WILLIAM DEAN HOWELLS. Library Edition. 6
vols. published of 32 projected. New York and London: Harper, 1911.

    See 12 for details.

Letters

831.   LIFE IN LETTERS OF WILLIAM DEAN HOWELLS. Ed. Mildred Howells.
New York: Doubleday, Doran, 1928.

832.   MARK TWAIN-HOWELLS LETTERS ... 1872-1910. Ed. Henry Nash
Smith and William M. Gibson. 2 vols. Cambridge, Mass.: Harvard
University Press, 1960.

833.   Note: In a letter to me, Professor George Arms has written that a six-
volume edition of the SELECTED LETTERS OF W. D. HOWELLS, edited
by himself, et al., will be published between 1974 and 1978.

834.   See 838 for other letters, mainly in periodicals.

Bibliography

835.   Gibson, William M. and George Arms. A BIBLIOGRAPHY OF WILLIAM
DEAN HOWELLS. New York: New York Public Library and Arno Press,
1971.

836.   See also 12. The definitive bibliography, scheduled for completion in
        1975, is being prepared by George Arms.

Checklist

837.   Beebe, Maurice. "Criticism of William Dean Howells: A Selected
        Checklist." MFS, 16 (1970), 395-419.

        Like all the MFS checklists, this one has the special virtue of
        a section in which studies of individual works are listed sepa-
        rately under the titles of the works.

838.   Fortenberry, George. "William Dean Howells." In FIFTEEN AMERICAN
        AUTHORS BEFORE 1900, ed. Robert A. Rees and Earl N. Harbert.
        Madison: University of Wisconsin Press, 1971.

        A useful bibliographical essay which covers bibliography,
        editions, manuscripts and letters, biography, and criticism.

839.   Kirk, Clara and Rudolf. "Selected Bibliography." In WILLIAM DEAN
        HOWELLS, REPRESENTATIVE SELECTIONS. New York: Hill and Wang,
        1961.

840.   Lydenberg, John and Edwin Cady. "The Howells Revival: Rounds Two
        and Three." NEQ, 32 (1959), 394-407.

        A discussion of some recent books on Howells and an attempt
        to place him in American literary history.

841.   Woodress, James. "The Dean's Comeback: Four Decades of Howells
        Scholarship." TSLL, 2 (1960), 115-23.

        A discussion of the writer-as-growth-stock ("today he is traded
        briskly").

842.   Woodress, James L. and Stanley P. Anderson, comps. "A Bibliography
        of Writings about W. D. Howells." ALR, 1969 Special Supplement,
        1-133.

        An indispensable annotated listing of critical studies on Howells
        from 1860 to the present.

Biography

843.   Brooks, Van Wyck. HOWELLS, HIS LIFE AND WORLD. New York:
        E. P. Dutton, 1959.

        A reliable biography, though smaller in scope than Cady's.
        See 844.

844.   Cady, Edwin. THE ROAD TO REALISM: THE EARLY YEARS 1837-
        1885 OF WILLIAM DEAN HOWELLS (1956) and THE REALIST AT WAR:

THE MATURE YEARS 1885-1920 OF WILLIAM DEAN HOWELLS (1958). Syracuse, N.Y.: Syracuse University Press.

This two-volume study is the best biography to date.

845. Lynn, Kenneth [S.]. WILLIAM DEAN HOWELLS: AN AMERICAN LIFE. New York: Harcourt Brace Jovanovich, 1971.

A readable critical biography, though little new material is included.

846. Wagenknecht, Edward. WILLIAM DEAN HOWELLS: THE FRIENDLY EYE. New York: Oxford University Press, 1969.

A detailed "psychography" of Howells.

Critical Studies

847. Arms, George. "The Literary Background of Howells' Social Criticism." AL, 14 (1942), 260-76.

Cites two influences on Howells' novels of social criticism: his work for the ATLANTIC and the writings of Bjorstjerne Bjornson.

848. Arvin, Newton. "The Usableness of Howells." NR, June 30, 1937, 227-28.

A balanced assessment of Howells' achievement.

849. Bennett, George N. WILLIAM DEAN HOWELLS, THE DEVELOPMENT OF A NOVELIST. Norman: University of Oklahoma Press, 1959.

Bennett makes a point of treating the major novels as works of art, not social documents.

850. Budd, Louis J. "Altruism Arrives in America." AQ, 8 (1956), 40-52.

A study of Howells in the broad context of nineteenth-century American altruism.

851. _____. "Howells and the ATLANTIC and Republicanism." AL, 24 (1952), 139-56.

An examination of Howells' political thinking during his editorship of the ATLANTIC.

852. Cady, Edwin H. and David L. Frazier, eds. THE WAR OF THE CRITICS OVER WILLIAM DEAN HOWELLS. Evanston, Ill.: Row, Peterson, 1962.

Sixty-eight articles and reviews by various hands.

853. Carrington, George C., Jr. THE IMMENSE COMPLEX DRAMA: THE WORLD AND ART OF THE HOWELLS NOVEL. Columbus: Ohio State

University Press, 1966.

A controversial "psychological" reading of the novels.

854. Carter, Everett. HOWELLS AND THE AGE OF REALISM. Philadelphia, Pa.: Lippincott, 1954; Hamden, Conn.: Archon Books, 1966.

Places Howells within the cultural context of his time.

855. Carter, Paul J., Jr. "The Influence of William Dean Howells upon Mark Twain's Social Satire." UNIVERSITY OF COLORADO STUDIES, SERIES IN LANGUAGE AND LITERATURE, 4 (1953), 93-100.

A vindication of Howells, whose social criticism could only have served as a stimulus to Twain, not a hindrance (as Van Wyck Brooks [see 341] and others have charged).

856. Clark, Harry Hayden. "The Role of Science in the Thought of W. D. Howells." TWA, 42 (1953), 263-303.

"In literary theory and practice, as well as in criticism, his passion for truth, for freedom of discussion, and for a realism based not on the exceptional or the erratic but on the law of averages owed much to science."

857. Commager, Henry Steele. "Return to Howells." SPECTATOR, May 28, 1948, 642-43.

Commager repudiates Howells as a critic of the economic order while praising him as a novelist of manners.

858. Cooke, Delmar. WILLIAM DEAN HOWELLS: A CRITICAL STUDY. New York: E. P. Dutton, 1922.

First genuine critical study of Howells.

859. Cowie, Alexander. "William Dean Howells." In THE RISE OF THE AMERICAN NOVEL. New York: American Book Co., 1951.

A general commentary which describes Howells as "an apostle of moderation."

860. Dean, James L. HOWELLS' TRAVELS TOWARD ART. Albuquerque: University of New Mexico Press, 1970.

A sensitive study of the growth of Howells' ideas as revealed in his travel books.

861. Eble, Kenneth E., ed. HOWELLS, A CENTURY OF CRITICISM. Dallas, Tex.: Southern Methodist University Press, 1962.

Essays by various hands, divided into two sections: studies written between 1860 and 1920 and studies since 1920.

862. Falk, Robert. "The Rise of Realism, 1871-91." In TRANSITIONS IN

AMERICAN LITERARY HISTORY, ed. Harry H. Clark. Durham, N.C.:
Duke University Press, 1953.

A long essay on American literary realism and Howells' contribution to the movement.

863. Firkins, Oscar W. WILLIAM DEAN HOWELLS. Cambridge, Mass.:
Harvard University Press, 1924.

An early study of Howells; valuable largely for its inclusiveness.

864. Fischer, William C., Jr. "William Dean Howells: Reverie and the
Nonsymbolic Aesthetic." NCF, 25 (1970), 1-30.

A detailed consideration of Howells' use of the reverie convention in his works and his resistance to "symbolic-metaphoric
language."

865. Foster, Richard. "The Contemporaneity of Howells." NEQ, 32 (1959),
54-78.

An important essay on two Howells themes that are still important in American thought and art: the severance of the
commercial present from the traditional past and the displace-
ment and isolation of the intellectual.

866. Fryckstedt, Olov W. IN QUEST OF AMERICA, A STUDY OF HOWELLS'
EARLY DEVELOPMENT AS A NOVELIST. Cambridge, Mass.: Harvard
University Press, 1958.

Treats Howells' career through 1882. Fryckstedt writes especially well on A MODERN INSTANCE.

867. Gibson, William M. WILLIAM DEAN HOWELLS. Minneapolis: University of Minnesota Press, 1967.

A perceptive brief introduction; includes a selected bibliography
and a checklist of critical works.

868. Gohdes, Clarence. "Realism for the Middle Class." In THE LITERATURE
OF THE AMERICAN PEOPLE, ed. Arthur Hobson Quinn. New York:
Appleton-Century-Crofts, 1951.

A brief but insightful general commentary.

869. Hough, Robert L. THE QUIET REBEL, WILLIAM DEAN HOWELLS AS
SOCIAL COMMENTATOR. Lincoln: University of Nebraska Press,
1959.

Deals with Howells' impact on American social thought. See
872.

870. Kazin, Alfred. "The Opening Struggle for Realism." In ON NATIVE
GROUNDS. New York: Reynal & Hitchcock, 1942.

The basic premise is that modern American literature begins with "the great symbolic episode in the early history of American realism--the move from Boston to New York of William Dean Howells, the Brahmins' favorite child but the first great champion of the new writers."

871. Kirk, Clara M. W. D. HOWELLS AND ART IN HIS TIME. New Brunswick, N.J.: Rutgers University Press, 1965.

A study of Howells' relation to the visual arts.

872. _____. W. D. HOWELLS, TRAVELER FROM ALTRURIA, 1889-1894. New Brunswick, N.J.: Rutgers University Press, 1962.

"An interpretation of Howells' view of the American scene between 1889 and 1894...." Treats aspects of Howells' social thought not covered by 869.

873. Kirk, Clara M. and Rudolf Kirk. WILLIAM DEAN HOWELLS. New York: Twayne, 1962.

A comprehensive treatment of Howells' work. Includes a useful "Selected Bibliography" of works by and about Howells.

874. McMurray, William. THE LITERARY REALISM OF WILLIAM DEAN HOWELLS. Carbondale: Southern Illinois University Press, 1967.

A discussion of the relation of Howells' realism to William James's pragmatism as evidenced in twelve major novels.

875. _____. "Point of View in Howells' THE LANDLORD AT LION'S HEAD." AL, 34 (1962), 207-214.

The "subject-object relationship" is dynamically interactive, both in the novel as well as in Howells' view of reality.

876. Morgan, H. Wayne. "William Dean Howells: The Realist as Reformer." In AMERICAN WRITERS IN REBELLION FROM TWAIN TO DREISER. New York: Hill and Wang, 1965.

A general treatment of Howells' life and works.

877. Parrington, Vernon L. "The Development of Realism." In THE REIN-TERPRETATION OF AMERICAN LITERATURE, ed. Norman Foerster. New York: Harcourt, Brace, 1928.

On the disjunction between Howells' realism of the commonplace and his radical ideas of social justice.

878. Pizer, Donald. "The Evolutionary Foundation of W. D. Howells' CRITICISM AND FICTION." PQ, 40 (1961), 91-103.

Howells' attitudes toward both criticism and fiction "are coherent in their common reference to a conception of the evolution of literature" from a romantic to a more realistic basis.

879. Pritchard, John Paul. "The Realists." In CRITICISM IN AMERICA. Norman: University of Oklahoma Press, 1956.

Deals with theories of literary realism held by Howells, James, and others.

880. ———. "William Dean Howells." In RETURN TO THE FOUNTAINS. Durham, N.C.: Duke University Press, 1942.

Classical influences on Howells' critical theories.

881. Quinn, Arthur Hobson. "William Dean Howells and the Establishment of Realism." In AMERICAN FICTION: AN HISTORICAL AND CRITICAL SURVEY. New York: Appleton-Century-Crofts, 1936.

General commentary.

882. Ratner, Marc L. "Howells and Boyesen: Two Views of Realism." NEQ, 35 (1962), 376-90.

An examination of the Howells-Boyesen correspondence and other documents indicates some differences between European and American concepts of realism.

883. Reeves, John K. "The Way of a Realist: A Study of Howells' Use of the Saratoga Scene." PMLA, 65 (1950), 1035-52.

Deals mainly with AN OPEN-EYED CONSPIRACY.

884. ———. "The Limited Realism of Howells' THEIR WEDDING JOURNEY." PMLA, 77 (1962), 617-28.

The novel marks the midpoint in Howells' conversion from romantic poet to realistic novelist.

885. Tanselle, G. Thomas. "The Architecture of THE RISE OF SILAS LAPHAM." AL, 37 (1966), 430-57.

A detailed argument for the success of the novel's structure.

886. Trilling, Lionel. "W. D. Howells and the Roots of Modern Taste." PR, 18 (1951), 516-36. Reprinted in THE OPPOSING SELF (New York: Viking, 1955).

Largely an appreciation of Howells' "muted, stubborn passion."

887. Vanderbilt, Kermit. "THE UNDISCOVERED COUNTRY: Howells' Version of American Pastoral." AQ, 17 (1965), 634-55.

Howells' first "big" novel can be seen as an "updated BLITHEDALE ROMANCE."

888.   . THE ACHIEVEMENT OF WILLIAM DEAN HOWELLS. Princeton,
N.J.: Princeton University Press, 1968.

Analyses of THE UNDISCOVERED COUNTRY, A MODERN
INSTANCE, THE RISE OF SILAS LAPHAM, and A HAZARD
OF NEW FORTUNES.

889. White, Morton G. and Lucia White. "The Ambivalent Urbanite:
William Dean Howells." In THE INTELLECTUAL VERSUS THE CITY.
Cambridge, Mass.: Harvard University Press and the M.I.T. Press, 1962.

Howells' changing attitudes toward the city.

890. WILLIAM DEAN HOWELLS SPECIAL NUMBER. MFS, 16 (1970), 271-
419.

Essays by various hands and a useful checklist of criticism.

891. Woodress, James L. HOWELLS AND ITALY. Durham, N.C.: Duke
University Press, 1952.

A perceptive study of the influence of Italy on Howells'
writings.

WASHINGTON IRVING (1783-1859)

Principal Works

SALMAGUNDI, 1807-8   Satirical Miscellanies (written with James Kirke
    Paulding and others)
A HISTORY OF NEW YORK, 1809   (pseudonym Diedrich Knickerbocker)
    Burlesque
THE SKETCH BOOK OF GEOFFREY CRAYON, GENT., 1819-20   Tales and
    Essays (includes THE LEGEND OF SLEEPY HOLLOW and RIP VAN WINKLE)
BRACEBRIDGE HALL, 1822   Romantic Sketches
TALES OF A TRAVELLER, 1824   Stories and Sketches
A HISTORY OF THE LIFE AND VOYAGES OF CHRISTOPHER COLUMBUS, 1828
A CHRONICLE OF THE CONQUEST OF GRANADA, 1829   History
VOYAGES AND DISCOVERIES OF THE COMPANIONS OF COLUMBUS, 1831
    History
THE ALHAMBRA, 1832   Sketches
THE CRAYON MISCELLANY, 1835   Essays
ASTORIA, 1836   History
THE ROCKY MOUNTAINS, 1837   History
OLIVER GOLDSMITH, 1849   Biography
A BOOK OF THE HUDSON, 1849   Sketches
MAHOMET AND HIS SUCCESSORS, 1850   Biography
WOLFERT'S ROOST, 1855   Sketches
LIFE OF GEORGE WASHINGTON, 1855-59   Biography
SPANISH PAPERS AND OTHER MISCELLANIES, 1866   Stories
THE WILD HUNTSMAN, 1924   Play
ABU HASSAN, 1924   Play

Irving's diaries and journals, all of which were published posthumously, are
listed in 29.

Collected Works

892.   THE COMPLETE WRITINGS OF WASHINGTON IRVING. 28 vols.
       projected. Ed. Henry A. Pochmann, Herbert Kleinfield, et al.
       Madison: University of Wisconsin Press, 1969- .

       See 898 for a description of this project.

893. THE WORKS OF WASHINGTON IRVING. Author's Uniform Revised
Edition. 21 vols. New York: G. P. Putnam's Sons, 1860-61.

The most readily available of more than forty editions.

Letters

894. Irving, Pierre M. THE LIFE AND LETTERS OF WASHINGTON IRVING.
4 vols. New York: G. P. Putnam's Sons, 1862-64.

The largest single collection of Irving's letters; others are listed
in 898.

895. McClary, Ben Harris, ed. WASHINGTON IRVING AND THE HOUSE
OF MURRAY. Knoxville: University of Tennessee Press, 1969.

The correspondence of Irving and his principal British publisher;
includes extensive commentary.

Bibliography

896. Langfeld, William R. and Philip C. Blackburn. WASHINGTON IRVING:
A BIBLIOGRAPHY. New York: New York Public Library, 1933. Reprinted from BNYPL, 36 (1932).

Includes details not found in the following work.

897. Williams, Stanley T. and Mary E. Edge. A BIBLIOGRAPHY OF THE
WRITINGS OF WASHINGTON IRVING. New York: Oxford University Press, 1936.

Also covers biographical and critical items.

Checklist

898. Pochmann, Henry A. "Washington Irving." In FIFTEEN AMERICAN
AUTHORS BEFORE 1900, ed. Robert A. Rees and Earl N. Harbert.
Madison: University of Wisconsin Press, 1971.

Includes bibliography, manuscripts and letters, editions, biography, literary history and criticism.

899. See also 897.

Biography

900. Wagenknecht, Edward. WASHINGTON IRVING: MODERATION DIS-
PLAYED. New York: Oxford University Press, 1962.

An intelligent critical biography which adds few facts to
Williams's account (901), although Wagenknecht's insights are

new and valuable in their own right.

901. Williams, Stanley T. THE LIFE OF WASHINGTON IRVING. 2 vols.
New York: Oxford University Press, 1935.

The definitive biography. 898 lists other biographical items.

Critical Studies:

902. Aderman, Ralph M., ed. WASHINGTON IRVING RECONSIDERED.
Hartford, Conn.: Transcendental Books, 1969.

Essays by various hands.

903. Beach, Leonard B. "Washington Irving: The Artist in a Changing
World." UKCR, 14 (1948), 259-66.

A general study, the main concern of which is Irving's
"realism."

904. Brooks, Van Wyck. THE WORLD OF WASHINGTON IRVING. New
York: Doubleday, 1944.

More useful as a study of the period than of Irving himself.

905. Callow, James T. KINDRED SPIRITS: KNICKERBOCKER WRITERS AND
AMERICAN ARTISTS, 1807-1855. Chapel Hill: University of North
Carolina Press, 1967.

Explores the relations of the Knickerbocker group to visual
artists of the day; useful for an understanding of the cultural
context in which Irving worked.

906. Canby, Henry Seidel. "Washington Irving." In CLASSIC AMERICANS.
New York: Russell & Russell, 1959.

The influence of Federalism on Irving. See 908.

907. Durant, David. "Aeolism in KNICKERBOCKER'S A HISTORY OF NEW
YORK." AL, 41 (1970), 493-506.

The satirical thread which unifies the HISTORY is "Irving's
treatment of Aeolism--the inflation of empty subjects into
false importance through idle words."

908. Guttmann, Allen. "Washington Irving and the Conservative Imagination."
AL, 36 (1964), 165-73.

Irving, like Cooper, was explicitly committed to "an ordered
and hierarchical agrarian society." See 906.

909. Hedges, William L. WASHINGTON IRVING: AN AMERICAN STUDY,
1802-1832. Baltimore, Md.: Johns Hopkins Press, 1965.

A judicious study of Irving's "major contributions as a writer" as well as "his relation [to] his intellectual environment."

910. _____. "Washington Irving: THE SKETCH BOOK OF GEOFFREY CRAYON, GENT." In LANDMARKS OF AMERICAN WRITING. ed. Hennig Cohen. New York: Basic Books, 1969.

Deals largely with the relation of THE SKETCH BOOK to its social and cultural context as well as its influence on subsequent American thought and literature.

911. Hoffman, Daniel G. "Prefigurations: 'The Legend of Sleepy Hollow.'" In FORM AND FABLE IN AMERICAN FICTION. New York: Oxford University Press, 1961.

Irving's story is "the first important literary statement of the themes of native folk character and superstition."

912. Hoffman, Louise M. "Irving's Use of Spanish Sources in THE CONQUEST OF GRANADA." HISPANICA, 28 (1945), 483-98.

Irving's book has been criticized as inaccurate history, but a study of his sources reveals that he deliberately planned to embellish his chronicle romantically.

913. Laird, C. G. "Tragedy and Irony in KNICKERBOCKER'S HISTORY." AL, 12 (1940), 157-72.

A "brooding intellectuality and a sense of irony and tragedy" are to be associated with Irving's most creative work, especially KNICKERBOCKER'S HISTORY, "his most original and successful production."

914. Leary, Lewis. WASHINGTON IRVING. Minneapolis: University of Minnesota Press, 1963.

A compact introduction to Irving; includes a useful selected bibliography.

915. LeFevre, Louis. "Paul Bunyan and Rip Van Winkle." YR, 36 (1946), 66-76.

"American life may be symbolized as a continuing debate between Paul Bunyan and Rip Van Winkle."

916. Lloyd, Francis V., Jr. "Irving's RIP VAN WINKLE." EXPLICATOR, 4 (1946), item 26.

Irving's story is a satire on the small-town mind.

917. Martin, Terence. "Rip, Ichabod, and the American Imagination." AL, 31 (1959), 137-49.

Irving's work reflects the tension between what America wanted to be and what Irving had to pretend it to be.

918. Myers, Andrew B., ed. WASHINGTON IRVING: A TRIBUTE. Tarry-
town, N.Y.: Sleepy Hollow Restorations, 1972.

Eight essays by distinguished scholars on THE SKETCH BOOK
and other matters.

919. Pochmann, Henry A. "Irving's German Sources in THE SKETCH BOOK."
SP, 27 (1930), 477-507.

The influence of German romantic literature on "Rip Van
Winkle," "The Legend of Sleepy Hollow," and "The Spectre
Bridegroom." See 921.

920. _____. "Washington Irving: Amateur or Professional?" In ESSAYS
ON AMERICAN LITERATURE IN HONOR OF JAY B. HUBBELL, ed.
Clarence Gohdes. Durham, N.C.: Duke University Press, 1967.

An illuminating study of Irving's awareness of his own literary
potential and how he exploited it.

921. Reichart, Walter A. WASHINGTON IRVING IN GERMANY. Ann
Arbor: University of Michigan Press, 1957.

A study of Irving's travels in Germany and the subsequent
effect on his work. See 919.

922. Ringe, Donald A. "New York and New England: Irving's Criticism
of American Society." AL, 38 (1967), 455-67.

A significant but frequently overlooked element in Irving's
writings is the mutual hostility between New York and New
England.

923. Roth, Martin. "The Final Chapter of Knickerbocker's New York."
MP, 66 (1969), 248-55.

The most obvious approach to "Rip Van Winkle" is by way of
Irving's previous work, particularly KNICKERBOCKER'S
HISTORY.

924. Snell, George. "Washington Irving: A Revaluation." MLQ, 7 (1946),
303-10.

Irving's importance lies more in his influence than in his own
work.

925. Young, Philip. "Fallen from Time: The Mythic Rip Van Winkle." KR,
22 (1960), 547-73.

A detailing of the mythic and folkloric precedents of Irving's
story.

HENRY JAMES (1843-1916)

Principal Works

A PASSIONATE PILGRIM, AND OTHER TALES, 1875
TRANSATLANTIC SKETCHES, 1875   Travel Sketches
RODERICK HUDSON, 1876   Novel
THE AMERICAN, 1877   Novel
FRENCH POETS AND NOVELISTS, 1878   Critical Essays
DAISY MILLER, 1879   Short Novel
THE EUROPEANS, 1879   Novel
AN INTERNATIONAL EPISODE, 1879   Short Novel
THE MADONNA OF THE FUTURE AND OTHER TALES, 1879
HAWTHORNE, 1880   Critical Essay
CONFIDENCE, 1880   Novel
WASHINGTON SQUARE, 1881   Novel
THE PORTRAIT OF A LADY, 1882   Novel
THE SIEGE OF LONDON, 1883   Stories
PORTRAITS OF PLACES, 1884   Travel Essays
TALES OF THREE CITIES, 1884
A LITTLE TOUR IN FRANCE, 1885   Travel Essays
THE BOSTONIANS, 1886   Novel
THE PRINCESS CASAMASSIMA, 1886   Novel
PARTIAL PORTRAITS, 1888   Critical Essays
THE ASPERN PAPERS, 1888   Stories
THE REVERBERATOR, 1888   Short Novel
A LONDON LIFE, 1889   Stories
THE TRAGIC MUSE, 1890   Novel
THE LESSON OF THE MASTER, 1892   Stories
ESSAYS IN LONDON AND ELSEWHERE, 1893   Critical Essays
THE REAL THING AND OTHER TALES, 1893
THE PRIVATE LIFE, 1893   Stories
PICTURE AND TEXT, 1893   Art Criticism
THE WHEEL OF TIME, 1893   Stories
THEATRICALS, 1894-95   Plays
TERMINATIONS, 1895   Stories
EMBARRASSMENTS, 1896   Stories
THE OTHER HOUSE, 1896   Novel
THE SPOILS OF POYNTON, 1897   Novel

WHAT MAISIE KNEW, 1897   Novel
IN THE CAGE, 1898   Short Novel
THE TWO MAGICS, 1898   Two Short Novels   (includes THE TURN OF THE
    SCREW)
THE AWKWARD AGE, 1899   Novel
THE SOFT SIDE, 1900   Stories
THE SACRED FOUNT, 1901   Novel
THE WINGS OF THE DOVE, 1902   Novel
THE AMBASSADORS, 1903   Novel
THE BETTER SORT, 1903   Stories
WILLIAM WETMORE STORY AND HIS FRIENDS, 1903   Biography
THE GOLDEN BOWL, 1904   Novel
ENGLISH HOURS, 1905   Travel Essays
THE QUESTION OF OUR SPEECH [AND] THE LESSON OF BALZAC, 1905
    Two Lectures
THE AMERICAN SCENE, 1907   Travel Essays
VIEWS AND REVIEWS, 1908   Critical Essays
ITALIAN HOURS, 1909   Travel Essays
THE FINER GRAIN, 1910   Stories
A SMALL BOY AND OTHERS, 1913   Autobiography
NOTES OF A SON AND BROTHER, 1914   Autobiography
NOTES ON NOVELISTS, 1914   Critical Essays
THE MIDDLE YEARS, 1917   Unfinished Autobiographical Volume
THE SENSE OF THE PAST, 1917   Unfinished Novel
THE IVORY TOWER, 1917   Unfinished Novel
WITHIN THE RIM AND OTHER ESSAYS 1914-1915, 1919   Essays on the War
NOTES AND REVIEWS, 1921   Critical Essays

There are several other posthumous collections of writings by James, particularly
critical essays; see 929 and 992.

Collected Works

926.   THE. NOVELS AND TALES OF HENRY JAMES. New York Edition.
       24 vols. New York: Charles Scribner's Sons, 1907-9 (two additional
       volumes were published in 1918); London: Macmillan, 1908-9 (the
       two additional volumes are not included in the English edition). Re-
       printed by Charles Scribner's Sons, 1962-65.

       See 953.

927.   THE NOVELS AND STORIES OF HENRY JAMES: NEW AND COMPLETE
       EDITION. 35 vols. Ed. Percy Lubbock. London: Macmillan, 1921-
       23.

       A reprint of the New York Edition with other titles added,
       this collection does not take into account James's reasons for
       choosing and ordering the works as he did in the earlier
       edition. See 953.

928.   THE COMPLETE TALES OF HENRY JAMES. 12 vols. Ed. Leon Edel.

London: Rupert Hart-Davis, 1961-64; Philadelphia, Pa.: J. B. Lippincott, 1962-65.

929.　THE ART OF THE NOVEL: CRITICAL PREFACES BY HENRY JAMES. Ed. R. P. Blackmur. New York: Charles Scribner's Sons, 1934.

This is the most useful of the several collections of James's criticism. For others, see the bibliography included in Powers's HENRY JAMES: AN INTRODUCTION AND INTERPRETATION (992). Other important collections not listed in Powers include those edited by James E. Miller, Morris Roberts, and Morris Shapira.

930.　THE AMERICAN SCENE. London: Chapman & Hall, 1907; New York and London: Harper & Brothers, 1907.

This is the most important collection of James's travel books. For others, see the bibliography in 992.

931.　THE COMPLETE PLAYS OF HENRY JAMES. Ed. Leon Edel. Philadelphia, Pa., and New York: J. B. Lippincott, 1949.

932.　HENRY JAMES: AUTOBIOGRAPHY. Ed. F. W. Dupee. New York: Criterion Books, 1956.

A collection in a single volume of James's three autobiographical works: A SMALL BOY AND OTHERS, NOTES OF A SON AND BROTHER, and the unfinished THE MIDDLE YEARS.

933.　THE NOTEBOOKS OF HENRY JAMES. Ed. F. O. Matthiessen and Kenneth B. Murdock. New York: Oxford University Press, 1947.

Letters

934　LETTERS/HENRY JAMES. Ed. Leon Edel. Cambridge, Mass: Belknap Press of Harvard University Press, 1974- .

935.　THE LETTERS OF HENRY JAMES. 2 vols. Ed. Percy Lubbock. London: Macmillan, 1920; New York: Charles Scribner's Sons, 1920.

936.　SELECTED LETTERS OF HENRY JAMES. Ed. Leon Edel. New York: Farrar, Straus, & Giroux, 1955.

936a.　The above are the most important collections of James's letters; for others, see 937 and 992.

Bibliography

937.　Edel, Leon and Dan H. Laurence. A BIBLIOGRAPHY OF HENRY JAMES. Rev. ed. London: Rupert Hart-Davis, 1961.

938.　Phillips, Le Roy. A BIBLIOGRAPHY OF THE WRITINGS OF HENRY JAMES. New York: Coward-McCann, 1930.

Checklist

939. Foley, Richard N. CRITICISM IN AMERICAN PERIODICALS OF THE WORKS OF HENRY JAMES FROM 1866 TO 1916. Washington, D.C.: Catholic University of America Press, 1944.

940. MODERN FICTION STUDIES. 3 (1957), 73-96; revised, 12 (1966), 117-77.

> This indispensable checklist (compiled by Maurice Beebe and William T. Stafford) includes a section in which studies of individual works are grouped under the titles of the works, which are listed alphabetically.

Biography

941. The definitive biography of James is a five-volume work written by Leon Edel and published by J. B. Lippincott of Philadelphia, Pa. The separate titles and publication dates are HENRY JAMES: THE UNTRIED YEARS, 1843-1870 (1953); HENRY JAMES: THE CONQUEST OF LONDON, 1870-1881 (1962); HENRY JAMES: THE MIDDLE YEARS, 1882-1895 (1962); HENRY JAMES: THE TREACHEROUS YEARS, 1895-1901 (1969); and HENRY JAMES: THE MASTER, 1901-1916 (1972).

Critical Studies

942. Anderson, Quentin. THE AMERICAN HENRY JAMES. New Brunswick, N.J.: Rutgers University Press, 1957.

> A widely-acclaimed study of the influence of the elder Henry James on his son, particularly in the writing of the major novels.

943. Auchincloss, Louis. "A Strategy for James Readers." NATION, 190 (April 23, 1960), 364-67.

> Though this is not a scholarly article, the proposed "strategy" is nonetheless worth considering.

944. Beach, Joseph Warren. THE METHOD OF HENRY JAMES. New Haven, Conn.: Yale University Press, 1918.

> An early, comprehensive study of James that is still useful in parts.

945. Blackmur, R. P. "The Loose and Baggy Monsters of Henry James: Notes on the Underlying Classic Form in the Novel." ACCENT, 11 (1951), 129-46.

> How THE AMBASSADORS, THE WINGS OF THE DOVE, and THE GOLDEN BOWL succeed in spite of themselves.

946. Booth, Wayne. THE RHETORIC OF FICTION. Chicago, Ill.: University of Chicago Press, 1961, pp. 42-50 and 339-74.

The first section considers the technical means by which James achieves the effect of realism; the second (and more problematic) section deals with the Jamesian "unreliable narrator" in "The Liar" and "The Aspern Papers."

947. Buitenhuis, Peter. THE GRASPING IMAGINATION: THE AMERICAN WRITINGS OF HENRY JAMES. Toronto: University of Toronto Press, 1970.

A comprehensive treatment of its subject.

948. _____, comp. TWENTIETH CENTURY INTERPRETATIONS OF THE PORTRAIT OF A LADY. Englewood Cliffs, N.J.: Prentice-Hall, 1968.

Essays by various hands.

949. Cargill, Oscar. THE NOVELS OF HENRY JAMES. New York: Macmillan, 1961.

The sections on the individual novels include references to other critical studies as well as Cargill's own valuable commentaries.

950. Cary, Elizabeth Luther. THE NOVELS OF HENRY JAMES. New York and London: G. P. Putnam's Sons, 1905; New York: Haskell House, 1964.

First full-scale critique of James's work. Sensible character studies, though little of any depth.

951. Dupee, F. W. HENRY JAMES. Rev. ed. Garden City, N.Y.: Doubleday, 1956.

An excellent critical biography.

952. _____, ed. THE QUESTION OF HENRY JAMES. New York: Holt, Rinehart and Winston, 1945.

Reprints a number of valuable studies; should be supplemented by 956.

953. Edel, Leon. "The Architecture of James's 'New York Edition.'" NEQ, 24 (1951), 169-78.

A schematic which groups the twenty-four volumes of the New York Edition according to theme.

954. _____. HENRY JAMES. Minneapolis: University of Minnesota Press, 1960.

A useful introduction to James which includes a selected bibliography.

955. _____. "Henry James: The Americano-European Legend." UTQ, 36 (1967), 321-34.

> Attempts to define the cosmopolitan imagination of James.

956. _____, ed. HENRY JAMES: A COLLECTION OF CRITICAL ESSAYS. Englewood Cliffs, N.J.: Prentice-Hall, 1963.

> A collection of the best general essays on James; should be supplemented by 952.

957. _____. "The Point of View." In THE MODERN PSYCHOLOGICAL NOVEL. New York: Grosset & Dunlap, 1964.

> Emphasizes point of view in THE TURN OF THE SCREW and THE SACRED FOUNT.

958. Fergusson, Francis. "James's Idea of Dramatic Form." KR, 5 (1943), 495-507.

> How James incorporated dramatic techniques into his fiction.

959. Finn, C. M. "Commitment and Identity in THE AMBASSADORS." MLR, 66 (1971), 522-31.

> This novel's special value is that it is located, in a historical sense, between the novel of traditional realism and the modern, more naturalistic novel.

960. Franklin, Rosemary F. AN INDEX TO HENRY JAMES'S PREFACES TO THE NEW YORK EDITION. Charlottesville: Bibliographical Society of the University of Virginia, 1966.

> An indispensable index to works, critical and aesthetic ideas, and people discussed in the "tangled jungle" of the prefaces. This edition is keyed to Blackmur's edition of the prefaces (929).

961. Gale, Robert L. THE CAUGHT IMAGE: FIGURATIVE LANGUAGE IN THE FICTION OF HENRY JAMES. Chapel Hill: University of North Carolina Press, 1964.

> More useful as a catalog of Jamesian imagery than as a critical study. See also Alexander Holder-Barell, THE DEVELOPMENT OF IMAGERY AND ITS FUNCTIONAL SIGNIFICANCE IN HENRY JAMES'S NOVELS (New York: Haskell House, 1966).

962. _____. PLOTS AND CHARACTERS IN THE FICTION OF HENRY JAMES. Hamden, Conn.: Archon Books, 1965.

> An indispensable collection of plot summaries as well as a "dictionary" of James's characters.

963. Guedalla, Phillip. "The Crowner's Quest." NEW STATESMAN, 12 (1919), 421-22.

Not a scholarly essay, this article takes issue with Pound's comments on James in THE LITTLE REVIEW (991). Guedalla divides James's career into three reigns--James I, James II, and James the Old Pretender--and prefers the second.

964. Habegger, Alfred.   "Reciprocity and the Market Place in THE WINGS OF THE DOVE and WHAT MAISIE KNEW." NCF, 25 (1971), 455-73.

"As WHAT MAISIE KNEW and also THE WINGS OF THE DOVE suggest, the principle of reciprocity--of freely giving in return--was an important part of Henry James's moral sensibility."

965. HENRY JAMES NUMBER. KR, 5 (1943), 481-617.

Essays by various hands, including Fergusson (958).

966. HENRY JAMES NUMBER. THE LITTLE REVIEW. 5 (August 1918), 1-64.

Essays by various hands, including Pound and Eliot. See 991.

967. HENRY JAMES SPECIAL NUMBER. MFS, 3 (1957), 1-196.

Essays by various hands and a useful checklist of selected criticism.

968. HENRY JAMES SPECIAL NUMBER. MFS, 12 (1966), 1-180.

Essays by various hands and an updated checklist of selected criticism.

969. Hoffman, Frederick. "Henry James, William Dean Howells and the Art of Fiction." In THE MODERN NOVEL IN AMERICA, 1900-1950. Chicago, Ill.: Henry Regnery, 1950.

James's contribution to the modern novel is twofold: he reminds the novelist of his responsibility toward the discipline of his craft, and he makes "intelligence of character" as important as "external fact."

970. "Homage to Henry James." HOUND AND HORN, 6 (1934), 361-562.

An important collection of essays, including Edmund Wilson's "The Ambiguity of Henry James," revised and reprinted in THE TRIPLE THINKERS (New York: Oxford University Press, 1948).

971. "In Honor of William and Henry James." NEW REPUBLIC, 108 (February 15, 1943), 215-30.

Essays on both men by various hands.

972. Kelley, Cornelia Pulsifer. THE EARLY DEVELOPMENT OF HENRY JAMES. Rev. ed. Urbana, Ill.: University of Illinois Press, 1965.

A study of James's writings through THE PORTRAIT OF A LADY.

973. Kirby, David K. "Henry James: Art and Autobiography." DR, 52 (1972-73), 637-44.

Discusses the technical means that James uses in his autobiography to compensate for the vagaries of an unreliable memory.

974. _____. "Henry James's THE OTHER HOUSE: From Novel to Play." MARKR, 3 (1972), 49-53.

A comparison and contrast of the different versions of THE OTHER HOUSE, a novel by James which he later made into a play. "Whereas the novel fails as a novel, the play succeeds as a play...."

975. _____. "Two Modern Versions of the Quest." SHR, 5 (1971), 387-95.

The governess of THE TURN OF THE SCREW, like the heroine of Thomas Pynchon's THE CRYING OF LOT 49 (to which the greater part of this article is devoted), is typical of the modern fictional character who is involved in a terrifying quest that has both epistemological and moral implications.

976. Krook, Dorothea. THE ORDEAL OF CONSCIOUSNESS IN HENRY JAMES. New York: Cambridge University Press, 1962.

A persuasive study of the Jamesian idea of consciousness as treated in most of the major novels. See also Krook's well-reasoned reconsideration of her book in "The Madness of Art: Further Reflections on the Ambiguity of Henry James," HEBREW UNIVERSITY STUDIES IN LITERATURE, 1 (1973), 25-38.

977. Leavis, F. R. THE GREAT TRADITION: GEORGE ELIOT, HENRY JAMES, JOSEPH CONRAD. New York: New York University Press, 1963.

Like Eliot and Conrad, James belongs to the tradition of great English [sic] novelists that begins with Jane Austen.

978. Lebowitz, Naomi, ed. DISCUSSIONS OF HENRY JAMES. Boston, Mass.: D. C. Heath, 1962.

Thirteen separate items by various hands (from Howells to date). The common theme is James's "moral vision."

979. _____. THE IMAGINATION OF LOVING: HENRY JAMES'S LEGACY TO THE NOVEL. Detroit, Mich.: Wayne State University Press, 1965.

A study of character relationships in the major novels.

980. Lubbock, Percy. THE CRAFT OF FICTION. London: J. Cape, 1921; New York: Charles Scribner's Sons, 1921; New York: Viking, 1957.

James perfected "the art of dramatizing the picture of somebody's experience"; Lubbock explores THE AMBASSADORS and THE WINGS OF THE DOVE (and works by other authors) in terms of this technique. This book is one of the foundations of James scholarship.

981. McCarthy, Harold T. HENRY JAMES: THE CREATIVE PROCESS. New York: Thomas Yoseloff, 1958.

Deals with "all the major aspects of James's aesthetics."

982. McElderry, Bruce R., Jr. HENRY JAMES. New York: Twayne, 1965.

A good introduction to James and his work.

983. Matthiessen, F. O. HENRY JAMES: THE MAJOR PHASE. New York: Oxford University Press, 1944.

Perceptive critical examination of THE AMBASSADORS, THE WINGS OF THE DOVE, THE GOLDEN BOWL, and THE IVORY TOWER.

984. _____. THE JAMES FAMILY. INCLUDING SELECTIONS FROM THE WRITINGS OF HENRY JAMES, SENIOR, WILLIAM, HENRY, & ALICE JAMES. New York: Alfred A. Knopf, 1947.

This "biography not of an individual but of a family" provides "a fairly full index to American literary history from the time of Emerson to that of the first World War."

985. Morris, Wright. THE TERRITORY AHEAD. New York: Harcourt, Brace & World, 1958. Pp. 93-112, 187-214.

Two indispensable essays on James's consciousness, his desire to be one on whom nothing is lost: "He was the first American of unquestioned genius to escape from the consolations of the past, without recourse to the endless vistas of optimism."

986. Mulqueen, James E. "Perfection of a Pattern: The Structure of THE AMBASSADORS, THE WINGS OF THE DOVE, and THE GOLDEN BOWL." ARQ, 27 (1971), 133-42.

Each novel describes a pattern of deception, discovery, and resolution, but only in THE GOLDEN BOWL is the resolution perfect.

987. Norton, Rictor. "THE TURN OF THE SCREW: Coincidentia Oppositorum." AMERICAN IMAGO, 28 (1971), 373-90.

Predominantly a psychosexual interpretation, this provocative study deals with the several "unions of opposites" that account for much of the disturbing ambiguity of the story.

988. Nowell-Smith, Simon, comp. THE LEGEND OF THE MASTER. New
York: Charles Scribner's Sons, 1948.

A delightful and useful collection of anecdotes about James
from more than one hundred and fifty sources.

989. Poirier, Richard. THE COMIC SENSE OF HENRY JAMES. New York:
Oxford University Press, 1960.

Examines the first six full-length novels (from RODERICK HUD-
SON to THE PORTRAIT OF A LADY) in terms of their characters. "Comedy exposes and evaluates the difference between
'free' and 'fixed' characters, while melodrama results from the
self-assertions of would-be 'free' characters whose ambitions
are being thwarted...."

990. Poulet, Georges. "Henry James." In STUDIES IN HUMAN TIME,
trans. Elliott Coleman. Baltimore, Md.: Johns Hopkins University
Press, 1956.

A succinct study of James's attitudes toward time, particularly
the "bygone future."

991. Pound, Ezra. "Henry James." In LITERARY ESSAYS OF EZRA POUND.
Norfolk, Conn.: New Directions, 1954.

Begins with a succinct and perceptive discussion of James's
politics, his attempts "to make two continents understand each
other....I am tired of hearing pettiness talked about
Henry James's style....I have heard no word of the
major James, of the hater of tyranny." What follows are some
"elliptical notes" on each of James's books (in order of publication). This article originally appeared in LITTLE REVIEW
(see 966 and 963).

992. Powers, Lyall H. HENRY JAMES: AN INTRODUCTION AND INTER-
PRETATION. New York: Holt, Rinehart and Winston, 1970.

Chapters on James's life, his fiction, his aesthetics. Useful
bibliography.

993. _____. HENRY JAMES AND THE NATURALIST MOVEMENT. East
Lansing: Michigan State University Press, 1971.

Discusses THE BOSTONIANS, THE PRINCESS CASAMASSIMA,
THE TRAGIC MUSE, and THE AMBASSADORS from the point
of view of naturalism.

994. _____, ed. THE MERRILL STUDIES IN THE PORTRAIT OF A LADY.
Columbus, Ohio: Charles E. Merrill, 1970.

Essays by various hands.

995. Putt, S. Gorley. A READER'S GUIDE TO HENRY JAMES. Ithaca,

N.Y.: Cornell University Press, 1966; London: Thames and Hudson, 1966.

A readable guide to (literally) all of James's novels and tales.

996. Rahv, Philip. IMAGE AND IDEA: TWENTY ESSAYS ON LITERARY THEMES. Rev. ed. London: Weidenfeld and Nicolson, 1957.

Contains two essays on James: "The Heiress of All the Ages" (which deals with the Jamesian heroine) and "Attitudes Toward Henry James" (a balanced study of James's achievement and reputation).

997. Reilly, Robert J. "Henry James and the Morality of Fiction." AL, 39 (1967), 1-30.

A provocative if sometimes irritating commentary on the moral direction of James's work.

998. Roberts, Morris. HENRY JAMES'S CRITICISM. Cambridge, Mass.: Harvard University Press, 1929.

Treats James's major critical works in chronological order; see also 1014.

999. Rowe, John Carlos. "The Symbolization of Milly Theale: Henry James's THE WINGS OF THE DOVE." ELH, 40 (1973), 131-64.

A stimulating discussion of Milly's symbolic function, which is, ultimately, "to disclose differences and manifest the ambiguity of human relations."

1000. Samuels, Charles Thomas. THE AMBIGUITY OF HENRY JAMES. Urbana: University of Illinois Press, 1971.

A challenging if, in places, irritating revaluation of James's achievements.

1001. Snow, Lotus. "The Disconcerting Poetry of Mary Temple: A Comparison of the Imagery of THE PORTRAIT OF A LADY and THE WINGS OF THE DOVE." NEQ, 31 (1958), 312-39.

"To compare the imagery of the two novels ... is to compare James's youthful and his mature vision of the qualities of life."

1002. Spender, Stephen. THE DESTRUCTIVE ELEMENT. London: J. Cape, 1935. Pp. 23-110, 189-200.

One of the best surveys of James's career.

1003. Stafford, William T., comp. THE MERRILL STUDIES IN THE AMERICAN. Columbus, Ohio: Charles E. Merrill, 1971.

Essays by various hands.

1004. _____, ed. PERSPECTIVES ON JAMES'S "THE PORTRAIT OF A LADY." New York: New York University Press, 1967.

Includes twenty items: James's own comments on the novel, reviews, the major critical studies.

1005. Stone, Albert E., ed. TWENTIETH CENTURY INTERPRETATIONS OF THE AMBASSADORS. Englewood Cliffs, N.J.: Prentice-Hall, 1969.

Essays by various hands.

1006. Tanner, Tony. "Henry James." In THE REIGN OF WONDER: NAIVITY AND REALITY IN AMERICAN LITERATURE. New York: Cambridge University Press, 1965.

A study of "the naive wondering vision" in James's works, especially WHAT MAISIE KNEW.

1007. Tompkins, Jane P., comp. TWENTIETH CENTURY INTERPRETATIONS OF THE TURN OF THE SCREW AND OTHER TALES. Englewood Cliffs, N.J.: Prentice Hall, 1970.

Essays by various hands on "The Pupil," "The Real Thing," "The Figure in the Carpet," "The Madonna of the Future," "The Beast in the Jungle," "The Jolly Corner," and THE TURN OF THE SCREW.

1008. Vaid, Krishna Baldev. TECHNIQUE IN THE TALES OF HENRY JAMES. Cambridge, Mass.: Harvard University Press, 1964.

A technical study of twenty-two tales.

1009. Van Ghent, Dorothy. "On THE PORTRAIT OF A LADY." In THE ENGLISH NOVEL: FORM AND FUNCTION. New York: Harper & Row, 1961.

Deals with the motif of "seeing" in THE PORTRAIT.

1010. Ward, Joseph A. THE SEARCH FOR FORM: STUDIES IN THE STRUC-TURE OF JAMES'S FICTION. Chapel Hill: University of North Carolina Press, 1967.

The best single work on James's form. Treats seven novels in all.

1011. Warren, Austin. "Henry James: Symbolic Imagery in the Later Novels." In RAGE FOR ORDER, ESSAYS IN CRITICISM, Chicago, Ill.: University of Chicago Press, 1948.

In his later fiction, James uses two devices borrowed from the dramatists he admired: close conversation (his characters are given to "close, minute, unwearying analysis") and metaphor. These devices correspond to "two modes of knowing: dialectic and myth."

1012. Watt, Ian. "The First Paragraph in THE AMBASSADORS: An Explication." EIC, 10 (1960), 250-74.

A model study in close reading which illuminates the subtleties
of James's prose.

1013. Weinstein, Philip M. HENRY JAMES AND THE REQUIREMENTS OF
THE IMAGINATION. Cambridge, Mass.: Harvard University Press,
1971.

An intelligent discussion of six James novels.

1014. Wellek, Rene. "Henry James's Literary Theory and Criticism." AL, 30
(1958), 293-321.

An essential study of James's critical views. See also 998.

1015. Willen, Gerald, ed. A CASEBOOK ON HENRY JAMES'S THE TURN
OF THE SCREW. 2nd ed. New York: Crowell, 1969.

Includes the best critical studies as well as letters, notebook
entries by James, etc.

1016. Winner, Viola Hopkins. HENRY JAMES AND THE VISUAL ARTS.
Charlottesville: University Press of Virginia, 1970.

A comprehensive treatment of its subject which concludes with
a perceptive analysis of THE GOLDEN BOWL.

1017. Winters, Yvor. "Maule's Well of Henry James and the Relation of
Morals to Manners." In IN DEFENSE OF REASON. Denver, Col.:
Alan Swallow, 1947. (Reprinted from MAULE'S CURSE, Norfolk, Conn.:
New Directions, 1938).

Although Winters feels that James is one of the five or six
greatest novelists, he finds that James "had too much moral
sense, but was insufficiently a moralist."

SARAH ORNE JEWETT (1849-1909)

Principal Works

DEEPHAVEN, 1877   Sketches
A COUNTRY DOCTOR, 1884   Novel
A MARSH ISLAND, 1885   Novel
A WHITE HERON, 1886   Stories
THE KING OF FOLLY ISLAND, 1888   Stories
A NATIVE OF WINBY, 1893   Stories
THE LIFE OF NANCY, 1895   Stories
THE COUNTRY OF THE POINTED FIRS, 1896   Sketches
THE TORY LOVER, 1901   Novel
VERSES, 1916

Jewett also wrote three books for children.

Collected Works

1018. THE BEST STORIES OF SARAH ORNE JEWETT. Ed. Willa Cather.
2 vols. Boston, Mass.: Houghton Mifflin, 1925.

1019. STORIES AND TALES. 7 vols. Boston, Mass.: Houghton Mifflin, 1910.

Letters

1020. LETTERS OF SARAH ORNE JEWETT. Ed. Annie Fields. Boston, Mass.
and New York: Houghton Mifflin, 1911.

1021. SARAH ORNE JEWETT LETTERS. Ed. Richard Cary. 2nd ed., rev. and
enlarged. Waterville, Me.: Colby College Press, 1967.

1022. See also 1034 and 1041.

Bibliography

1023. Frost, John Eldridge. "Sarah Orne Jewett Bibliography: 1949-1963."

CLQ, Series 6, 10 (1964), 405–17.

Includes checklists and bibliographies, dissertations and theses, works by Jewett, and works about her.

1024. Weber, Clara Carter and Carl J. Weber. A BIBLIOGRAPHY OF THE PUBLISHED WRITINGS OF SARAH ORNE JEWETT. Waterville, Me.: Colby College Library, 1949.

Checklist

1025. Eichelberger, Clayton L., comp. "Sarah Orne Jewett (1849–1909): A Critical Bibliography of Secondary Comment." ALR, 2 (1969), 189–262.

An indispensable annotated listing of books and articles about Jewett and her writings.

1026. See also 1023.

Biography

1027. Frost, John Eldridge. SARAH ORNE JEWETT. Kittery Point, Me.: Gundalow Club, 1960.

Provides details that are missing in Matthiessen.

1028. Matthiessen, F. O. SARAH ORNE JEWETT. Boston, Mass.: Houghton Mifflin, 1929; Gloucester, Mass.: Peter Smith, 1965.

A readable but essentially nonscholarly treatment of Jewett's life.

Critical Studies

1029. Berthoff, Warner. "The Art of Jewett's POINTED FIRS." NEQ, 32 (1959), 31–53.

A discussion of Jewett's development as an artist, culminating in a thorough analysis of her best-known work.

1030. Bishop, Ferman. "Henry James Criticizes THE TORY LOVER." AL, 27 (1955), 262–64.

Reprints a James letter which criticizes not only Jewett's novel but the historical novel in general.

1031. _____. "Sarah Orne Jewett's Idea of Race." NEQ, 30 (1957), 243–49.

Despite her admiration of Whittier and Harriet Beecher Stowe, Jewett maintained "an aristocratic emphasis upon the racial inequalities of mankind."

1032. _____. THE SENSE OF THE PAST IN SARAH ORNE JEWETT. Wichita, Kan.: University Of Wichita, 1959.

Deals with the effect of Jewett's sense of the past on her realistic literary method.

1033. Buchan, Alexander McIntosh. "OUR DEAR SARAH"; AN ESSAY ON SARAH ORNE JEWETT. St. Louis, Mo.: Washington University, 1953.

Though somewhat mawkish, this brief study is nonetheless interesting because of its remarks on Jewett's theory of literary creation, which is likened to Wordsworth's.

1034. Cary, Richard. "Jewett's Literary Canons." CLQ, Series 7, 2 (1965), 82-87.

Extracts from Jewett's letters indicate that she had a viable literary credo.

1035. _____. SARAH ORNE JEWETT. New York: Twayne, 1962.

First full-length critical study of Jewett's works.

1036. Cather, Willa. "Miss Jewett." In NOT UNDER FORTY. New York: Alfred A. Knopf, 1936.

A temperate assessment of Jewett's achievements by her fellow writer and friend.

1037. Chapman, Edward M. "The New England of Sarah Orne Jewett." YR, 3 (1913), 157-72.

Interesting for its occasional contrasting of Jewett with Thomas Hardy.

1038. Chase, Mary Ellen. "Sarah Orne Jewett as a Social Historian." In THE WORLD OF DUNNET LANDING, ed. David B. Green. Lincoln: University of Nebraska Press, 1962.

Discusses Jewett's value as a historian and an etymologist in terms of THE COUNTRY OF THE POINTED FIRS.

1039. Eakin, P. J. "Sarah Orne Jewett and the Meaning of Country Life." AL, 38 (1967), 508-31.

A careful examination of Jewett's development as a writer and her increasingly skillful use of the "visit pattern" which is present in most of her major work.

1040. Green, David Bonnell. "The World of Dunnet Landing." NEQ, 34 (1961), 514-17.

A brief discussion of the relation of THE COUNTRY OF THE POINTED FIRS to other sketches that deal with the same fictional world. Reprinted in THE WORLD OF DUNNET LANDING (see 1038).

1041. JEWETT ISSUE. CLQ, Series 5, 3 (1959).

Essays by various hands plus a checklist of Jewett letters.

1042. JEWETT ISSUE. CLQ, Series 6, 10 (1964).

Essays by various hands and a bibliography.

1043. JEWETT ISSUE. CLQ, Series 8, 3 (1968).

Essays by various hands.

1044. Magowan, Robin. "Pastoral and the Art of Landscape in THE COUNTRY OF THE POINTED FIRS." NEQ, 36 (1963), 229-40.

In her novel Jewett reconciles "forms as seemingly disparate as pastoral and local color, the ideal landscape and the regional style."

1045. Rhode, Robert D. "Sarah Orne Jewett and the 'Palpable Present Intimate.'" CLQ, Series 8, 3 (1968), 146-55.

A thoughtful examination of Jewett's use of setting as an element in narration.

1046. Short, Clarice. "Studies in Gentleness." WHR, 11 (1957), 387-93.

A perceptive comparison of THE COUNTRY OF THE POINTED FIRS to Mrs. Gaskell's CRANFORD.

1047. Smith, Eleanor M. "The Literary Relationship of Sarah Orne Jewett and Willa Sibert Cather." NEQ, 29 (1956), 472-92.

A thorough consideration of the relationship which concludes that Jewett "paints a tiny segment in the broad landscape of Willa Cather's works and that in this fragment there is the same essential touch."

1048. Thompson, Charles M. "The Art of Miss Jewett." ATLANTIC MONTHLY, 94 (1904), 485-97.

A nonscholarly but interesting attempt to account for the various shaping forces in Jewett's artistic development.

1049. Thorp, Margaret Farrand. SARAH ORNE JEWETT. Minneapolis: University of Minnesota Press, 1966.

A brief, sensible introduction to Jewett and her works. Includes a useful selected bibliography.

1050. Toth, Susan A. "The Value of Age in the Fiction of Sarah Orne Jewett." SSF, 8 (1971), 433-41.

In almost every story Jewett introduces the reader to men and women who are seventy years old or older, but she "has never

been given full credit for her wise and sensitive attitude
towards the very old."

1051. Waggoner, Hyatt H. "The Unity of THE COUNTRY OF THE POINTED
FIRS." TCL, 5 (1959), 67-73.

Previous commentators have not recognized that the book is
organized in terms of the archetypal symbols discussed here.

1052. Weber, Carl J. "Whittier and Sarah Orne Jewett." NEQ, 18 (1945),
401-7.

An account of their friendship and mutual influence; includes
a Jewett poem dedicated to Whittier and heretofore unpublished.

JOHN PENDLETON KENNEDY (1795-1870)

Principal Works

THE RED BOOK, 1819-21   Satirical Periodical   (Kennedy wrote the prose
  for this publication, and Peter Hoffman Cruse the poetry.)
SWALLOW BARN, 1832   Novel (although usually classified as a novel,
  Kennedy insisted that it was only a series of sketches.)
HORSE SHOE ROBINSON, 1835   Novel
ROB OF THE BOWL, 1838   Novel
QUODLIBET, 1840   Political Satire
DEFENCE OF THE WHIGS, 1844   History
MEMOIRS OF THE LIFE OF WILLIAM WIRT, 1849   Biography
MR. AMBROSE'S LETTERS ON THE REBELLION, 1865   Essays
AT HOME AND ABROAD, 1872   Essays and Miscellanea

Collected Works

1053. THE COLLECTED WORKS OF JOHN PENDLETON KENNEDY. 10 vols.
  New York: G.P. Putnam's Sons, 1871.

Bibliography

1054. See 1069 and 1076.

Checklist

1055. See 1069 and 1076.

Biography

1056. Bohner, Charles H. JOHN PENDLETON KENNEDY: GENTLEMAN
  FROM BALTIMORE. Baltimore, Md.: Johns Hopkins Press, 1961.

The definitive biography to date. (Note: Items 1059-62 are versions of material contained in this book.)

1057. Gwathmey, Edward M. JOHN PENDLETON KENNEDY. New York: Thomas Nelson, 1931.

Adds little to Tuckerman (1058) and is occasionally inaccurate.

1058. Tuckerman, Henry T. THE LIFE OF JOHN PENDLETON KENNEDY. New York: G.P. Putnam's Sons, 1871.

The authorized biography; now largely superseded by Bohner (1056).

Critical Studies

1059. Bohner, Charles H. "'As Much History as ... Invention': John P. Kennedy's ROB OF THE BOWL." WMQ, 17 (1960), 329-40.

An analysis of the factual background of the novel and its relation to the purely fictional elements.

1060. _____. "J. P. Kennedy's QUODLIBET: Whig Counterattack." AQ, 13 (1961), 84-92.

A discussion of the book's background, its reception, and its place among Kennedy's other writings.

1061. _____. "THE RED BOOK, 1819-1821, a Satire on Baltimore Society." MHM, 51 (1956), 175-87.

Kennedy's first important literary endeavor was THE RED BOOK, a satirical periodical written entirely by himself and Peter Hoffman Cruse.

1062. _____. "SWALLOW BARN: John P. Kennedy's Chronicle of Virginia Society." VMHB, 68 (1960), 317-30.

A study of the novel's sources and social context.

1063. Campbell, Killis. "The Kennedy Papers." SR, 25 (1917), 1-19, 193-208, 348-60.

Publication for the first time of various documents, mainly letters to Kennedy from Irving, Dickens, Cooper, Henry Clay, and others.

1064. Cowie, Alexander. "John Pendleton Kennedy (1795-1870)." In THE RISE OF THE AMERICAN NOVEL. New York: American Book Co., 1951.

Useful general commentary.

1065. Ellison, Rhoda Coleman. "An Interview with Horse-Shoe Robinson."

AL, 31 (1959), 329-32.

An account of an interview between Robinson, upon whom Kennedy's fictional hero is based, and the Alabama belle-lettrist Beaufort Meek.

1066. Forman, Henry C. "The Rose Croft in Old St. Mary's." MHM, 35 (1940), 26-31.

Of no direct critical value, this essay relates the history of the plantation where ROB OF THE BOWL was set.

1067. Griffin, Lloyd W. "The John Pendleton Kennedy Manuscripts." MHM, 48 (1953), 327-36.

A description of the papers in the Peabody Institute Library in Baltimore.

1068. Hubbell, Jay B. "Introduction" to SWALLOW BARN. New York: Harcourt, Brace, 1929.

A general introduction to Kennedy's life, works, and relation-ships with other authors (particularly Thackeray and Poe).

1069. Leisy, Ernest E. "Introduction" to HORSE-SHOE ROBINSON. New York: American Book Co., 1937; New York: Hafner, 1962.

A helpful guide to the background of the novel. Includes a "Selected Bibliography" of works by and about Kennedy.

1070. Moore, John R. "Kennedy's HORSE-SHOE ROBINSON: Fact or Fiction?" AL, 4 (1932), 160-66.

The novel is more than an elaboration of one old veteran's recollections, as has been commonly assumed.

1071. Osborne, William S. "Introduction" to ROB OF THE BOWL. New Haven, Conn.: College and University Press, 1965.

A thoroughly-documented essay which deals with the critical reception of the novel, its characters, and other matters.

1072. _____. "Introduction" to SWALLOW BARN. New York: Hafner, 1962.

A knowledgeable and comprehensive study of Kennedy's "close portrait of Southern life."

1073. _____. "John Pendleton Kennedy's HORSE-SHOE ROBINSON: A Novel with 'the Utmost Historical Accuracy.'" MHM, 59 (1964), 286-96.

A careful study of the novel's sources.

1074. _____. "'The Swiss Traveller' Essays: Earliest Literary Writings of John Pendleton Kennedy." AL, 30 (1958), 228-33.

These five essays are notable chiefly for their expression of the young Kennedy's ardent nationalism.

1075. Parrington, Vernon L. "John Pendleton Kennedy: A Southern Whig." In MAIN CURRENTS IN AMERICAN THOUGHT, vol. 2. New York: Harcourt, Brace, 1930.

A general commentary; valuable mainly for bringing Kennedy's work to the attention of the literary historians who had formerly overlooked him.

1076. Ridgely, J. V. JOHN PENDLETON KENNEDY. New York: Twayne, 1966.

The greater part of this book is devoted to SWALLOW BARN, HORSE-SHOE ROBINSON, and ROB OF THE BOWL. Includes a useful "Selected Bibliography" of works by and about Kennedy.

1077. Roberts, Warren E. "Some Folksong References in Kennedy's SWALLOW BARN." SFQ, 17 (1953), 249-54.

A number of songs referred to in the novel were current in the Virginia-West Virginia border region around 1800 and survive to the present day.

1078. Rose, Alan H. "The Image of the Negro in the Pre-Civil-War Novels of John Pendleton Kennedy and William Gilmore Simms." JAMS, 4 (1970), 217-26.

As social tensions increased with the approach of the Civil War, Kennedy and Simms employed unique strategems in order to avoid presenting potentially disturbing visions of southern life.

1079. Taylor, William R. "A Squire of Change Alley." In CAVALIER AND YANKEE. New York: George Braziller, 1963.

A useful discussion of Kennedy, who "probed the significance of the South's mixed cultural heritage," mainly through SWALLOW BARN and HORSE-SHOE ROBINSON.

1080. Uhler, John Earle. "Kennedy's Novels and His Posthumous Works." AL, 3 (1932), 471-79.

The three posthumous volumes of essays, speeches, etc., that appeared in 1872 are helpful to an understanding of Kennedy's novels, and they require the reader to broaden his notion of Kennedy as a literary man.

1081. Wermuth, Paul C. "SWALLOW BARN: A Virginia Idyll." VIRGINIA CAVALCADE, 9 (Summer 1959), 30-34.

A nonscholarly commentary; illustrated.

GRACE ELIZABETH KING (1852-1932)

Principal Works

MONSIEUR MOTTE, 1888   Novel
TALES OF A TIME AND PLACE, 1892
BALCONY STORIES, 1893
THE PLEASANT WAYS OF ST. MEDARD, 1916   Novel

King also wrote several historical and biographical works.

Collected Works

1082. GRACE KING OF NEW ORLEANS: A SELECTION OF HER WRITINGS. Ed. Robert Bush. Baton Rouge: Louisiana State University Press, 1973.

> Selections from her fiction, historical writings, and autobiography; also notebook excerpts and letters. Bush provides notes and a useful introduction.

Letters

1083. See 1082.

Bibliography

1084. Vaughan, Bess, comp. "A Bio-Bibliography of Grace Elizabeth King." LAHISTQ, 17 (1934), 752-70.

> A more complete bibliography of King's writings than that of William Beers, LAHISTQ, 6 (1923), 378-79. Also includes works about King as well as reviews of her books.

Checklist

1085. See 1084.

Biography

1086. Kendall, John S. "A New Orleans Lady of Letters." LAHISTQ, 19
(1936), 436-65.

    A fairly detailed biographical memoir by an acquaintance of
King.

1087. King, Grace Elizabeth. MEMORIES OF A SOUTHERN WOMAN OF
LETTERS. New York: Macmillan, 1932.

    An autobiographical memoir.

1088. Note: Professor Robert Bush is now writing the definitive biography of
King.

Critical Studies

1089. Bush, Robert. "Grace King and Mark Twain." AL, 44 (1972), 31-51.

    An account of their literary relationship and their friendship;
based on the Grace King papers at Louisiana State University.

1090. Cocks, Reginald S. "The Fiction of Grace King." LAHISTQ, 6 (1923),
353-59.

    Brief, nonscholarly remarks on King's fiction.

1091. Dart, Henry P. "The Ideals of Grace King." LAHISTQ, 15 (1932),
339-44.

    Brief discussions of what the author considers to be King's
greatest achievements.

1092. _____. "Miss King's Historical Works." LAHISTQ, 6 (1923), 347-53.

    Impressionistic comments on four historical works by King.

1093. Guyol, Louise Hubert. "A Southern Author in Her New Orleans Home."
LAHISTQ, 6 (1923), 365-74.

    Based on an interview in which King comments on her own work,
other contemporary literati, and other matters.

1094. Kirby, David K. GRACE KING. New York: Twayne, forthcoming.

    A study of King's life, works, cultural milieu, and place in
American literary history.

1095. Pattee, Fred Lewis. In THE DEVELOPMENT OF THE AMERICAN SHORT
STORY. New York and London: Harper & Brothers, 1923.

    Concise general commentary.

1096. _____. In A HISTORY OF AMERICAN LITERATURE SINCE 1870.

New York: Century Co., 1915.

Concise general commentary.

1097. Snyder, Henry N. "Miss Grace Elizabeth King." In William Malone Baskervill's SOUTHERN WRITERS: BIOGRAPHICAL AND CRITICAL STUDIES, vol. II. Nashville, Tenn. and Dallas, Tex.: Publishing House of the M. E. Church, South, 1903.

A general introduction to King's writings.

JOSEPH KIRKLAND (1830-1894)

Principal Works

ZURY: THE MEANEST MAN IN SPRING COUNTY, 1887   Novel
THE MCVEYS, 1888   Novel (sequel to ZURY)
THE CAPTAIN OF COMPANY K, 1891   Novel

Bibliography

1098. See 1105.

Checklist

1099. Eichelberger, Clayton L. "Edgar Watson Howe and Joseph Kirkland:
       More Critical Comment." ALR, 4 (1971), 279-90.

       Mainly incidental items which supplement 1100.

1100. Eichelberger, Clayton L. and Frank L. Stallings, Jr. "Joseph Kirkland
       (1830-1894): A Critical Bibliography of Secondary Comment." ALR, 2
       (1969), 51-69.

       An indispensable annotated listing of books and articles about
       Kirkland and his writings.

Biography

1101. There is no definitive biography, although Henson's study (1105) contains
       much useful biographical information.

Critical Studies

1102. Duffey, Bernard. In THE CHICAGO RENAISSANCE IN AMERICAN
       LETTERS: A CRITICAL HISTORY. East Lansing: Michigan State College
       Press, 1954.

Discussion of the main features of Kirkland's writings.

1103. Flanagan, John T. "Introduction" to ZURY: THE MEANEST MAN IN
SPRING COUNTY, Urbana: University of Illinois Press, 1956.

A general introduction to Kirkland and the novel.

1104. _____. "Joseph Kirkland, Pioneer Realist." AL, 11 (1939), 273-84.

A useful introduction to Kirkland and his works.

1105. Henson, Clyde E. JOSEPH KIRKLAND. New York: Twayne, 1962.

The only book-length study of Kirkland. Includes separate
chapters on the major works as well as a useful "Selected
Bibliography" of works by and about Kirkland.

1106. _____. "Joseph Kirkland's Influence on Hamlin Garland." AL, 23
(1952), 458-63.

The Garland-Kirkland correspondence reveals that Kirkland
was instrumental in the shaping of Garland's career.

1107. Holaday, Clayton A. "Kirkland's CAPTAIN OF COMPANY K: A Twice-
Told Tale." AL, 25 (1953), 62-68.

An illuminating discussion of the composition of the novel and
its relation to ZURY and THE MCVEYS.

1108. La Budde, Kenneth J. "A Note on the Text of Joseph Kirkland's
ZURY." AL, 20 (1949), 452-55.

A comparison of different printings of the novel indicates a
change in Kirkland's conception of the character of Anne.

1109. Lease, Benjamin. "Realism and Joseph Kirkland's ZURY." AL, 23
(1952), 464-66.

A succinct discussion of Kirkland whose place in literary
history is determined by the fact that, in ZURY, he "plunged
beneath the surface of sentimental regionalism to new, profound depths of psychological realism."

1110. Solomon, Eric. "Another Analogue for THE RED BADGE OF COURAGE."
NCF, 13 (1958), 63-67.

Plot similarities between THE CAPTAIN OF COMPANY K and
Crane's novel.

HERMAN MELVILLE (1819-1891)

Principal Works

TYPEE, 1846   Novel
OMOO, 1847   Novel
MARDI, 1849   Novel
REDBURN, 1849   Novel
WHITE-JACKET, 1850   Novel
MOBY-DICK, 1851   Novel
PIERRE, 1852   Novel
ISRAEL POTTER, 1855   Novel
PIAZZA TALES, 1856 (includes "Benito Cereno" and "Bartleby the Scrivener")
THE CONFIDENCE-MAN, 1857   Novel
BATTLE-PIECES, 1866   Poems
CLAREL, 1876   Poem
JOHN MARR AND OTHER SAILORS, 1888 Poems
TIMOLEON, 1891   Poems
THE APPLE-TREE TABLE AND OTHER SKETCHES, 1922
BILLY BUDD, 1924   Short Novel
JOURNAL UP THE STRAITS, 1935 (diary of the trip to the Holy Land which
    resulted in CLAREL)
JOURNAL OF A VISIT TO LONDON AND THE CONTINENT, 1948
JOURNAL OF A VISIT TO EUROPE AND THE LEVANT, 1955

Collected Works

1111. COMPLETE WORKS OF HERMAN MELVILLE. Ed. Howard P. Vincent,
    et al. Chicago, Ill. and New York: Hendricks House, 1948- .

1112. THE WORKS OF HERMAN MELVILLE. Standard Edition. 16 vols.
    London: Constable, 1922-24; New York: Russell & Russell, 1963.

    The most complete edition to date.

1113. THE WRITINGS OF HERMAN MELVILLE, THE NORTHWESTERN-NEW-
    BERRY EDITION. Ed. Harrison Hayford, et al. 15 vols. projected.
    Evanston, Ill.: Northwestern University Press, 1968- .

When completed, this will be the definitive edition.

Letters

1114. FAMILY CORRESPONDENCE OF HERMAN MELVILLE, 1830-1904, Ed. V. H. Palsits. New York: New York Public Library, 1929.

1115. THE LETTERS OF HERMAN MELVILLE. Ed. Merrell R. Davis and William H. Gilman. New Haven, Conn.: Yale University Press, 1960.

Bibliography

1116. Ricks, Beatrice and Joseph Adams. HERMAN MELVILLE: A REFERENCE BIBLIOGRAPHY. Boston, Mass.: G. K. Hall, 1973.

Includes works by and about Melville.

Checklist

1117. Beebe, Maurice, et al. "Criticism of Herman Melville: A Selected Checklist." MFS, 8 (1962), 312-46.

General studies are included as well as studies of individual works (which are grouped under the titles of the individual works). Extremely useful.

1118. Bowen, James K. and Richard VanDerBeets. A CRITICAL GUIDE TO HERMAN MELVILLE: ABSTRACTS OF FORTY YEARS OF CRITICISM. Glenview, Ill.: Scott, Foresman, 1971.

Abstracts of over one hundred critical essays from 1928 to 1969 (most of the essays were published between 1950 and 1970).

1119. Gross, Theodore L. "Herman Melville." In HAWTHORNE, MELVILLE, STEPHEN CRANE: A CRITICAL BIBLIOGRAPHY, by Theodore L. Gross and Stanley Wertheim. New York: Free Press, 1971.

An indispensable research guide which includes abstracts of more than 170 critical books and articles.

1120. See 1152 and 1172.

Biography

1121. The following works are the principal biographical volumes; critical works with a biographical orientation are listed under CRITICAL STUDIES (below).

1122. Allen, Gay Wilson. MELVILLE AND HIS WORLD. New York: Viking, 1971.

A biographical sketch accompanied by more than one hundred and thirty reproductions of photographs, drawings, and paintings which depict Melville's world.

1123. Howard, Leon. HERMAN MELVILLE: A BIOGRAPHY. Berkeley: University of California Press, 1951.

The definitive biography to date.

1124. Leyda, Jay. THE MELVILLE LOG: A DOCUMENTARY LIFE OF HERMAN MELVILLE, 1819-1891. 2 vols. New York: Harcourt, Brace, 1951.

A source book which provided most of the materials upon which Howard's biography (1123) is based.

1125. Metcalf, Eleanor Melville. HERMAN MELVILLE: CYCLE AND EPI-CYCLE. Cambridge, Mass.: Harvard University Press, 1953.

A biography of the Melville family.

1126. Weaver, Raymond. HERMAN MELVILLE, MARINER AND MYSTIC. New York: George H. Doran, 1921.

The first full-length biography.

Critical Studies

1127. Anderson, Charles R. MELVILLE IN THE SOUTH SEAS. New York: Columbia University Press, 1939.

The definitive account of Melville's experiences in the South Seas and their influence on his writings.

1128. Arvin, Newton. HERMAN MELVILLE. New York: William Sloane, 1950; New York: Compass Books, 1957.

A useful introduction to the life and works.

1129. Auden, W. H. THE ENCHAFED FLOOD OR THE ROMANTIC ICONOG-RAPHY OF THE SEA. New York: Random House, 1950.

An examination of Romantic fascination with the sea, concluding with an essay on MOBY-DICK and BILLY BUDD.

1130. Barrett, Laurence. "The Differences in Melville's Poetry." PMLA, 70 (1955), 606-23.

The "violences of form" in Melville's poetry are virtues as well as difficulties.

1131. Berthoff, Warner. THE EXAMPLE OF MELVILLE. Princeton, N.J.: Princeton University Press, 1962.

A study of Melville's development and ultimate achievement as a literary craftsman. Includes separate chapters on settings, narrators, characters, etc.

1132. Bewley, Marius. "Melville." In THE ECCENTRIC DESIGN. New York: Columbia University Press, 1959.

A study of Melville's "profound disillusionment with American democracy" as indicated by MOBY-DICK, PIERRE, and THE CONFIDENCE-MAN.

1133. Brooks, Van Wyck. THE TIMES OF MELVILLE AND WHITMAN. New York: E. P. Dutton, 1947.

A study of the era in which Melville lived rather than of the writer himself. See 1170.

1134. Canaday, Nicholas, Jr. MELVILLE AND AUTHORITY. Gainesville: University of Florida Press, 1968.

Considers "whether a long life spent in subordination to external authority might have resulted in a dominant theme in Melville's fiction." See 1149.

1135. _____. "Harry Bolton and Redburn: The Old World and the New." In ESSAYS IN HONOR OF ESMOND LINWORTH MARILLA, ed. Thomas A. Kirby and William J. Olive. Baton Rouge: Louisiana State University Press, 1971.

A study of REDBURN in terms of its two contrasting main characters: "Redburn as New World democrat and Harry Bolton as Old World aristocrat."

1136. Chase, Richard, ed. MELVILLE: A COLLECTION OF CRITICAL ESSAYS. Englewood Cliffs, N.J.: Prentice-Hall, 1962.

Eleven essays, by various hands, on the major works.

1137. _____. "Melville and Moby-Dick." In THE AMERICAN NOVEL AND ITS TRADITION. Garden City, N.Y.: Doubleday, 1957.

Treats the novel as an "epic romance." For a refutation which argues that the novel succeeds as epic but not romance, see Martin Green, "Melville and the American Romance," in REAPPRAISALS: SOME COMMONSENSE READINGS IN AMERICAN LITERATURE, New York: W. W. Norton, 1965.

1138. Cowie, Alexander. "Herman Melville." In THE RISE OF THE AMERICAN NOVEL. New York: American Book Co., 1951.

A useful general survey.

1139. Davis, Merrell R. MELVILLE'S MARDI, A CHARTLESS VOYAGE. New Haven, Conn.: Yale University Press, 1952.

"The literary and biographical background, the genesis, writing, and meaning of Herman Melville's MARDI."

1140. Dryden, Edgar A. MELVILLE'S THEMATICS OF FORM: THE GREAT ART OF TELLING THE TRUTH. Baltimore, Md.: Johns Hopkins Press, 1968.

A study of Melville's "search for a form which will allow him safely to explore and reveal a destructive and maddening Truth."

1141. Feidelson, Charles, Jr. SYMBOLISM AND AMERICAN LITERATURE. Chicago, Ill.: University of Chicago Press, 1953.

"Emerson and Melville were the polar figures of the American symbolist movement.... Emerson represented the upsurge of a new capacity, Melville the relapse into doubt."

1142. Fiedler, Leslie A. In LOVE AND DEATH IN THE AMERICAN NOVEL. Rev. ed. New York: Stein and Day, 1966.

"MOBY DICK can be read ... as a love story, perhaps the greatest love story in our fiction, cast in the peculiar American form of innocent homosexuality."

1143. Fogle, R. H. MELVILLE'S SHORTER TALES. Norman: University of Oklahoma Press, 1960.

A close examination of fifteen tales and sketches.

1144. Forster, E. M. In ASPECTS OF THE NOVEL. New York: Harcourt, Brace, 1927.

A discussion of MOBY-DICK and BILLY BUDD in terms of "prophecy" (which, for Forster, is a "tone of voice," not the ability to foresee the future).

1146. Franklin, H. Bruce. THE WAKE OF THE GODS: MELVILLE'S MYTHOLOGY. Stanford, Calif.: Stanford University Press, 1963.

A discussion of Melville's conscious use of myth in his major writings.

1147. Gale, Robert L. PLOTS AND CHARACTERS IN THE FICTION AND NARRATIVE POETRY OF HERMAN MELVILLE. Hamden, Conn.: Archon Books, 1969.

Faithful summaries of Melville's plots and brief character sketches.

1148. Gilman, W. H. MELVILLE'S EARLY LIFE AND REDBURN. New York: New York University Press, 1951.

An examination of Melville's life from 1819 to 1841 as well as an attempt to separate autobiography from fiction in REDBURN.

1149. Gross, Theodore L. "Herman Melville: The Nature of Authority." COLQ, 16 (1968), 397–412.

> Melville's works reveal his distrust of authority. BILLY BUDD is a "prayer" which "speaks of the authority that ought to be." See 1134.

1150. Guetti, James. "The Languages of MOBY-DICK." In THE LIMITS OF METAPHOR: A STUDY OF MELVILLE, CONRAD, AND FAULKNER. Ithaca, N.Y.: Cornell University Press, 1967.

> The three languages of MOBY-DICK are technical language, the language of allusion (what others have said about whales and Moby-Dick), and unresolved figurative language which reveals the narrator's mystification.

1151. Hayman, Allen. "The Real and the Original: Herman Melville's Theory of Prose Fiction." MFS, 8 (1962), 211–33.

> "As Melville developed as a writer, he became progressively less concerned with the techniques of realism"; for him, "surface verisimilitude" was less important than the "vital truth," as this detailed study shows.

1152. HERMAN MELVILLE NUMBER. MFS, 8 (1962), 211–346.

> Essays by various hands and an indispensable checklist of critical studies.

1153. Hetherington, Hugh W. MELVILLE'S REVIEWERS, BRITISH AND AMERICAN, 1846-1891. Chapel Hill: University of North Carolina Press, 1961.

> A useful study of the contemporary reception of Melville's works.

1154. Hillway, Tyrus. HERMAN MELVILLE. New York: Twayne, 1963.

> A reliable brief account of the life and works. Includes a useful "Selected Bibliography" of works by and about Melville.

1155. Hillway, Tyrus and Luther S. Mansfield, eds. MOBY-DICK CENTENNIAL ESSAYS. Dallas, Tex.: Southern Methodist University Press, 1953.

> Nine essays by various hands.

1156. Hoffman, Daniel G. "Melville." In FORM AND FABLE IN AMERICAN FICTION. New York: Oxford University Press, 1961.

> Mythic and folkloric elements in MOBY-DICK and THE CONFIDENCE-MAN.

1157. Howard, Leon. HERMAN MELVILLE. Minneapolis: University of Minnesota Press, 1961.

A useful brief introduction which includes a "Selected Bibliography."

1158. Humphreys, A. R. HERMAN MELVILLE. Edinburgh: Oliver and Boyd, 1962.

A useful survey of the life and works.

1159. Kaplan, Sidney. "Herman Melville and the American National Sin." JOURNAL OF NEGRO HISTORY, 41 (1956), 311-38; 42 (1957), 11-37. Reprinted in THE IMAGE OF THE NEGRO IN AMERICAN LITERATURE, edited by Seymour Gross and John Edward Hardy (Chicago, Ill.: University of Chicago Press, 1966).

A perceptive examination of Melville's conflicting attitudes toward slavery.

1160. Kaul, A. N. "Herman Melville: The New-World Voyageur." In THE AMERICAN VISION: ACTUAL AND IDEAL SOCIETY IN NINETEENTH-CENTURY FICTION. New Haven, Conn., and London: Yale University Press, 1963.

A study of the "ideal community" in Melville, its various permutations throughout the works, and its ultimate, though qualified, failure.

1161. Levin, Harry. THE POWER OF BLACKNESS: HAWTHORNE, POE, AND MELVILLE. New York: Alfred A. Knopf, 1958.

A study of "the symbolic character of our greatest fiction and the dark wisdom of our deeper minds." The last two chapters are devoted to Melville.

1162. Lewis, R. W. B. "Melville: The Apotheosis of Adam." In THE AMERICAN ADAM: INNOCENCE, TRAGEDY, AND TRADITION IN THE NINETEENTH CENTURY. Chicago, Ill.: University of Chicago Press, 1955.

How "the one novelist in nineteenth-century America gifted with a genuinely myth-making imagination" elevated the story of Adam to the status of myth.

1163. McCarthy, Harold T. "Melville's REDBURN and the City." MQ, 12 (1971), 395-410.

How Melville uses Redburn to dramatize his own attitudes toward the "secular cities" of Liverpool and New York.

1164. Marx, Leo. In THE MACHINE IN THE GARDEN, TECHNOLOGY AND THE PASTORAL IDEAL IN AMERICA. New York: Oxford University Press, 1964.

A consideration of MOBY-DICK in terms of Ishmael's "complex pastoralism."

1165. Mason, Ronald. THE SPIRIT ABOVE THE DUST. London: John Lehmann, 1951.

Melville's works constitute "a single, deeply impressive record" of "the search for the rediscovery of that innocence in the human soul of which contact with worldly experience has deprived it."

1166. Matthiessen, F. O. AMERICAN RENAISSANCE: ART AND EXPRESSION IN THE AGE OF EMERSON AND WHITMAN. London: Oxford University Press, 1941.

Chapters 5 and 9-12 constitute an important study of Melville (which concludes that he "could endure to the end in the belief that though good goes to defeat and death, its radiance can redeem life").

1167. Maxwell, D. E. S. "The Tragic Phase: Melville and Hawthorne." In AMERICAN FICTION, THE INTELLECTUAL BACKGROUND. New York: Columbia University Press, 1963.

Examines WHITE-JACKET, THE CONFIDENCE-MAN, MOBY-DICK, and BILLY BUDD.

1168. MELVILLE SPECIAL NUMBER. SNNTS. 1 (1969), 393-535.

Eight essays concerning various aspects of Melville and his works and a checklist of selected Melville criticism, 1958-1968.

1169. Miller, James E., Jr. "Melville's Search for Form." BuR, 8 (November 1958), 260-76.

Melville has been misjudged by those who analyze his works in terms of traditional genres; his "inventive genius" constantly pushed beyond the usual formal limitations.

1170. Miller, Perry. THE RAVEN AND THE WHALE: THE WAR OF WORDS AND WITS IN THE ERA OF POE AND MELVILLE. New York: Harcourt, Brace, 1956.

A study of the literary world in which Melville lived and worked; see also 1133.

1171. Norman, Liane. "Bartleby and the Reader." NEQ, 44 (1971), 22-39.

Though "Bartleby the Scrivener" makes rigorous demands on the reader, "Melville's rhetorical mechanisms provide the reader with subtle and precise means of evaluating a potentially unintelligible experience."

1171a. Olson, Charles. CALL ME ISHMAEL. New York: Reynal & Hitchcock, 1947.

On Shakespeare's influence and other matters. Holman (in 21) calls this book "eccentric in style, invaluable in content." See Ann Charters, OLSON/MELVILLE: A STUDY IN AFFIN- ITY, New York: Oyez, 1968; see also 1174 and 1188.

1172. Parker, Hershel, comp. MOBY-DICK AS DOUBLOON: ESSAYS AND EXTRACTS (1851-1970). New York: W. W. Norton, 1970.

Seventy reviews and perhaps twice as many critical studies of MOBY-DICK. Includes "An Annotated Bibliography" of critical studies.

1173. _____, ed. THE RECOGNITION OF HERMAN MELVILLE, SELECTED CRITICISM SINCE 1846. Ann Arbor: University of Michigan Press, 1967.

A collection of "the criticism essential for understanding Melville's gradual recognition."

1174. Pommer, Henry Francis. MILTON AND MELVILLE. Pittsburgh, Pa.: University of Pittsburgh Press, 1950.

A detailed study of a third major literary influence on Melville (after Shakespeare and the Bible). See also 1171a and 1188.

1175. Rosenberry, Edward H. "The Problem of BILLY BUDD." PMLA, 80 (1965), 489-98.

The author favors a "straightforward" reading of the tale which respects "the author's sensitively wrought image of a tragically belittered world."

1176. Sealts, Merton M. MELVILLE AS LECTURER. Cambridge, Mass.: Harvard University Press, 1957.

A study of Melville's career as a lecturer, 1857-1860. The texts of the lectures are included.

1177. _____. MELVILLE'S READING, A CHECK-LIST OF BOOKS OWNED AND BORROWED. Madison: University of Wisconsin Press, 1966.

1178. Seelye, John. MELVILLE: THE IRONIC DIAGRAM. Evanston, Ill.: Northwestern University Press, 1970.

"There is no absolute center of value in Melville's work to which one may refer.... Truth, for Melville, is a question not an answer."

1179. Short, R. W. "Melville as Symbolist." UKCR, 15 (1948), 38-46. Reprinted in INTERPRETATIONS OF AMERICAN LITERATURE, ed. Charles Feidelson, Jr. and Paul Brodtkorb. New York: Oxford University Press, 1959.

Argues against the strictly allegorical interpretation of MOBY- DICK.

1180. Springer, Haskell S., comp. THE MERRILL STUDIES IN BILLY BUDD. Columbus, Ohio: Charles E. Merrill, 1970.

Essays by various hands. See also 1181 and 1186.

1181. Stafford, William T., ed. MELVILLE'S BILLY BUDD AND THE CRITICS. Rev. ed. San Francisco, Calif.: Wadsworth Publishing Co., 1968.

Includes texts of the story and the play, essays by various hands, and an annotated checklist of critical studies. See also 1180 and 1186.

1182. Stern, Milton, ed. DISCUSSIONS OF MOBY-DICK. Boston, Mass.: D. C. Heath, 1960.

Essays by various hands.

1183. Stone, Geoffrey. MELVILLE. New York: Sheed and Ward, 1949.

A study of the life and works which closely examines Melville's fundamental Calvinism.

1184. Vincent, Howard P., comp. THE MERRILL STUDIES IN MOBY-DICK. Columbus, Ohio: Charles E. Merrill, 1969.

Contemporary reviews and essays and tributes by various hands.

1185. _____. THE TAILORING OF MELVILLE'S WHITE-JACKET. Evanston, Ill.: Northwestern University Press, 1970.

A study of the genesis of WHITE-JACKET.

1186. _____, ed. TWENTIETH CENTURY INTERPRETATIONS OF BILLY BUDD. Englewood Cliffs, N.J.: Prentice-Hall, 1971.

Essays and excerpts from longer studies; by various hands. See 1180 and 1181.

1187. Widmer, Kingsley. THE WAYS OF NIHILISM: A STUDY OF HERMAN MELVILLE'S SHORT NOVELS. Los Angeles: The Ward Ritchie Press for the California State Colleges, 1970.

On BILLY BUDD, "Benito Cereno," and "Bartleby the Scrivener." Melville is "an American existential nihilist."

1188. Wright, Nathalia. MELVILLE'S USE OF THE BIBLE. Durham, N.C.: Duke University Press, 1949.

A thorough examination of one of the two major influences on Melville's writings (the other being Shakespeare). See also 1171a and 1174.

S. WEIR MITCHELL (1829-1914)

Principal Works

IN WAR TIME, 1885   Novel
ROLAND BLAKE, 1886   Novel
CHARACTERISTICS, 1892   Novel
HUGH WYNNE, FREE QUAKER, 1897   Novel
THE ADVENTURES OF FRANCOIS, 1898   Novel
DR. NORTH AND HIS FRIENDS, 1900   Novel   (sequel to CHARACTER-
    ISTICS)
CIRCUMSTANCE, 1901   Novel
CONSTANCE TRESCOT, 1905   Novel
THE RED CITY, 1908   Novel
JOHN SHERWOOD, IRON MASTER, 1911   Novel
WESTWAYS, 1913   Novel

> Mitchell was also the author of several volumes of poetry and children's stories as well as a great number of medical treatises.

Collected Works

1189. AUTHOR'S DEFINITIVE EDITION. 16 vols. 1901-1914.

Letters

1190. There is no separate collection of the letters, although Burr (1195) reproduces numerous letters and Earnest (1196) quotes others.

Bibliography

1191. A CATALOGUE OF THE SCIENTIFIC AND LITERARY WORK OF S. WEIR MITCHELL. Philadelphia, Pa.: Privately printed, 1894.

> Compiled by Mitchell himself.

1192. Mumey, Nolie. SILAS WEIR MITCHELL: THE VERSATILE PHYSICIAN. Denver, Col.: Range Press, 1934.

Of little value in the critical sense, this book nonetheless contains the most comprehensive bibliography of Mitchell's writings.

Checklist

1193. Hayne, Barrie. "S[ilas]. Weir Mitchell (1829-1914)." ALR, 2 (1969), [149]-55.

A brief overview of the current status of Mitchell scholarship; includes suggestions for further study.

1194. See 1199.

Biography

1195. Burr, Anna Robeson. WEIR MITCHELL: HIS LIFE AND LETTERS. New York: Duffield, 1929.

A eulogistic and nonscholarly biography.

1196. Earnest, Ernest. S. WEIR MITCHELL: NOVELIST AND PHYSICIAN. Philadelphia: University of Pennsylvania Press, 1950.

The definitive biography to date.

Critical Studies

1197. Earnest, Ernest. "Weir Mitchell As Novelist." ASCH, 17 (1948), 314-22.

General commentary on the novels.

1198. Griffith, Kelley, Jr. "Weir Mitchell and the Genteel Romance." AL, 44 (1972), 246-61.

Defines the chief characteristics of Mitchell's romances and the genteel romance in general.

1199. Lovering, Joseph P. S. WEIR MITCHELL. New York: Twayne, 1971.

Deals primarily with the novels, which "are of historical interest, even though...his artistic merits are quite limited in comparison with the major writers of the century." Includes a useful "Selected Bibliography" of works by and about Mitchell.

1200. Quinn, Arthur Hobson. "Weir Mitchell, Pioneer and Patrician." In AMERICAN FICTION, AN HISTORICAL AND CRITICAL SURVEY. New

York: Appleton-Century-Crofts, 1936.

General commentary on the major works.

1201. Rein, Donald. S. WEIR MITCHELL AS A PSYCHIATRIC NOVELIST. New York: International Universities Press, 1952.

A psychoanalytic study of Mitchell's characters.

1202. Richardson, Lyon N. "S. Weir Mitchell at Work." AL, 11 (1939), 58-65.

A study of Mitchell's revisions of ROLAND BLAKE.

MARY NOAILLES MURFREE
("CHARLES EGBERT CRADDOCK") (1850-1922)

Principal Works

IN THE TENNESSEE MOUNTAINS, 1884   Stories
WHERE THE BATTLE WAS FOUGHT, 1884   Novel
DOWN THE RAVINE, 1885   Stories
THE PROPHET OF THE GREAT SMOKY MOUNTAINS, 1885   Novel
THE MYSTERY OF WITCH-FACE MOUNTAIN, 1895   Stories
THE YOUNG MOUNTAINEERS, 1897   Stories
THE STORY OF OLD FORT LOUDON, 1899   Novel
A SPECTRE OF POWER, 1903   Novel
THE FRONTIERSMEN, 1904   Novel
THE STORM CENTRE, 1905   Novel
THE AMULET, 1906   Novel

Bibliography

1203. See 1208.

Checklist

1204. Cary, Richard. "Mary Noailles Murfree (1850-1922)." ALR, 1 (1967), 79-83.

Biography

1205. Parks, Edd Winfield. CHARLES EGBERT CRADDOCK (MARY NOAILLES MURFREE). Chapel Hill: University of North Carolina Press, 1941.

The definitive biography to date.

Critical Studies

1206. Adkins, Milton T. "The Mountains and Mountaineers of Craddock's

Fiction." MAGAZINE OF AMERICAN HISTORY, 24 (1890), 305-09.

Plaudits for Murfree's powers of observation.

1207. Baskervill, William Malone. "Charles Egbert Craddock." In SOUTHERN WRITERS: BIOGRAPHICAL AND CRITICAL STUDIES, vol. I. Nashville, Tenn. and Dallas, Tex.: Publishing House of the M. E. Church, South, 1897.

An impressionistic and nonscholarly survey.

1208. Cary, Richard. MARY N. MURFREE. New York: Twayne, 1967.

First book-length analysis of her fiction. Includes a useful "Selected Bibliography" of works by and about Murfree.

1209. Loyd, Dennis. "Tennessee's Mystery Woman Novelist." THQ, 29 (1970), 272-77.

General commentary.

1210. Pattee, Fred Lewis. In THE DEVELOPMENT OF THE AMERICAN SHORT STORY. New York and London: Harper & Brothers, 1923.

A succinct and largely negative evaluation of Murfree's achievement as a writer of stories.

1211. Toulmin, Harry A., Jr. "Charles Egbert Craddock (Mary Noailles Murfree)." In SOCIAL HISTORIANS. Boston, Mass.: R. G. Badger, 1911.

Murfree as a literary historian of mountain life.

1212. Warfel, Harry R. "Local Color and Literary Artistry: Mary Noailles Murfree's IN THE TENNESSEE MOUNTAINS." SLJ, 3 (1970), 154-63.

A discussion of elements of local color and romanticism in Murfree's stories.

1213. Wright, Nathalia. "Introduction" to IN THE TENNESSEE MOUNTAINS. Knoxville: University of Tennessee Press, 1970.

A perceptive introduction to the stories.

FRANK NORRIS (1870-1902)

Principal Works

YVERNELLE A LEGEND OF FEUDAL FRANCE, 1892   Poem
MORAN OF THE LADY LETTY, 1898   Novel
MCTEAGUE, 1899   Novel
BLIX, 1899   Novel
A MAN'S WOMAN, 1900   Novel
THE OCTOPUS, 1901   Novel (first novel of a projected trilogy which was
    to include THE PIT and an unwritten work, THE WOLF)
A DEAL IN WHEAT, 1903   Stories
THE PIT, 1903   Novel
THE RESPONSIBILITIES OF THE NOVELIST, 1903   Essays
THE JOYOUS MIRACLE, 1906   Novel
THE THIRD CIRCLE, 1909   Stories
VANDOVER AND THE BRUTE, 1914   Novel

Collected Works

1214. COLLECTED WRITINGS. 10 vols. Garden City, N.Y.: Doubleday,
      Doran, 1928. Reprinted 1967 by Kennikat Press.

      Identical to the more expensive ARGONAUT MANUSCRIPT
      LIMITED EDITION (also published by Doubleday, Doran in
      1928).

1215. FRANK NORRIS OF "THE WAVE." San Francisco, Calif.: Westgate
      Press, 1931.

      Stories and sketches originally published in the San Francisco
      magazine between 1893 and 1897.

1216. THE LITERARY CRITICISM OF FRANK NORRIS. Ed. Donald Pizer.
      Austin: University of Texas Press, 1964.

Letters

1217. THE LETTERS OF FRANK NORRIS. Ed. Franklin Walker. San Francisco: Book Club of California, 1956.

Bibliography

1218. Lohf, Kenneth and Eugene Sheehy, eds. FRANK NORRIS BIBLIOGRAPHY. Los Gatos, Calif.: Talisman Press, 1959.

Certain items not listed here may be found in William White's "Frank Norris: Bibliographical Addenda," BB, 22 (1959), 227-28.

Checklist

1219. Dillingham, William B. "Frank Norris." In FIFTEEN AMERICAN AUTHORS BEFORE 1900, ed. Robert A. Rees and Earl N. Harbert. Madison: University of Wisconsin Press, 1971.

An indispensable essay which covers bibliography, texts and editions, manuscripts and letters, biography, and criticism.

1220. French, Warren. "Frank Norris (1870-1902)." ALR, 1 (1967), 84-89.

Discusses Norris criticism and biography as well as locations and editions of his writings.

1221. Hill, John S. CHECKLIST OF FRANK NORRIS. Columbus, Ohio: Charles E. Merrill, 1970.

Norris's book-length publications, editions of his work, and letters; bibliographies and checklists, biographies, scholarship and criticism of Norris; reviews of his work.

1222. Crisler, Jesse S. and Joseph R. McElrath, Jr. FRANK NORRIS: A REFERENCE GUIDE. Boston, Mass.: G.K. Hall, 1974.

An annotated checklist of writings (1891-1972) about Norris and his works; includes dissertations.

Biography

1223. Walker, Franklin D. FRANK NORRIS: A BIOGRAPHY. Garden City, N.Y.: Doubleday, Doran, 1932.

The only full-length biography to date.

Critical Studies

1224. Ahnebrink, Lars. THE BEGINNINGS OF NATURALISM IN AMERICAN FICTION. New York: Russell & Russell, 1961.

Dillingham (1219) reports that although Norris is treated in several chapters, the most useful is Chapter 10, which establishes Zola's influence on Norris.

1225. Berthoff, Warner. "Frank Norris, Stephen Crane." In THE FERMENT OF REALISM: AMERICAN LITERATURE, 1884-1919. New York: Free Press, 1965.

"With Norris in particular the impression is strong of a writer who never got beyond the synthetic ambitions of his apprenticeship."

1226. Cargill, Oscar. "A Robber Baron Revises THE OCTOPUS." In TOWARD A PLURALISTIC CRITICISM. Carbondale: Southern Illinois University Press, 1965.

An interesting account of how Norris may have been influenced to shift the emphasis of his novel.

1226a. _____. "American Naturalism." In INTELLECTUAL AMERICA: IDEAS ON THE MARCH. New York: Macmillan, 1941.

Cargill's treatment of Norris's writings in this chapter is comprehensive and largely unfavorable.

1227. Chase, Richard. "Norris and Naturalism." In THE AMERICAN NOVEL AND ITS TRADITION. Garden City, N.Y.: Doubleday, 1957.

In Norris's works, which are romances as well as naturalistic novels, we see "the glories and perils of naturalism in their sheerest form." Concerning the romance, see also 1240.

1228. Collins, Carvel. "Introduction" to MCTEAGUE. New York: Holt, Rinehart and Winston, 1950.

A general essay which comments on naturalism and Norris's life as well as the novel itself.

1229. Cooperman, Stanley. "Frank Norris and the Werewolf of Guilt." MLQ, 20 (1959), 252-58.

American naturalism results from the imposition of traditional Calvinist determinism on the new scientific determinism. The discussion focuses on two Norris novels, MCTEAGUE and VANDOVER AND THE BRUTE.

1230. Dillingham, William B. "Frank Norris and the Genteel Tradition." TSL, 5 (1960), 15-24.

Norris's break with the genteel tradition is less pronounced than had been thought previously.

1231. _____. FRANK NORRIS: INSTINCT AND ART. Lincoln: University of Nebraska Press, 1969.

A study of the life and works. Includes a useful "Selected Bibliography" of works about Norris.

1232. Folsom, James K. "Social Darwinism or Social Protest? The 'Philosophy' of THE OCTOPUS." MFS, 8 (1962-63), 393-400.

The solution to the conflict posed in the novel is to be found in its appeal for social justice, not social Darwinism.

1233. French, Warren. FRANK NORRIS. New York: Twayne, 1962.

Sees Norris not as a convert to European naturalism but as an ingenuous heir of the transcendentalists and one who borrowed the latest techniques to give new impetus to the tradition of American romanticism. Includes a useful "Selected Bibliography" of works by and about Norris.

1234. Frohock, W. M. FRANK NORRIS. Minneapolis: University of Minnesota Press, 1968.

A useful brief introduction to the life and works.

1235. Geismar, Maxwell. "Frank Norris: AND THE BRUTE." In REBELS AND ANCESTORS: THE AMERICAN NOVEL, 1890-1915. Boston, Mass.: Houghton Mifflin, 1953.

A psychological study of Norris.

1236. Goldsmith, Arnold L. "The Development of Frank Norris's Philosophy." In STUDIES IN HONOR OF JOHN WILCOX, ed. A. Doyle Wallace and Woodburn O. Ross. Detroit, Mich.: Wayne State University Press, 1958.

Because of his optimism, Norris is neither romantic nor naturalistic but should be thought of as somewhere between the two positions.

1237. Hicks, Granville. "Frank Norris." In THE GREAT TRADITION. Rev. ed. New York: Biblo and Tannen, 1967.

A general and largely deprecatory essay, originally published in 1933.

1238. Hoffman, Charles G. "Norris and the Responsibility of the Novelist." SAQ, 54 (1955), 508-15.

Norris's novels do not indicate a steady development on his part, but they reflect his belief in the novelist's responsibility to a "realistic fidelity to life" and "a seriousness and complexity of theme, character, and content." A useful article; see also 1244.

1239. Howells, William Dean. "Frank Norris." NAR, 175 (1902), 769-78.

A sympathetic overview of Norris's works; written shortly after his death.

1240. Johnson, George W. "Frank Norris and Romance." AL, 33 (1961), 52-63.

Deals with Norris's attempt "to reconstitute romance in American letters." See also 1227.

1241. Kaplan, Charles. "Fact into Fiction in MCTEAGUE." HLB, 8 (1954), 381-85.

How Norris drew on a dentistry text for many of the details in MCTEAGUE.

1242. _____. "Norris's Use of Sources in THE PIT." AL, 25 (1953), 75-84.

The factual basis for Norris's novel.

1243. Kazin, Alfred. In ON NATIVE GROUNDS. New York: Reynal & Hitchcock, 1942.

The key to Norris's mind is "a naive, open-hearted, and essentially unquenchable joy" which is "eager to absorb every flicker of life."

1244. Kwiat, Joseph J. "Frank Norris: The Novelist as Social Critic and Literary Theorist." ARQ, 18 (1962), 319-28.

It is impossible to reconcile Norris's aesthetic theories with his social theories. See also 1238.

1245. Marchand, Ernest. FRANK NORRIS, A STUDY. Stanford, Calif.: Stanford University Press, 1942.

The first extensive study of Norris. Still useful.

1246. Martin, Jay. "Frank Norris." In HARVESTS OF CHANGE: AMERICAN LITERATURE, 1865-1914. Englewood Cliffs, N.J.: Prentice-Hall, 1967.

A compact introduction to Norris. Martin identifies four key elements in Norris's work: romance, Zolaesque naturalism, an updated version of chivalry, and the ethic of social Darwinism.

1247. Meyer, George W. "A New Interpretation of THE OCTOPUS." CE, 4 (1943), 351-59.

Meyer discusses three purposes that Norris had in writing THE OCTOPUS and reconciles what are usually described as disparate thematic elements of the novel.

1248. Millgate, Michael. In AMERICAN SOCIAL FICTION: JAMES TO COZZENS. New York: Barnes and Noble, 1964.

Norris reflects a new sense of excitement about American
society; his work represents a transition between the restraint
of Howells and the violence of Dreiser. (This essay deals
mainly with THE PIT.)

1249. Pizer, Donald. THE NOVELS OF FRANK NORRIS. Bloomington:
Indiana University Press, 1966.

Norris's novels are of a piece: they arise out of "a coherent
conception of man, nature, and God, though they derive from
different parts of that conception."

1250. _____. In REALISM AND NATURALISM IN NINETEENTH-CENTURY
AMERICAN LITERATURE. Carbondale and Edwardsville: Southern
Illinois University Press, 1966.

Includes chapters on Norris's definition of Naturalism, his
literary criticism, and THE OCTOPUS.

1251. Taylor, Walter Fuller. "Frank Norris." In THE ECONOMIC NOVEL
IN AMERICA. Chapel Hill: University of North Carolina Press, 1942.

Taylor concludes that Norris's faults are negligible when com-
pared to his achievements.

1252. Vance, William L. "Romance in THE OCTOPUS." GENRE, 3 (1970),
111-36.

The book is a failure because Norris's "preoccupation with
literary types--with the epic, the romantic, the tragic, the
realistic, the naturalistic, and the melodramatic--evidently
so obsessed him that he indulged himself in all of them,
oblivious to incompatibilities."

1253. Walcutt, Charles Child. "Frank Norris and the Search for Form." In
AMERICAN LITERARY NATURALISM, A DIVIDED STREAM. Minneapolis:
University of Minnesota Press, 1956.

Many of Norris's works are failures; but if the novelist is more
"reckless" than his successors, he is also more "powerful."

THOMAS NELSON PAGE (1853-1922)

Principal Works

IN OLE VIRGINIA, 1887   Stories
BEFO' DE WAR, 1888   Dialect Verse
TWO LITTLE CONFEDERATES, 1888   Novel
ELSKET AND OTHER STORIES, 1891
ON NEWFOUND RIVER, 1891   Novel
THE OLD SOUTH, 1892   Essays
THE BURIAL OF THE GUNS, 1894   Stories
THE OLD GENTLEMAN OF THE BLACK STOCK, 1897   Novel
RED ROCK, 1898   Novel
GORDON KEITH, 1903   Novel
BRED IN THE BONE, 1904   Stories
THE OLD DOMINION, 1908   Essays
JOHN MARVEL ASSISTANT, 1909   Novel
ROBERT E. LEE MAN AND SOLDIER, 1911   Biography
THE RED RIDERS, 1924   Novel (finished by his brother, Rosewell Page)

Collected Works

1254. THE NOVELS, STORIES, SKETCHES, AND POEMS OF THOMAS NELSON
PAGE. Plantation Edition. 18 vols. New York: Charles Scribner's
Sons, 1906–1918.

Bibliography

1255. See 1257.

Biography

1256. Page, Rosewell. THOMAS NELSON PAGE: A MEMOIR OF A VIR-
GINIA GENTLEMAN. New York: Charles Scribner's Sons, 1923.

A eulogistic biography by Page's brother.

Critical Studies

1257. Gross, Theodore L. THOMAS NELSON PAGE. New York: Twayne, 1967.

> First full-length study of Page that has been published; includes bibliography. Gross cites Harriet Holman's 1947 Duke University dissertation, "The Literary Career of Thomas Nelson Page, 1884-1910" (unpublished), as "the only complete account of his life and work."

1258. _____. "Thomas Nelson Page: Creator of a Virginia Classic." GaR, 20 (1966), 338-51.

> A general introduction to Page which deals with "Marse Chan" and other stories; parts of this essay are reprinted in Gross (1257).

1259. Holman, Harriet R. "Attempt and Failure: Thomas Nelson Page as Playwright." SLJ, 3 (1970), 72-82.

> An authoritative account of Page's unsuccessful attempts at playwriting.

1260. Hubbell, Jay B. "Thomas Nelson Page." In THE SOUTH IN AMERICAN LITERATURE, 1607-1900. Durham, N.C.: Duke University Press, 1954.

> A general introduction to Page.

1261. Kent, Charles W. "Thomas Nelson Page." SAQ, 6 (1907), 263-71.

> Largely a review of the Plantation Edition of Page's collected works.

1262. Mims, Edwin. "Thomas Nelson Page." ATLANTIC, 100 (1907), 109-15.

> Treats Page primarily as an interpreter to the nation of Virginia aristocracy.

1263. Quinn, Arthur Hobson. "Place and Race in American Fiction." In AMERICAN FICTION: AN HISTORICAL AND CRITICAL SURVEY. New York: Appleton-Century-Crofts, 1936.

> Includes some useful insights into Page's novels.

1264. Wilson, Edmund. "Novelists of the Post-War South: Albion W. Tourgee, George W. Cable, Kate Chopin, Thomas Nelson Page." In PATRIOTIC GORE: STUDIES IN THE LITERATURE OF THE AMERICAN CIVIL WAR. New York: Oxford University Press, 1962.

> The section on Page includes a realistic appraisal of his social attitudes as revealed in his fiction.

JAMES KIRKE PAULDING (1778-1860)

Principal Works

SALMAGUNDI, 1807-8   Satirical Miscellanies (written with Washington
    Irving and others; Paulding published a second series alone, 1819-20.)
THE DIVERTING HISTORY OF JOHN BULL AND BROTHER JONATHAN, 1812
    Satire
THE LAY OF THE SCOTTISH FIDDLE, 1813   Burlesque Poem
LETTERS FROM THE SOUTH, 1817   Sketches
THE BACKWOODSMAN, 1818   Poem
A SKETCH OF OLD ENGLAND, 1822   Sketches
KONINGSMARKE, 1823   Novel
JOHN BULL IN AMERICA, 1825   Satire
THE MERRY TALES OF THE THREE WISE MEN OF GOTHAM, 1826   Stories
TALES OF THE GOOD WOMAN, 1829   Stories
THE DUTCHMAN'S FIRESIDE, 1831   Novel
WESTWARD HO!, 1832   Novel
A LIFE OF WASHINGTON, 1835   Biography
SLAVERY IN THE UNITED STATES, 1836   Essay
THE OLD CONTINENTAL, 1846   Novel
THE PURITAN AND HIS DAUGHTER, 1849   Novel

Collected Works

1265. COLLECTED WORKS. 14 vols. New York: Harper & Brothers, 1835-37.

Letters

1266. THE LETTERS OF JAMES KIRKE PAULDING. Ed. Ralph M. Aderman.
    Madison: University of Wisconsin Press, 1962.

Bibliography

1267. See 1268.

James Kirke Paulding

Biography

1268. Herold, Amos L. JAMES KIRKE PAULDING: VERSATILE AMERICAN.
New York: Columbia University Press, 1926.

> The only modern critical biography. Includes a bibliography of
> Paulding's works.

1269. Paulding, William I. LITERARY LIFE OF JAMES K. PAULDING. New
York: Charles Scribner, 1867.

> By Paulding's son. Based largely on letters and excerpts from
> his works.

Critical Studies

1270. Aderman, Ralph M. "James Kirke Paulding as Social Critic." PLL, 1
(1965), 217-29.

> Paulding "admired equality in a democratic society, but at the
> same time he recognized and defended the differences in in-
> tellect and wealth in that society."

1271. _____. "James Kirke Paulding on Literature and the West." AL, 27
(1955), 97-101.

> An 1835 letter (printed here) to Dr. Daniel Drake expresses
> Paulding's belief that Americans should forsake Europe as a
> source of literary materials and turn to the American West.

1272. Davidson, Frank. "Paulding's Treatment of the Angel of Hadley." AL,
7 (1935), 330-32.

> A note on THE PURITAN AND HIS DAUGHTER.

1273. Dondore, Dorothy. "The Debt of Two Dyed-in-the-Wool Americans
to Mrs. Grant's MEMOIRS: Cooper's SATANSTOE, Paulding's THE
DUTCHMAN'S FIRESIDE." AL, 12 (1940), 52-58.

> THE DUTCHMAN'S FIRESIDE owes much to Mrs. Grant's book.

1274. Gerber, Gerald H. "James Kirke Paulding and the Image of the
Machine." AQ, 22 (1970), 736-41.

> Paulding may be the first important American writer to use the
> machine image as a negative sign of the times.

1275. O'Donnell, Thomas F. "Introduction" to THE DUTCHMAN'S FIRESIDE.
New Haven, Conn.: College and University Press, 1966.

> The background and critical reception of Paulding's most
> successful work.

1276. Turner, Arlin. "James K. Paulding and Timothy Flint." MVHR, 34

(1947), 105-11.

The influence of Flint's RECOLLECTIONS on Paulding's
WESTWARD HO!

1277. Watkins, Floyd C. "James Kirke Paulding and the South." AQ, 5
(1953), 219-30.

Paulding's progress from Unionism to support of the idea of
secession.

1278. _____. "James Kirke Paulding's Creole Tale." LAHISTQ, 33 (1950),
364-79.

A brief introduction to "The Creole's Daughter" (printed here)
notes that it may be the first fiction in English about Creoles.

EDGAR ALLAN POE (1809-1849)

Principal Works

TAMERLANE AND OTHER POEMS, 1827
AL AARAAF, TAMERLANE, AND MINOR POEMS, 1829
POEMS, 1831
THE NARRATIVE OF ARTHUR GORDON PYM, 1838   Novel
TALES OF THE GROTESQUE AND ARABESQUE, 1840
TALES, 1845
THE RAVEN AND OTHER POEMS, 1845
EUREKA: A PROSE POEM, 1848

Collected Works

1279. COLLECTED WORKS OF EDGAR ALLAN POE. Ed. Thomas Ollive Mabbott. Cambridge, Mass.: Harvard University Press, 1969- .

1280. THE COMPLETE WORKS OF EDGAR ALLAN POE. Virginia Edition. 17 vols. Ed. James A. Harrison. New York: Thomas Y. Crowell, 1902.

> The best of the early editions of Poe.

Letters

1281. THE LETTERS OF EDGAR ALLAN POE. Ed. John W. Ostrom. Cambridge, Mass.: Harvard University Press, 1948. Reprinted with supplement, New York: Gordian Press, 1966.

> To date, three more supplements have been printed, all in AL: 24 (1952), 358-66; 29 (1957), 79-86; and 45 (1974), 513-36.

Journals

1282. POE STUDIES. 1971- .

Essays, book reviews, bibliography dealing with Poe's life and works. Supersedes POE NEWSLETTER (1968-1971). Published 2-3 times per year by Washington State University Press, Pullman, Washington. 99163.

Bibliography

1283. Heartman, Charles F. and James R. Canny. A BIBLIOGRAPHY OF FIRST PRINTINGS OF THE WRITINGS OF EDGAR ALLAN POE. Rev. ed. Hattiesburg, Miss.: The Book Farm, 1943.

A review by James Southall in AL, 13 (May 1941), 176-77 indicates shortcomings of this book.

1284. Robbins, J. Albert. CHECKLIST OF EDGAR ALLAN POE. Columbus, Ohio: Charles E. Merrill, 1969.

Books and major separate publications by Poe, editions of his work and letters, bibliographies and checklists, biographies and memoirs, scholarship and criticism.

1285. Robertson, John W. BIBLIOGRAPHY OF THE WRITINGS OF EDGAR ALLAN POE. 2 vols. San Francisco, Calif.: Privately printed, 1934.

For additions and corrections by David Randall, see PW, 125 (April 21, 1934), 1540-43.

Checklist

1286. Cauthen, Irby B., Jr. "A Descriptive Bibliography of Criticism of Edgar Allan Poe, 1827-1941." Unpublished master's thesis, University of Virginia, 1942.

1287. Dameron, J. Lesley. EDGAR ALLAN POE: A CHECKLIST OF CRITICISM, 1942-1960. Charlottesville: Bibliographical Society of the University of Virginia, 1966.

1288. Hubbell, Jay B. "Poe." In EIGHT AMERICAN AUTHORS, ed. Floyd Stovall. Rev. ed. New York: W. W. Norton, 1971.

Biography

1289. Quinn, Arthur Hobson. EDGAR ALLAN POE: A CRITICAL BIOGRAPHY. New York: Appleton-Century-Crofts, 1941.

There are a number of highly romanticized and unreliable biographies of Poe, but this well-researched book separates the true from the false and is considered definitive.

1290. Wagenknecht, Edward. EDGAR ALLAN POE--THE MAN BEHIND THE LEGEND. New York: Oxford University Press, 1963.

A sensible, readable biography, though Quinn's is preferred.

Critical Studies

Note: Because of their number, studies dealing exclusively with Poe's poetry
are not included.

1291. Abel, Darrel. "Edgar Poe: A Centennial Estimate." UKCR, 16 (1949), 77-96.

Abel prefers Poe's critical writings to his poems and argues
that the short stories are that part of Poe's work which is
"most likely to endure."

1292. Alexander, Jean. AFFIDAVITS OF GENIUS: EDGAR ALLAN POE AND
THE FRENCH CRITICS, 1847-1924. Port Washington, N.Y.: Kennikat,
1971.

Translations of 17 essays (by Baudelaire, Valery, Mallarme,
and others) plus an introductory discussion of the French view
of Poe. See also 1295, 1300, 1303, 1320.

1293. Allen, Michael. POE AND THE BRITISH MAGAZINE TRADITION.
Cambridge, Mass.: Harvard University Press, 1969.

A study of the substantial influence of British journals and
journalists on Poe's career.

1294. Asselineau, Roger. EDGAR ALLAN POE. Minneapolis: University of
Minnesota Press, 1970.

A brief but useful treatment of the paradoxes and contradictions
of Poe's life and works. Includes "Selected Bibliography."

1295. Baudelaire, Charles. BAUDELAIRE ON POE: CRITICAL PAPERS, trans.
Lois Hyslop and Francis E. Hyslop, Jr. State College, Pa.: Bald Eagle
Press, 1952.

Baudelaire's essays on and introductions to works by Poe. Includes a list of Poe's works translated by Baudelaire. See also
1292, 1300, 1303, 1320.

1296. Benton, Richard P., ed. "Poe Symposium." ESQ, 60 (1970), 3-91.

Essays on "Ligeia," "William Wilson," THE NARRATIVE OF
ARTHUR GORDON PYM, and other works.

1297. Bonaparte, Marie. THE LIFE AND WORKS OF EDGAR ALLAN POE,
trans. John Rodker. London: Imago, 1949.

A ponderous (749 pp.) but interesting reading of Poe from a
rather limited, largely psychosexual viewpoint. Includes a
brief foreword by Sigmund Freud.

1298. Buranelli, Vincent. EDGAR ALLAN POE. New York: Twayne, 1961.

A useful introduction to Poe's life and works; includes a "Selected Bibliography" of works by and about Poe.

1299. Campbell, Killis. THE MIND OF POE AND OTHER STUDIES. Cambridge, Mass.: Harvard University Press, 1933.

Seven essays, all significant contributions to Poe scholarship.

1300. Carlson, Eric W., ed. THE RECOGNITION OF EDGAR ALLAN POE:
SELECTED CRITICISM SINCE 1829. Ann Arbor: University of Michigan
Press, 1966.

Contains essays (of uneven quality, though a number of them
are excellent) by American, British, and French critics of
Poe. Concerning the French view of Poe, see also 1292,
1295, 1303, 1320.

1301. Cobb, Palmer. THE INFLUENCE OF E. T. A. HOFFMANN ON THE
TALES OF E. A. POE. Chapel Hill: University of North Carolina
Press, 1908.

How Hoffman's fascination with the grotesque and the gruesome
influenced Poe.

1302. Davidson, Edward H. POE: A CRITICAL STUDY. Cambridge, Mass.:
Harvard University Press, 1957.

A philosophic inquiry into the mind and writings of Poe based
on the critical and metaphysical theories of Coleridge.

1303. Eliot, T. S. "From Poe to Valery." HUDR, 2 (1949), 327-43.

"I find that by trying to look at Poe through the eyes of
Baudelaire, Mallarme and most of all Valery, I become more
thoroughly convinced of his importance." See also 1292, 1295,
1300, 1320.

1304. Fagin, N. Bryllion. THE HISTRIONIC MR. POE. Baltimore, Md.:
John Hopkins Press, 1949.

Poe was an actor manque who acted through his stories; thus
his characters are not people but masks of the real Poe.

1305. Fiedler, Leslie A. "The Blackness of Darkness: Edgar Allan Poe and
the Development of the Gothic." In LOVE AND DEATH IN THE
AMERICAN NOVEL. Rev. ed. New York: Stein and Day, 1966.

THE NARRATIVE OF ARTHUR GORDON PYM is "the archetypal American story, which would be recast in MOBY DICK
and HUCKLEBERRY FINN."

1306. Gale, Robert L. PLOTS AND CHARACTERS IN THE FICTION AND

POETRY OF EDGAR ALLAN POE. Hamden, Conn.: Archon Books, 1970.

An indispensable handbook.

1307. Hoffman, Daniel. POE POE POE POE POE POE POE. Garden City, N.Y.: Doubleday, 1972.

An admittedly unconventional attempt, by a poet and literary critic, to substitute subjective responses for Olympian judgments.

1308. Howarth, William L., comp. TWENTIETH CENTURY INTERPRETATIONS OF POE'S TALES. Englewood Cliffs, N.J.: Prentice-Hall, 1971.

Nearly fifty of Poe's tales are discussed in this very useful collection.

1309. Jacobs, Robert D. POE: JOURNALIST AND CRITIC. Baton Rouge: Louisiana State University Press, 1969.

A distinguished work of scholarship; the definitive book on Poe's literary criticism. See 1317.

1310. Krutch, Joseph Wood. EDGAR ALLAN POE: A STUDY IN GENIUS. New York: Alfred A. Knopf, 1926.

An attempt to trace "Poe's art to an abnormal condition of the nerves and his critical ideas to a rationalized defense of the limitations of his own taste."

1311. Lawrence, D. H. In STUDIES IN CLASSIC AMERICAN LITERATURE. New York: Viking, 1964.

A rambling but provocative discourse on Poe's main themes: "love, intense vibrations and heightened consciousness."

1312. Levin, Harry. THE POWER OF BLACKNESS: HAWTHORNE, POE, AND MELVILLE. New York: Alfred A. Knopf, 1958.

An enlightening examination of Poe and the other authors in terms of Levin's thesis that "our most perceptive minds have distinguished themselves from our popular spokesmen by concentrating on the dark other half of the situation."

1313. Liebman, Sheldon W. "Poe's Tales and His Theory of the Poetic Experience." SSF, 7 (1970), 582-96.

A study of the tales in which Poe dramatizes his aesthetics indicates that Poe believed in "the second fall": because he rejects the terms of earthly existence (which are the consequences of the fall of Adam), the artist is fated to suffer a continuous process of birth, death, and rebirth.

1314. Miller, Perry. THE RAVEN AND THE WHALE: THE WAR OF WORDS

AND WITS IN THE ERA OF POE AND MELVILLE. New York: Harcourt, Brace, 1956.

Only indirectly concerned with the literary works of Poe and other writers of the day, this book describes in detail the professional and intellectual milieu in which they lived.

1315. Moldenhauer, Joseph J. "Imagination and Perversity in THE NARRATIVE OF ARTHUR GORDON PYM." TSLL, 13 (1971), 267-80.

This work illustrates "with unusual clarity" a principle which operates in almost all of Poe's fiction: "the coincidence or even equation of perversity and creative imagination."

1316. Moskowitz, Sam, ed. THE MAN WHO CALLED HIMSELF POE. Garden City, N.Y.: Doubleday, 1969.

A collection of stories and poems in which Poe appears as a character or which were written in imitation of Poe.

1317. Parks, Edd W. EDGAR ALLAN POE AS LITERARY CRITIC. Athens: University of Georgia Press, 1964.

A short introduction to Poe's critical theories; see also 1309.

1318. Pollin, Burton R. DICTIONARY OF NAMES AND TITLES IN POE'S COLLECTED WORKS. New York: Da Capo, 1968.

Keyed to the Virginia Edition (17 vols.; New York: T.Y. Crowell, 1902).

1319. _____. DISCOVERIES IN POE. Notre Dame, Ind.: University of Notre Dame Press, 1970.

Essays which deal with Poe's sources and other matters.

1320. Quinn, Patrick F. THE FRENCH FACE OF POE. Carbondale: Southern Illinois University Press, 1957.

Originally lukewarm toward Poe, Quinn finds that an examination of the French veneration for him leads to an increased appreciation of his works. See also 1292, 1295, 1300, 1303.

1321. Rans, Geoffrey. EDGAR ALLAN POE. Edinburgh and London: Oliver and Boyd, 1965.

A short introduction to the life and works.

1322. Regan, Robert, ed. POE: A COLLECTION OF CRITICAL ESSAYS. Englewood Cliffs, N.J.: Prentice-Hall, 1967.

Includes a number of the best essays on Poe's works.

1323. Seelye, John. "Edgar Allan Poe: TALES OF THE GROTESQUE AND ARABESQUE." In LANDMARKS OF AMERICAN WRITING, ed. Hennig Cohen. New York and London: Basic Books, 1969.

Poe's "compressed, closed-in" art is explained by (1) his
claustrophobic sense of space and (2) his fascination with the
idea of attraction and repulsion. When attraction-repulsion
breaks down, as in the case of Roderick Usher, the result is
"a perfect unity of annihilation"--the claustrophobe's ultimate
nightmare. An illuminating essay.

1324. Shulman, Robert.   "Poe and the Powers of the Mind." ELH, 37 (1970),
245-62.

A psychocritical approach to Poe which, happily, discovers
genuine psychological insights in his writings, not just more
necrophilia and incest.

1325. Tate, Allen.   "The Angelic Imagination: Poe and the Power of Words."
KR, 14 (Summer 1952), 455-75. Reprinted in THE FORLORN DEMON
(Chicago, Ill.: Regnery, 1953) as "The Angelic Imagination: Poe as God."

An examination of Poe's theology.

1326. _____. "Our Cousin, Mr. Poe." In THE FORLORN DEMON. Chicago, Ill.: Regnery, 1953. Also in COLLECTED ESSAYS (Denver, Col.:
Alan Swallow, 1959).

A highly readable essay which counters the notion that Poe's
works are somehow unrelated to the mainstream of American
literature. See also 1328.

1327. Thompson, G. R.   POE'S FICTION: ROMANTIC IRONY IN THE
GOTHIC TALES. Madison: University of Wisconsin Press, 1973.

The emphasis is on an important and heretofore ignored aspect
of Romanticism (the European school of Romantic Irony) which
"provides a historical context for reading Poe as an ironist
instead of a completely serious Gothicist."

1328. Williams, William Carlos.   "Edgar Allan Poe." In IN THE AMERICAN
GRAIN. Norfolk, Conn.: New Directions, 1925.

Poe is no "bizarre, isolate writer....On the contrary, in
him American literature is anchored, in him alone, on solid
ground." See also 1326.

1329. Winters, Yvor.   "Edgar Allan Poe: A Crisis in the History of American
Obscurantism." In MAULE'S CURSE. Norfolk, Conn.: New Directions,
1938.

Although Poe's theory agrees with his practice, he is "excep-
tionally bad in both."

1330. Woodson, Thomas, comp. TWENTIETH CENTURY INTERPRETATIONS OF
THE FALL OF THE HOUSE OF USHER. Englewood Cliffs, N.J.:
Prentice-Hall, 1969.

Essays by various hands.

WILLIAM GILMORE SIMMS (1806-1870)

Principal Works

MARTIN FABER, 1833   Novel
GUY RIVERS, 1834   Novel
THE YEMASSEE, 1835   Novel
THE PARTISAN, 1835   Novel
MELLICHAMPE, 1836   Novel (sequel to THE PARTISAN; see also
    KATHARINE WALTON)
RICHARD HURDIS, 1838   Novel
PELAYO, 1838   Novel
THE DAMSEL OF DARIEN, 1839   Novel
BORDER BEAGLES, 1840   Novel (sequel to RICHARD HURDIS)
THE KINSMEN, 1841   Novel (revised as THE SCOUT)
BEAUCHAMPE, 1842   Novel
COUNT JULIAN, 1845   Novel (sequel to PELAYO)
HELEN HALSEY, 1845   Novel
THE WIGWAM AND THE CABIN, 1845   Stories
KATHARINE WALTON, 1851   Novel (sequel to THE PARTISAN)
THE SWORD AND THE DISTAFF, 1852   Novel (revised as WOODCRAFT)
VASCONSELOS, 1853   Novel
THE FORAYERS, 1855   Novel
EUTAW, 1856   Novel (sequel to THE FORAYERS)
CHARLEMONT, 1856   Novel (expansion of the first part of BEAUCHAMPE)
THE CASSIQUE OF KIAWAH, 1859   Novel

Simms also published books about South Carolina, poetry, plays, and several biographies--in all, about eighty volumes.

Collected Works

1331. THE WORKS OF WILLIAM GILMORE SIMMS. 20 vols. New York: J. S. Redfield, 1853-59.

1332. THE WRITINGS OF WILLIAM GILMORE SIMMS. Centennial Edition. 24 vols. projected. Columbia: University of South Carolina Press, 1969- .

In progress.

Letters

1333. THE LETTERS OF WILLIAM GILMORE SIMMS. Ed. Mary C. Simms
Oliphant, et al. 5 vols. Columbia: University of South Carolina Press,
1952-56.

Bibliography

1334. Morris, J. Allen. "The Stories of William Gilmore Simms." AL, 14
(1942), 20-35.

A list of fifty-eight stories and their appearances, including
periodical appearances not listed in Salley and Wegelin (1335
and 1336). There is also a useful brief essay which catego-
rizes the stories according to character, setting, etc.

1335. Salley, Alexander S. CATALOGUE OF THE SALLEY COLLECTION OF
THE WORKS OF WILLIAM GILMORE SIMMS. Columbia, S.C.: Privately printed, 1943.

1336. Wegelin, Oscar. A BIBLIOGRAPHY OF THE SEPARATE WRITINGS OF
WILLIAM GILMORE SIMMS, 1806-1870. 3rd ed. Hattiesburg, Miss.:
Privately printed, 1941.

Biography

1337. Salley, A. S. "William Gilmore Simms." In THE LETTERS OF WILLIAM
GILMORE SIMMS, vol. 1, ed. Mary C. Simms Oliphant, et al. Columbia: University of South Carolina Press, 1952.

A brief but thoroughly reliable biographical sketch.

1338. Trent, William P. WILLIAM GILMORE SIMMS. Boston, Mass.:
Houghton Mifflin, 1892.

Though not definitive, this is the only full-length biography of
Simms to date.

Critical Studies

1339. Brooks, Van Wyck. "Charleston and the Southwest: Simms." In THE
WORLD OF WASHINGTON IRVING. New York: E. P. Dutton, 1944.

A readable if somewhat impressionistic essay on Simms and his
milieu.

1340. Cecil, L. Moffitt. "Functional Imagery in Simms' THE PARTISAN."

In STUDIES IN MEDIEVAL, RENAISSANCE, AMERICAN LITERATURE: A FESTSCHRIFT, ed. Betsy F. Colquitt. Fort Worth: Texas Christian University Press, 1971.

> The dominant images depict nature in violent conflict with itself; thus Simms "makes more poignant the fratricidal struggle of the Revolutionary armies."

1341. Current-Garcia, Eugene. "Simms's Short Stories: Art or Commercialism?" MISSQ, 15 (1962), 56-67.

> The latter.

1342. Duvall, S. P. C. "W. G. Simms's Review of Mrs. Stowe." AL, 30 (1958), 107-17.

> How Simms used critical theory "to reinforce proslavery argument and sectional prejudice." See also 1357.

1343. Guilds, John C. "The Literary Criticism of William Gilmore Simms." SCR, 2 (November 1969), 49-56.

> As a literary critic, Simms is "second only to Poe in the first period of American literature."

1344. _____. "Simms's Views on National and Sectional Literature, 1825-1845." NCHR, 34 (1957), 393-405.

> Simms believed that an artist's faithful depiction of one section of the country would be the most useful contribution he could make to a national literature.

1345. Higham, John W. "The Changing Loyalties of William Gilmore Simms." JSH, 9 (1943), 210-23.

> A study of the events which brought about Simms's transformation "from American into Southerner."

1346. Holman, C. Hugh. "The Influence of Scott and Cooper on Simms." AL, 23 (1951), 203-18.

> Both Cooper and Simms modified Scott's pattern for the historical novel to fit their own needs and "their modifications turned their work in opposing directions."

1347. _____. "Introduction" to Simms's VIEWS AND REVIEWS IN AMERICAN LITERATURE, HISTORY AND FICTION, FIRST SERIES. Cambridge, Mass.: Harvard University Press, 1962.

> A thorough consideration of Simms's participation in "the first major radical democratic movement in American letters" and the importance of VIEWS AND REVIEWS as an expression of the Young America viewpoint.

1348. _____. "Simms and the British Dramatists." PMLA, 65 (1950), 346-59.

Treats Simms's debt to the English dramatists, particularly in his creation of Porgy (of the Revolutionary romances), a character "Elizabethan in attitudes and attributes."

1349. _____. "William Gilmore Simms's Picture of the Revolution as a Civil Conflict." JSH, 15 (1949), 441-62.

Examines seven novels by Simms and finds in them "a clear and realistic picture of social conditions" in South Carolina during the American Revolution.

1350. Howell, Elmo. "The Concept of Character in Simms' Border Romances." MISSQ, 22 (1969), 303-12.

Simms's Southerners pursue "a concept of manhood, which in their own eyes gives them dignity and sets them apart from the rest of the country."

1351. Hubbell, Jay B. In THE SOUTH IN AMERICAN LITERATURE, 1607-1900. Durham, N.C.: Duke University Press, 1954.

A general introduction which compares Simms to such contemporaries as Cooper and Poe.

1352. Miller, Perry. THE RAVEN AND THE WHALE: THE WAR OF WORDS AND WITS IN THE ERA OF POE AND MELVILLE. New York: Harcourt, Brace, 1956.

Numerous references to Simms's role in "the war of words and wits in the era of Poe and Melville."

1353. Parks, Edd W. WILLIAM GILMORE SIMMS AS LITERARY CRITIC. Athens: University of Georgia Press, 1961.

As a critic, Simms wrote vigorously and provocatively, through hurriedly and without allowing sufficient time for revision; thus he is "a good but not a great critic."

1354. Parrington, Vernon L. In MAIN CURRENTS IN AMERICAN THOUGHT, vol. 2. New York: Harcourt, Brace, 1930.

A brief and insightful, if perhaps overly laudatory, study of Simms's literary craft and his place in American letters.

1355. Ridgely, Joseph V. "Simms's Concept of Style in the Historical Romance." ESQ, 60 (1970), 16-23.

Although epical, dramatic, and poetic in nature, Simms's style was rhetorical as well.

1356. _____. WILLIAM GILMORE SIMMS. New York: Twayne, 1962.

Sees Simms as a myth-maker: "the creator through fiction of the vision of an ideal Southern social structure." Includes a useful "Selected Bibliography" of works by and about Simms.

1357. _____. "WOODCRAFT: Simms's First Answer to UNCLE TOM'S CABIN." AL, 31 (1960), 421-33.

In WOODCRAFT, Simms tried to portray accurately a region and an era which he thought had been misrepresented in Mrs. Stowe's novel. See also 1342.

1358. Rose, Alan H. "The Image of the Negro in the Pre-Civil-War Novels of John Pendleton Kennedy and William Gilmore Simms." JAMS, 4 (1970), 217-26.

As social tensions increased with the approach of the Civil War, Kennedy and Simms employed unique strategems in order to avoid presenting potentially disturbing visions of Southern life.

1359. Taylor, William R. In CAVALIER AND YANKEE. New York: George Braziller, 1961.

Concerned largely with the Revolutionary novels and how they reflect Simms's changing attitudes toward the South.

1360. Vandiver, Edward P., Jr. "Simms's Border Romances and Shakespeare." SHAKESPEARE QUARTERLY, 5 (1954), 129-39.

Details six ways in which Shakespeare influenced the border romances.

1361. Welsh, John R. "William Gilmore Simms, Critic of the South." JSH, 26 (1960), 201-14.

Contrary to a notion which has its basis in Trent's biography (see 1338), Simms was not blind to the faults of the South and criticized many of them.

1362. Wimsatt, Mary A. "Simms and Irving." MISSQ, 20 (1967), 25-37.

Though their works are ultimately rather different, it is illuminating to note the ways in which the interests of Irving and Simms converged at several points during their careers.

HARRIET BEECHER STOWE (1811-1896)

Principal Works

UNCLE TOM'S CABIN, 1852   Novel
A KEY TO UNCLE TOM'S CABIN, 1853   A Defense of the Novel
SUNNY MEMORIES OF FOREIGN LANDS, 1854   Travel
DRED; A TALE OF THE GREAT DISMAL SWAMP, 1856   Novel
THE MINISTER'S WOOING, 1859   Novel
THE PEARL OF ORR'S ISLAND, 1862   Novel
AGNES OF SORRENTO, 1862   Novel
RELIGIOUS POEMS, 1867
OLDTOWN FOLKS, 1869   Novel
LADY BYRON VINDICATED, 1870   Essay
PINK AND WHITE TYRANNY, 1871   Novel
MY WIFE AND I, 1871   Novel
SAM LAWSON'S OLDTOWN FIRESIDE STORIES, 1872
PALMETTO-LEAVES, 1873   Sketches
WE AND OUR NEIGHBORS, 1875   Novel (sequel to MY WIFE AND I)
POGANUC PEOPLE, 1878   Novel

Collected Works

1363. THE WRITINGS OF HARRIET BEECHER STOWE. 16 vols. Cambridge, Mass.: The Riverside Press, 1896.

Bibliography

1364. Johnson, Merle. "American First Editions: Harriet (Elizabeth) Beecher Stowe." PW, 121 (April 16, 1932), 1738-40.

   A complete listing of all of Stowe's book publications, including pamphlets and books to which she contributed or wrote introductions.

1365. Kirkham, E. Bruce. "The First Editions of UNCLE TOM'S CABIN: A Bibliographical Study." PBSA, 65 (1971), 365-82.

1366. Randall, David A. and John T. Winterich. "One Hundred Good Novels: Stowe, Harriet Beecher: UNCLE TOM'S CABIN." PW, 137 (May 18, 1940), 1931-33.

> Bibliographical information on the first edition plus a note on the serialization of the novel.

1367. Talbot, William. "UNCLE TOM'S CABIN: First English Editions." ABC, 3 (1933), 292-97.

Checklist

1368. Adams, John R. "Harriet Beecher Stowe (1811-1896)." ALR, 2 (1969), 160-64.

> A brief overview of the current status of Stowe scholarship; includes suggestions for further study.

Biography

1369. Gilbertson, Catherine. HARRIET BEECHER STOWE. New York: Grosset & Dunlap, 1937.

> Although this biography contains little previously unknown material, it is less biased than its predecessors.

1370. Wagenknecht, Edward Charles. HARRIET BEECHER STOWE: THE KNOWN AND THE UNKNOWN. New York: Oxford University Press, 1965.

> A "psychograph" which sees Stowe as a family member first and then a storyteller; "her services as ... reformer come in a bad third."

1371. Wilson, Forrest. CRUSADER IN CRINOLINE: ·THE LIFE OF HARRIET BEECHER STOWE. Philadelphia, Pa.: Lippincott, 1941.

> A well-written and well-documented biography, its silly title notwithstanding. Preferable to Gilbertson.

Critical Studies

1372. Adams, John R. HARRIET BEECHER STOWE. New York: Twayne, 1963.

> A balanced view of Stowe's fiction which concludes that, though "more levels of meaning" may be found in a single story by Poe or Hawthorne than in an entire novel by Stowe, still she offers (particularly in OLDTOWN FOLKS, her best book) "a wealth of information about our earlier United States and some of the curious kinds of people who were involved in making it what it is." Includes a "Selected Bibliography" of works by and about Stowe.

1373. Beatty, Lillian. "The Natural Man Versus the Puritan." PERSONALIST, 40 (Winter 1959), 22-30.

A comparison of Stowe's THE MINISTER'S WOOING TO Santayana's THE LAST PURITAN.

1374. Bradford, Gamaliel. "Portraits of American Women: Harriet Beecher Stowe." ATLANTIC, 122 (July 1918), 84-94. Reprinted in Bradford's PORTRAITS OF AMERICAN WOMEN (Boston, Mass.: Houghton Mifflin, 1919).

A pleasant causerie on Stowe's character, particularly her missionary zeal and its relation to her literary works.

1375. Brown, Herbert Ross. "Uncle Tom's and Other Cabins." In THE SENTIMENTAL NOVEL IN AMERICA 1789-1860. Durham, N.C.: Duke University Press, 1940.

An interesting sketch of the post-Civil War literary milieu. Both pro- and anti-slavery novelists (including Stowe) "reveal a fertile ingenuity in the contrivance of incidents designed to illustrate their arguments and to substantiate their charges."

1376. Burns, Wayne and Emerson Grant Sutcliffe. "Uncle Tom and Charles Reade." AL, 17 (1946), 334-47.

The influence of Stowe's novel on the career of the English author.

1377. Crozier, Alice C. THE NOVELS OF HARRIET BEECHER STOWE. New York: Oxford University Press, 1969.

"This book points out two main features of Mrs. Stowe's work that ... typify what was generally expected ... in the fiction of her time. The first is that her novels are historical novels, in the tradition of Scott. The second and more important factor is the paramount importance of Byron."

1378. Davis, Richard Beale. "Mrs. Stowe's Characters-in-Situations and a Southern Literary Tradition." In ESSAYS ON AMERICAN LITERATURE IN HONOR OF JAY B. HUBBELL, ed. Clarence Gohdes. Durham, N.C.: Duke University Press, 1967.

The relation of Stowe's two anti-slavery novels (UNCLE TOM'S CABIN and DRED) to the writings of Cable, Twain, Faulkner, and Robert Penn Warren.

1379. Duvall, S. P. C. "W. G. Simms's Review of Mrs. Stowe." AL, 30 (1958), 107-17.

A long unsigned review (attributed to Simms) of A KEY TO UNCLE TOM'S CABIN also attacks the novel itself. The review is unusual, however, in that it ostensibly approaches UNCLE TOM'S CABIN from the standpoint of critical theory rather than sectionalism.

1380. Duvall, Severn. "UNCLE TOM'S CABIN: The Sinister Side of the Patriarchy." NEQ, 36 (1963), 3-22.

A penetrating analysis of UNCLE TOM'S CABIN in terms of the dominant pro-slavery theses, particularly the belief in the planter as pseudo-biblical patriarch.

1381. Fletcher, Edward G. "Illustrations for Uncle Tom." TQ, 1 (1958), 166-80.

Interesting details concerning the staging of UNCLE TOM'S CABIN (e. g., Eliza's prop child was stuffed with meat to encourage the pursuit of the hounds); includes illustrations, largely of actors who appeared in Aiken's 1853 dramatization of the novel.

1382. Foster, Charles H. THE RUNGLESS LADDER: HARRIET BEECHER STOWE AND NEW ENGLAND PURITANISM. Durham, N.C.: Duke University Press, 1954.

Foster's thesis is that the theology and morality of New England Puritanism account for most of what is significant in Stowe's work.

1383. Furnas, J. C. GOODBYE TO UNCLE TOM. New York: William Sloane, 1956.

An attempt to attribute modern racial stereotypes to UNCLE TOM'S CABIN.

1384. Hale, Nancy. "What God Was Writing." TQ, 1 (1958), 35-40.

A psychological reading of UNCLE TOM'S CABIN.

1385. Hudson, Benjamin F. "Another View of 'Uncle Tom.'" PHYLON, 24 (1963), 79-87.

Stowe's character was admirable and noble; therefore Tom's name should signify dignity and self-respect instead of being synonymous with grovelling and cowardliness, as it is today.

1386. Jackson, Frederick H. "UNCLE TOM'S CABIN in Italy." SYMPOSIUM, 7 (1953), 323-32.

A survey of the reception of the novel in Italy in 1852-53. See also 1393 and 1398.

1387. Klingberg, Frank J. "Harriet Beecher Stowe and Social Reform in England." AHR, 43 (1938), 542-52.

"Her books were seized upon as arguments for the emancipation of the white laborer in England as well as of the Black slave in America."

1388. McDowell, Tremaine. "The Use of Negro Dialect by Harriet Beecher

Stowe." ASP, 6 (1931), 322-26.

A technical analysis of the dialogue in Stowe's novels indicates that she was an inaccurate reporter of black dialect.

1389. Maxfield, E. K. "'Goody Goody' Literature and Mrs. Stowe." ASP, 4 (1929), 189-202.

Like other juvenile novels of the day, UNCLE TOM'S CABIN is merely "a Sunday School story about a good little girl who died and went to heaven."

1390. Nicholas, Herbert G. "UNCLE TOM'S CABIN, 1852-1952." GAR, 8 (1954), 140-48.

A short history of the novel's reception in this and other countries; includes three illustrations from the 1852 edition.

1391. Nichols, Charles. "The Origins of UNCLE TOM'S CABIN." PHYLON, 19 (1958), 328-34.

A comparison of Stowe's novel to its chief source, Richard Hildreth's THE SLAVE (1836), reveals that UNCLE TOM'S CABIN is largely derivative hack work; on the other hand, it is to be praised for its anti-slavery influence.

1392. Roppolo, Joseph P. "Harriet Beecher Stowe and New Orleans: A Study in Hate." NEQ, 30 (1957), 346-62.

The Southern hatred for Stowe was especially virulent in New Orleans, as indicated by the published attacks which serve as the basis for this essay.

1393. Rossi, Joseph. "UNCLE TOM'S CABIN and Protestantism in Italy." AQ, 11 (1959) 416-24.

This essay adds to the information contained in Jackson's study (see 1386) and, in particular, elaborates on the hostility of the Italian clerical press to Stowe's novel. See also 1398.

1394. Stone, Harry. "Charles Dickens and Harriet Beecher Stowe." NCF, 12 (1957), 188-202.

The story of a relationship which began amicably and ended when Dickens, outraged by Stowe's speculations concerning the sex life of Lord Byron, suggested that someone "'knock Mrs. Beecher Stowe on the head.'"

1395. Strout, Cushing. "UNCLE TOM'S CABIN and the Portent of Millenium." YR, 57 (1968), 375-85.

An answer to James Baldwin's attack on the novel ("Everybody's Protest Novel," PR, 16 [1949], 578-85), this essay argues that the novel's "confused anxieties and emotional power, as well as its intellectual limitations, stem not from racial prej-

udice but from the ambivalent encounter of the American
Protestant imagination with history."

1396. Suchow, Ruth. "An Almost Lost American Classic." CE, 14 (1953),
315-25.

On OLDTOWN FOLKS.

1397. Wilson, Edmund. "Harriet Beecher Stowe." In PATRIOTIC GORE:
STUDIES IN THE LITERATURE OF THE AMERICAN CIVIL WAR. New
York: Oxford University Press, 1962.

A readable essay which presents a balanced view of Stowe's
literary achievements.

1398. Woodress, James. "UNCLE TOM'S CABIN in Italy." In ESSAYS ON
AMERICAN LITERATURE IN HONOR OF JAY B. HUBBELL, ed. Clarence
Gohdes. Durham, N.C.: Duke University Press, 1967.

"Italian readers have always felt the vitality of UNCLE TOM'S
CABIN, while American readers have had to rediscover the
book.... It is probably safe to say that every Italian
with a high school education has read the book." Includes
a bibliography of Italian editions of UNCLE TOM'S CABIN.
See also 1386 and 1393.

1399. Wyman, Margaret. "Harriet Beecher Stowe's Topical Novel on Woman
Suffrage." NEQ, 25 (1952), 383-91.

On MY WIFE AND I.

MAURICE THOMPSON (1844-1901)

Principal Works

HOOSIER MOSAICS, 1875   Sketches
A TALLAHASSEE GIRL, 1881   Novel
HIS SECOND CAMPAIGN, 1883   Novel
SONGS OF FAIR WEATHER, 1883   Poems
AT LOVE'S EXTREMES, 1885   Novel
POEMS, 1892
ALICE OF OLD VINCENNES, 1900   Novel

Thompson is also the author of several nature books.

Bibliography

1400. Banta, Richard E., ed. INDIANA AUTHORS AND THEIR BOOKS. Crawfordsville, Ind.: Wabash College, 1949.

>   Biographical essay and short bibliography.

1401. Russo, Dorothy R. and Thelma L. Sullivan. In SEVEN AUTHORS OF CRAWFORDSVILLE, INDIANA. Indianapolis: Indiana Historical Society, 1952.

>   First editions (books, ephemera, contributions) and periodical appearances. More detailed than Banta (above).

Biography

1402. A number of the critical studies are at least partly biographical; see particularly 1409.

Critical Studies

1403. Baskervill, William Malone. "Maurice Thompson." In SOUTHERN WRITERS: BIOGRAPHICAL AND CRITICAL STUDIES, vol. 1. Nashville,

Tenn. and Dallas, Tex.: Publishing House of the M. E. Church, South, 1897.

A brief, personal look at Thompson's life and works.

1404. Fertig, Walter L. "Maurice Thompson's Primitive Baptist Heritage." IMH, 64 (1968), 1-12.

Thompson's paradoxical character (he seemed genteel Victorian one moment, energetic progressive the next) is explained in terms of the family history.

1405. Flanagan, John T., ed. "A Letter from Maurice Thompson." IMH, 64 (1968), 13-14.

To Thomas Wentworth Higginson; indicates Thompson's attitude toward New England.

1406. _____. "Introduction" to HOOSIER MOSAICS. Gainesville, Fla.: Scholars' Facsimiles & Reprints, 1956.

Thompson failed as a fiction writer because he abandoned the realism that HOOSIER MOSAICS, his first book, embodies.

1407. Nicholson, Meredith. In THE HOOSIERS. New York: Macmillan, 1916.

A brief, largely biographical treatment.

1408. Tracy, Henry C. In AMERICAN NATURISTS. New York: E. P. Dutton, 1930.

A wordy but colorful treatment of Thompson's writings on nature and archery.

1409. Wheeler, Otis B. THE LITERARY CAREER OF MAURICE THOMPSON. Baton Rouge: Louisiana State University Press, 1965.

The definitive biographical-critical work on Thompson, whose work is seen as thoroughly representative of the genteel tradition in American literature from 1875 to 1900.

ALBION WINEGAR TOURGEE (1838-1905)

Principal Works

TOINETTE, 1874   Novel (republished as A ROYAL GENTLEMAN in 1881)
FIGS AND THISTLES, 1879   Novel
A FOOL'S ERRAND, 1879   Novel
BRICKS WITHOUT STRAW, 1880   Novel (sequel to A FOOL'S ERRAND)
JOHN EAX AND MAMELON, 1882   Novel
HOT PLOWSHARES, 1883   Novel
PACTOLUS PRIME, 1890   Novel

Bibliography

1410. Keller, Dean H. "A Checklist of the Writings of Albion W. Tourgee."
SB, 18 (1965), 269-79.

Checklist

1411. See 1413.

Biography

1412. Dibble, Roy Floyd. ALBION W. TOURGEE. New York: Lemcke &
Buechner, 1921.

The only biography of Tourgee before Olsen's; generally accurate, though far from definitive.

1413. Olsen, Otto H. CARPETBAGGER'S CRUSADE: THE LIFE OF ALBION
WINEGAR TOURGEE. Baltimore, Md.: Johns Hopkins Press, 1965.

A balanced, well-researched, and definitive biography. The
bibliography, which includes works both by and about Tourgee,
is extremely useful.

Critical Studies

1414. Becker, George J. "Albion W. Tourgee: Pioneer in Social Criticism."
AL, 19 (1947), 59-72.

Tourgee's novels "constitute our first large-scale venture into
the field of social criticism"; thus, argues this essay, an attempt
at literary resurrection, they "have a continuing relevance in
our own day."

1415. Gross, Theodore L. ALBION W. TOURGEE. New York: Twayne, 1963.

"An attempt to restore Tourgee as a significant interpreter and
remarkably powerful reporter of the Reconstruction era." Includes a "Selected Bibliography" of works by and about Tourgee.

1416. Magdol, Edward. "A Note of Authenticity: Eliab Hill and Nimbus
Ware in BRICKS WITHOUT STRAW." AQ, 22 (1970), 907-11.

How Tourgee used real persons as the bases for these two
characters.

1417. Wilson, Edmund. "Novelists of the Post-War South: Albion W.
Tourgee, George W. Cable, Kate Chopin, Thomas Nelson Page." In
PATRIOTIC GORE: STUDIES IN THE LITERATURE OF THE AMERICAN
CIVIL WAR. New York: Oxford University Press, 1962.

A relatively short but insightful treatment of Tourgee's literary
career.

CONSTANCE FENIMORE WOOLSON (1840-1894)

Principal Works

CASTLE NOWHERE: LAKE-COUNTRY SKETCHES, 1875
RODMAN THE KEEPER: SOUTHERN SKETCHES, 1880
ANNE, 1882   Novel
FOR THE MAJOR, 1883   Novel
EAST ANGELS, 1886   Novel
JUPITER LIGHTS, 1889   Novel
HORACE CHASE, 1894   Novel
THE FRONT YARD AND OTHER ITALIAN STORIES, 1895
DOROTHY AND OTHER ITALIAN STORIES, 1896

Letters

1418. CONSTANCE FENIMORE WOOLSON (vol. 2 of Benedict's FIVE
GENERATIONS ... OF THE COOPER, POMEROY, WOOLSON AND
BENEDICT FAMILIES). Ed. Claire Benedict. London: Ellis, 1932.

Includes letters and poems by Woolson as well as selections
from her notebooks and other materials.

1419. Hubbell, Jay B. "Some New Letters of Constance Fenimore Woolson."
NEQ, 14 (1941), 715-35.

Fifteen letters, all addressed to Paul Hamilton Hayne.

Bibliography

1420. See 1422.

Checklist

1421. Moore, Rayburn S. "Constance Fenimore Woolson (1840-1894)." ALR,
1 (1968), 36-38.

A brief overview of the current status of Woolson scholarship; includes suggestions for further study.

Biography

1422. Kern, John Dwight. CONSTANCE FENIMORE WOOLSON: LITERARY PIONEER. Philadelphia: University of Pennsylvania Press, 1934.

Only full-length critical biography of Woolson. Includes a reliable bibliography of her writings.

Critical Studies

1423. Brooks, Van Wyck. In THE TIMES OF MELVILLE AND WHITMAN. New York: E. P. Dutton, 1947.

On Woolson's treatment of the South in her fiction. See also 1427.

1424. Cowie, Alexander. In THE RISE OF THE AMERICAN NOVEL. New York: American Book Co., 1951.

A good brief introduction to Woolson's fiction.

1425. James, Henry. "Miss Constance Fenimore Woolson." HARPER'S WEEK-LY, 31 (February 12, 1887), 114–15. Reprinted in PARTIAL PORTRAITS (London and New York: Macmillan, 1888).

A penetrating analysis of Woolson's fiction, with emphasis on EAST ANGELS.

1426. Moore, Rayburn S. CONSTANCE FENIMORE WOOLSON. New York: Twayne, 1963.

Includes separate chapters on Woolson's life, short fiction, novels, literary theories, and literary reputation.

1427. Pattee, Fred L. "Constance Fenimore Woolson and the South." SAQ, 38 (1939), 130–141.

The best writing of this "feminine Henry James" is set in the South. See also 1423.

1428. Pattee, Fred Lewis. In THE DEVELOPMENT OF THE AMERICAN SHORT STORY. New York and London: Harper & Brothers, 1923.

A balanced view of Woolson's achievement as a writer of short stories.

1429. Quinn, Arthur Hobson. In AMERICAN FICTION: AN HISTORICAL AND CRITICAL SURVEY. New York: Appleton-Century-Crofts, 1936.

A good brief introduction to Woolson's fiction.

1430. Richardson, Lyon N. "Constance Fenimore Woolson, 'Novelist Laureate' of America." SAQ, 39 (1940), 18-36.

A good introduction to Woolson's life and works.

INDEX

This index includes all authors, editors, and translators mentioned in the text, as well as titles of scholarly and other books, novels, short stories, plays, and poems. Numbers refer to entry numbers. In the case of individual authors, underlined numbers refer to main entries. For a list of principal works by each author, the reader should refer to the text.

Index

M